Rhetorical Vectors of Memory in National and International Holocaust Trials

Rhetoric and Public Affairs Series

Eisenhower's War of Words: Rhetoric and Leadership
Martin J. Medhurst, editor

The Nuclear Freeze Campaign: Rhetoric and Foreign Policy in the Telepolitical Age
J. Michael Hogan

Mansfield and Vietnam: A Study in Rhetorical Adaptation
Gregory A. Olson

Truman and the Hiroshima Cult
Robert P. Newman

Post-Realism: The Rhetorical Turn in International Relations
Francis A. Beer and Robert Hariman, editors

Rhetoric and Political Culture in Nineteenth-Century America
Thomas W. Benson, editor

Frederick Douglass: Freedom's Voice, 1818–1845
Gregory P. Lampe

Angelina Grimké: Rhetoric, Identity, and the Radical Imagination
Stephen Howard Browne

Strategic Deception: Rhetoric, Science, and Politics in Missile Defense Advocacy
Gordon R. Mitchell

Rostow, Kennedy, and the Rhetoric of Foreign Aid
Kimber Charles Pearce

Visions of Poverty: Welfare Policy and Political Imagination
Robert Asen

General Eisenhower: Ideology and Discourse
Ira Chernus

The Reconstruction Desegregation Debate: The Politics of Equality and the Rhetoric of Place, 1870–1875
Kirt H. Wilson

Shared Land/Conflicting Identity: Trajectories of Israeli and Palestinian Symbol Use
Robert C. Rowland and David A. Frank

Darwinism, Design, and Public Education
John Angus Campbell and Stephen C. Meyer, editors

Religious Expression and the American Constitution
Franklyn S. Haiman

Christianity and the Mass Media in America: Toward a Democratic Accommodation
Quentin J. Schultze

Bending Spines: The Propagandas of Nazi Germany and the German Democratic Republic
Randall L. Bytwerk

Malcolm X: Inventing Radical Judgment
Robert E. Terrill

Metaphorical World Politics
Francis A. Beer and Christ'l De Landtsheer, editors

The Lyceum and Public Culture in the Nineteenth-Century United States
Angela G. Ray

The Political Style of Conspiracy: Chase, Sumner, and Lincoln
Michael William Pfau

The Character of Justice: Rhetoric, Law, and Politics in the Supreme Court Confirmation Process
Trevor Parry-Giles

Rhetorical Vectors of Memory in National and International Holocaust Trials

MAROUF A. HASIAN JR.

Michigan State University Press
East Lansing

∞ The paper used in this publication meets the minimum requirements of ANSI/NISO Z39.48-1992 (R 1997) (Permanence of Paper).

Michigan State University Press
East Lansing, Michigan 48823-5245
Printed and bound in the United States of America.

12 11 10 09 08 07 06 1 2 3 4 5 6 7 8 9 10

LIBRARY OF CONGRESS CATALOGING-IN-PUBLICATION DATA

Hasian, Marouf Arif
Rhetorical vectors of memory in national and international holocaust trials / Marouf A. Hasian Jr.
p. cm.—(Rhetoric and public affairs series)
Includes bibliographical references and index.
ISBN-13: 978-0-87013-784-6 (casebound 13dig : alk. paper)
ISBN-10: 0-87013-784-0 (casebound 10dig : alk. paper)
1. War crime trials—Europe. 2. Holocaust, Jewish (1939–1945)—Historiography. I. Title.
KZ1176.5.H37 2006
341.6′9—dc22

2006021698

Cover and book design by Sans Serif, Inc.
Front cover upper photo depicts camp survivors, soon after liberation, awaiting their ration of potato soup. Bergen-Belsen, Germany, April 28, 1945. Lower photo shows defendant John Demjanjuk as he crosses his heart upon hearing the pronouncement of his death sentence. Both photos are used courtesy of the Photo Archives of the United States Holocaust Memorial Museum, Washington D.C.

green press INITIATIVE Michigan State University Press is a member of the Green Press Initiative and is committed to developing and encouraging ecologically responsible publishing practices. For more information about the Green Press Initiative and the use of recycled paper in book publishing, please visit www.greenpressinitiative.org.

Visit Michigan State University Press on the World Wide Web at:
www.msupress.msu.edu

For Milun Doskovic, Helena Zdravkovic,
James P. Hedges, and Ann Bialowas

four young friends who accept my eccentricities
and pulled me back from the abyss

Contents

Acknowledgments

I would like to thank the many people who helped me think through the controversial ideas that appear in this book. For years, George Cheney, Lisa Flores, Len Hawes, Rick Rieke, and Helena Zdravkovic have supported me as I talked about many of my major contentions, and Marty Medhurst provided unflagging support as I dealt with dissenting opinions. The three readers who reviewed the manuscript for Michigan State often disagreed with some of my positions, but they nevertheless provided me with invaluable advice, and I have profited immensely from their suggestions. Ann Darling, the chair of the Department of Communication at the University of Utah, and Robert Newman, dean of the College of Humanities, provided me with sabbatical support so that I could write this book. For seven years, the staff of the interlibrary loan department at Utah's Marriott Library have graciously helped me track down key archival materials as I wrote parts of this manuscript. Several staff members working at the National Archives and Records Administration, the Library of Congress, and the U.S. Holocaust Memorial Museum helped me obtain the photographs that appear in the book. A very courteous staff for the Northern District of Ohio in Cleveland provided me with key information on the legal artifacts that appeared in the American Demjanjuk proceedings.

My editors at Michigan State University Press, including Marty Medhurst, Kristine M. Blakeslee and Martha Bates, helped me with the final preparation of this book, and my copyeditor, Robert Burchfield, made a number of changes that significantly improved the final product. I would also like to thank the production manager, Annette K. Tanner, for her help.

Several of the chapters in this book contain material that was previously published, and I would like to thank the publishers of the following essays for permission to incorporate parts of them in this book.

- Some of the arguments that appear in chapters 1 and 7 first appeared in "The 'Vichy Syndrome' and Legal Decision-Making in French Holocaust Trials," *Speaker and Gavel* 39 (2002): 1–22.
- Part of chapter 3 contains material from "Collective Amnesias: The Rudolph Kastner Trial and Holocaust Consciousness in Israel, 1948–1955," *Southern Communication Journal* 69 (2003): 136–156 Copyright 2003; reproduced by permission of Taylor & Francis

Group, LLC, http://www.taylorandfrancis.com; "In Search of 'Ivan the Terrible': John Demjanjuk and the Judicial Use of Ironic Argumentation," *Argumentation and Advocacy* 39 (2003): 231–253.

- Part of chapter 5 contains material from "Canadian Civil Liberties, Holocaust Denial, and the Zündel Trials," *Communications and Law* 21 (1999): 43–56.
- Part of chapter 6 contains material from "Holocaust Denial Debates: The Symbolic Significance of *Irving v. Penguin and Lipstadt,*" *Communication Studies* 53 (2002): 129–150 Copyright 2002; reproduced by permission of Taylor & Francis Group, LLC, http://www.taylorandfrancis.com.

1

The Role of Legal Trials in the Preservation of Select Holocaust Histories and Memories

There is a degree of insomnia, of rumination, of historical awareness, which injures and destroys a living thing.

—Friedrich Nietzsche, "History in the Service and Disservice of Life"

By now it has become a truism in many public and academic communities that societies need to maintain a healthy balance between remembering and forgetting, but given the symbolic rewards and costs that are attached to our recollections of select artifacts, people, events, dates, and places, this is no easy task. In concrete situations, rhetors and their audiences have to make choices about what will be recalled and what will become oblivious. If some individuals or collectives try to bury the past, they will be accused of using the "dubious coin of denial and amnesia," while too much congratulatory remembering will be treated as a shameful example of "nationalistic exhibitionism."[1]

In this book, I take up the question of how various national and international communities use judicial forums as a way of preserving—and erasing—particular memories of the Judeocide.[2] For more than half a century, the International Military Tribunal's (IMT's) Nuremberg trials and other judicial proceedings have been used strategically for a variety of normative and instrumental functions—the dispensation of retributive justice, the encapsulation of collective traumas,[3] the deterrence of future genocides,[4] the collection of evidence for economic restitution,[5] and the establishment of historical records.[6] In many circles, it is taken as a given that the preservation of Holocaust memories requires some type of legal intervention and that some symmetry needs to exist between the "judicial memory" and the "collective memory" of these catastrophic events.[7] In theory, the more legal memory that we have about the Nazi extermination policies that were perpetrated during the Holocaust, the better. Yes, there have been critics of these Holocaust trials, but as Gerry Simpson noted in 2001, "these various doubters have not been strong enough to derail the war crimes movement entirely."[8]

Through the deployment of a comparative, rhetorical approach that investigates popular national and international Holocaust trials,[9] I hope to tackle some of the descriptive and prescriptive questions that attend the use of these forums. Do the legal benefits of these trials outweigh their societal costs? Is Tzvetan Todorov missing something when he argues that these trials are based on the testimony of unreliable witnesses, that some participants in these proceedings lack the "intuitive understanding" of the facts that have been accumulated outside the courtroom, and that regimes should not be in charge of our judicial memories?[10]

At least since the Stalinist years, observers have openly worried about show trials, where the guilt or innocence of defendants seems to be predetermined. In these types of tutelary proceedings, governmental creeds take center stage in politicized trials. As Stephen Browne has recently observed, the accused has to suffer through what some have termed a "theatrical brand of political justice."[11] Courtrooms are then treated as commemorative events that are catalytic forums for public remembrance.[12]

Those who have inherited what Austin Sarat and Thomas Kearns call the "classical liberal" conceptions of justice worry about the preservation of "impartial adjudication."[13] Daphne Eviatar has similarly written: "The concept of a show trial is anathema to the traditional Western belief in a neutral justice system that objectively applies the letter of the law. Of course, the concern that a war crimes trial will become such a partisan spectacle dates back far before Eichmann, at least to the decision to try the major Nazi criminals at Nuremberg."[14] Sarat and Kearns note that to "talk about law and collective memory is almost immediately to conjure images of the show trial where individual rights were sacrificed in the service of political goals."[15] Even those who don't believe in "neutral" justice systems have complained about these types of proceedings.[16]

Yet in recent years, "a small but growing number" of interdisciplinary theorists have been making the "unsettling argument that a 'show trial' is precisely what a war crimes proceeding should be."[17] In their deployment of arguments that resemble those that have been advanced by advocates of victims' rights movements,[18] these defenders of pedagogical trials argue that these forums allow "survivor witnesses to unburden themselves in a courtroom," creating moments of "public catharsis."[19] Stiina Löytömäki explains how these proceedings "offer a public forum for groups that have been moved to the margins of the official collective memory and who now seek the world's attention through law."[20] These advocates contend that the problematics of the show trial come from the "rather deliberate and systematic misinterpretation of legally innocent acts" and not necessarily from their "didactic-political intent."[21] "The defensibility of the practice," notes Mark Osiel, "depends on the defensibility of the lessons being taught—that is, on the liberal nature of the stories being told."[22] In the words of one reviewer for the *Times Literary Supplement*, Holocaust trials can become instruments of "historical understanding and commemorative pedagogy."[23] In the ideal world, defenders of these types of Holocaust trials can make analytical distinctions between the historical facts that are circulated by prosecutors in laudable criminal proceedings and the falsehoods that are allegedly circulated by demagogues.[24]

Throughout this book, I question many of the basic legal and rhetorical assumptions that are made by these advocates of Holocaust show trials. Regardless of whether we believe in positivistic or postmodern notions of legal interpretation, the idea that we can somehow detach the *lessons* of classical liberalism from the liberal *processes* that are needed to achieve those lessons appears to me to be idealistic. Legal systems risk losing their legitimacy when pedagogical lessons become the raison d'être for these Holocaust trials. As Jamie Mayerfeld has recently observed, some of those who defend the pedagogical nature of these Holocaust trials sometimes provide the very evidence that leads to an "obvious" conclusion—that these proceedings "cannot adequately honor" all of the values that we associate with legal processes.[25]

My research—which focuses on both the intentions of speakers and writers and *audience* reactions—indicates that the debates surrounding the revival of interest in show trials are not simply academic affairs. Many national and international communities are writing about Holocaust trials, collective traumas, and the expansion of our traditional definitions of justice. For example, elites and ordinary citizens in Britain, Canada,[26]

Germany,[27] Israel, and the United States have engaged in extended conversations about the nature and scope of many post–World War II trials, and I will argue that national communities should not ask their judiciaries to act as the preservers of contentious historical remembrances.

This of course means that I need to defend a correlative claim: perhaps it is time that we openly admit the political nature of these trials, and that we don't need any more judicial proceedings that try World War II criminals. There comes a time when we can legally forgive and forget some acts—marching octogenarians and other older citizens into courtrooms reaches a point of diminishing returns. Even if one concedes that the thousands of prosecutions of Nazis or their collaborators in the postwar years were not instances of "victor's justice,"[28] the passage of time means that we need to reassess these situations.

Yehudah Elkana, an Israeli historian, once wrote a controversial article entitled "In Praise of Forgiveness," which was circulated at the same time that the Israeli public was hearing about the Demjanjuk case (chapter 4). Elkana—a survivor of Auschwitz—suggested that perhaps it was time that some communities engaged in acts of "national amnesia."[29] His reasoning was that preserving some types of Holocaust memories gave Hitler many belated victories—instead of focusing on constructive futures, too many of us were obsessed with an evil past.

While I don't agree with all of Elkana's arguments, there is much to be said for the idea that traumatic wounds need some type of judicial statute of limitations. When we hastily embrace some notions of collective guilt or collective innocence, we are put in a position where we gloss over too many historical complexities. As I note in the following chapters, what often start out as courtroom presentations that are supposed to contextualize historical facts get turned into rhetorical battles over comparative victimization. When prosecutorial and defense teams try to make their cases through their instantiation of "the" truth, they have to sift through the mounds of materials that come from the mutually exclusive materials that are presented by perpetrators, victims, and bystanders. The pragmatic nature of courtrooms means that judicial performers sometimes have to settle for some negotiated truths, but in the process this search for convergent meanings means that divergent histories and memories pass into oblivion.

When I first began this project, I thought that my comparative approach would lead me to conclude that all nations clearly benefited tremendously from most of the Holocaust trials, but I soon found that at best, most post-Nuremberg judicial proceedings provided us with only limited epistemic knowledge about the Judeocide. Several generations have used these trials for a host of presentist reasons, and we have had to sacrifice many due process safeguards as participants performed their roles in these complex "theaters" of justice.[30]

There are some perceptive writers, including Lawrence Douglas, who believe that Holocaust trials can balance the needs of both the defendants and the victims, and that these proceedings have much to tell us about both individual culpability and collective memories.[31] Douglas should be commended for clearly articulating and synthesizing the views of many of those who believe in expanding the horizons of judicial inquiry and for pointing out the rhetorical nature of these proceedings. Yet he perhaps goes too far when he claims that legal forums can provide a "salve" for "traumatic history."[32]

We do have a need for extrajudicial commentaries on the historiographies of the Holocaust,[33] but these arguments can be presented in extrajudicial forums. When governmental institutions defend select histories or memories as "the" correct way of thinking about collective traumas[34] or collective guilt, then these same institutions become Platonic guardians. These decision makers—whose readings, decodings, and arguments are the "very stuff of the law"—end up being treated as the crafters of some "uncontested history."[35]

In this book, I adopt a critical rhetorical posture that asks us to look at several diachronic and synchronic memories and histories, and I refuse to accept the position that scholars can put together any single apolitical history or Holocaust memory. Moreover, even if we assume that scholars can suture together this dominant and convergent objective history, that activity cannot be accomplished in legal forums. As a fallback position, I would argue that if national communities are going to keep asking for Holocaust trials, then at least these trials need to be transparent and conducted in front of international forums. If Holocaust consciousness-raising is going to be considered to be a part of legitimate judicial decision making, then we need to be able to see and hear many narrated histories and memories.[36]

While I do not share Hannah Arendt's views on the status of legal positivism, I do believe that we should be cautious in our adoption of positions that privilege communal memories of victims over the individual rights of a defendant. Arendt, who defended the use of international war crimes trials, remarked in *Eichmann in Jerusalem* that some nationalist proceedings weren't always preoccupied with the task of studying individual wrongdoing. Instead, jurists and audiences in these show trials often took on much larger metaquestions, involving, for example, "the suffering of the Jews," the culpability of "the German people or mankind," "anti-Semitism," or "racism."[37] Eichmann would be convicted, and his case would be used as precedent for other Holocaust trials in the following decades,[38] but many of the legal problematics that would be associated with that particular proceeding are still a part of many nationalistic judicial landscapes.

Douglas and others have defended some of the "spectacular proceedings" that tried to "submit unprecedented atrocities to legal judgment *and* to clarify the historical record,"[39] but we need to avoid the danger of ossification. For example, what happens when nationalist courts begin circulating lessons that we don't like, that critique rather than privilege the tales that are told by Holocaust victims? How will we feel when American soldiers fighting in places such as Afghanistan or Iraq are put on trial in faraway places for their alleged participation in new "holocausts"? Will we still argue that involving "courts in the social construction of collective memory does not threaten judicial legitimacy"?[40]

Even if we support the idea that Holocaust trials need to take on pedagogical roles, just how do we determine the relative value of competing narrative frameworks or Holocaust memories? Not all didactic lessons provide us with the same amount of edification about past misconduct.[41] Note, for example, the worries that have been voiced about the show trial arguments of Milosevic[42] and Hussein.[43] Hanna Yablonka reminds us that the Holocaust trials of various periods were conducted "according to the spirit and psychology of the times," and each "trial had its hidden agenda."[44]

In all fairness, Douglas has admitted that "to attempt fully to represent and explain the Holocaust is" to "risk spectacular failure,"[45] and yet he is willing to take these risks in the name of legal reformation. I share Vivian Curran's belief that the "need for collective memory and the responsibility of truth may be served better by mechanisms other than trials," and that Douglas may underestimate the significance of the "massive failings" of Holocaust proceedings.[46]

We now know a great deal about Auschwitz; we have thousands of testimonials in extensive video collections, and we have hundreds of monuments and museums that educate countless publics about the Holocaust. Peter Novick, in his provocative *The Holocaust in American Life*, argues that we now live in an era where we are very "Holocaust conscious."[47] Tim Cole similarly notes that by the end of the twentieth century, more than $168 million had been donated for the "building of the United States Holocaust Memorial

Museum, while Steven Spielberg's movie *Schindler's List* netted over $221 million at foreign box offices."[48] Popular histories have encouraged us to remember World War II and the greatest generation.[49]

What some have called our current "obsession" with the Holocaust is inextricably tied to earlier periods of historical forgetting and oblivion. As Yablonka has insightfully observed, during the late 1940s information about the "Holocaust was basically repressed, whereas World War II served as a nucleus for multi-faceted identification."[50] The politics of the cold war was just one of many factors that contributed to these cultural amnesias.[51] After Auschwitz, Nanking, and the dropping of the bombs at Hiroshima and Nagasaki, countless communities around the world sought succor and solace by rebuilding both their buildings and their memories,[52] and there was no shortage of characters or conditions to blame for the devastation—anti-Semitism, anticommunism, appeasement, Hitler, collaborators, oil shortages, bureaucracies, modernity, and so forth. It was also comforting to know that there were those who survived the war and lived "on the side of the angels."[53]

Key Argumentative Defenses of Holocaust Trials

There are many laypersons, scholars, and politicians who share the "conviction" that trials "should be given a greater role than the determination of individual guilt,"[54] but these defenders of pedagogical trials take for granted the fragility of our memories. Moreover, many of the contentions that are advanced in support of these trials focus on the "transnational" identity needs of present generations. At the same time, groups of people who suffered "injustice, injury or trauma" during World War II are "increasingly prepared to demand public recognition of their experience, testimony, and current status as 'victims' or 'survivors.'"[55] Now we have investigations that look at representations of previous representations.

In many ways, the rhetorical templates that created these linkages between trials and Holocaust memories were forged in the fires of the postwar years, when few questioned the need for either the summary execution of key Axis leaders or the trials of thousands of perpetrators.[56] While critics today engage in contentious debates about the Nuremberg tribunals' role in the preservation of Holocaust memories, there is still general agreement that these trials were necessary parts of the denazification process. Yet given the fact that these forums heard from very few survivors—and that these international tribunals underestimated the impact of the systematic planning of the Judeocide—many scholarly critiques moved in directions that defended the arrival of complementary Eichmann-type trials. Observers could defend both national and international types of Holocaust trials that supplied "potent and portable" signifiers.[57]

For the last half-century, however, scholars have also admitted that the more they studied the Holocaust, the more they encountered a series of crises of representation, where the very magnitude of the Holocaust created labyrinthian problems for those who wanted to preserve what Douglas has called "responsible collective memory."[58] A proliferation of historical and contemporary debates provide commentaries on the devastation in the death camps, and we have had vehement exchanges on the representativeness of various diaries, books, films, memorials, museums, and archives.[59] Oftentimes the question today is not whether we are going to remember the Holocaust, but how we are going to remember the Holocaust.[60]

Given our extensive documentary, testimonial, and archival records, do we really need more Holocaust trials? Osiel argues that didactic courtroom tales provide "social" solidarity,[61] but do we really have any empirical proof that holding these trials has made the world safer, contributed to genocidal deterrence, or altered the views of perpetrators or bystanders?[62] Is Douglas too idealistic when he claims that some of these proceedings "possessed greatness—as dramatic and necessary acts of social will—that fully justified their historical undertakings"?[63] Should academicians testify in some of these trials, and should they back legislative and judicial efforts at restricting hate speech and Holocaust revisionism?[64] Have the defenders of these trials inadvertently "trivialized Holocaust" crimes?[65]

These are not merely academic questions, because the defenses of the Nuremberg- and Eichmann-type trials are often tied to our modern decision-making processes that look at the the limits of freedom of expression or the legitimacy of academic methodologies. Note, for example, the ways that academic trends involving "political correctness" or "deconstruction" have been tied to the arrival of Holocaust "denial."[66] Or how the debates about "Holocaust legacies" may be tied to issues of national identity, the compensation of victims, and collective self-perceptions.[67] It is perhaps no coincidence that many of the defenses of Holocaust trials appear on a horizon filled with commentaries that explain the fragmentation of totalizing paradigms, the questioning of foundational truths, and the explosion of information that accompanied the arrival of the Internet.[68] When courts—even the mythic Nuremberg tribunals—adopt "intentionalist" types of frameworks,[69] they circumscribe the ways that we think or talk about the Holocaust. Moreover, for some, defending the Holocaust trials becomes another active form of vicarious witnessing.

Defenders also advance the argument that even imperfect epistemic vehicles provide some societal benefits. At one time, U.S. polls indicated that more than 20 percent of America's adults and children may have believed that the Holocaust did not happen.[70] Deborah Lipstadt claimed that these statistics provided positive proof that the Holocaust denial movement had contributed to the daily assault on both "truth and memory."[71] "Holocaust denial," noted Kenneth Stern, "although widely ridiculed, has appeared in many American institutions."[72] Belgium, Brazil, Cyprus, England, Italy, and the Netherlands all have laws that proscribe hate speech, while countries like Austria, Belgium, France, Germany, Israel, and Switzerland specifically prohibit "Holocaust denial."[73]

For the first several postwar decades, when people wrote about Holocaust trials, they were thinking about the trials of Nazis or their collaborators, but now writers can comment on Holocaust cases that might involve civil proceedings—perhaps a breach of contract or libel case. The arguments and forms of evidence that first appeared in the Nuremberg or Eichmann trials can now resurface in newer rhetorical controversies, and symbolic linkages are made between different types of Holocaust trials. The legal and ethical problems associated with these trials recede from view in discursive frameworks that take for granted the importance of Nazi hunting. For example, Irwin Cotler offered this intriguing insight:

> In my view, the whole question of bringing suspected Nazi war criminals to justice is inextricably bound up with the whole question of Holocaust Denial [*sic*] in this sense: Every time we bring a suspected Nazi war criminal to justice, we repudiate by the legal process the Holocaust Denial movement. Conversely, every time we abstain, for whatever reason, and do not bring suspected Nazi war criminals to justice, it allows the inference to be drawn that if there were no criminals, it's because there were no crimes.[74]

While I disagree with Cotler's assessment of the effectiveness of these proceedings, I appreciate the fact that many audiences do apparently symbolically link war crimes trials with the preservation or loss of particular Holocaust memories.

These issues grew in complexity as I collected information on the Nuremberg, Eichmann, Auschwitz, and Demjanjuk trials, and I began to sense the transnational nature of the arguments that were advanced by both the proponents and critics of these trials. Some of the same witnesses and experts appeared in several of these trials, and various governments were exchanging information that could be used in both criminal and civil suits. Moreover, these proceedings involved more than simply the retrieval of evidence that could be used in the prosecution of a single perpetrator of war crimes or crimes against humanity. I began to realize just how many outside observers who wrote about these trials viewed them as institutional vehicles that would "settle" debates about controversial facts, values, or interpretations.[75] Vivian Curran had this to say about the possibilities and limitations of these public spectacles:

> The trial can be an ideal medium for representing memory, so long as the concern is to control meaning according to present perspectives, to concretize a normative position. . . . Judicially imposed strictures limit both the questions posed and the answers permitted. Even the nature of the lawyers' questions to witnesses and parties becomes defined by the presiding judges' interpretations, for a judge's directions presuppose the judge's unimpeachable understanding of the questions. . . . [T]he emergent version of reality is determined by the judges' array of presuppositions and perspectives, operating within the particular formative framework of the judicial setting. . . . Trials offer resolution by purporting to supply the answer, while in fact producing merely one of many possible answers.[76]

In a nutshell, closing a legal case mandates that we shut off historical, political, economic, social, or other scholarly inquiry in the search for that "one" answer.

If we are ever going to understand the selective nature of these Holocaust representations, or the role that political power plays in the choice of these frameworks, then we need to pay attention to more than the valorized words of a famous lawyer, jurist, or witness who testifies in these controversial Holocaust trials. We need to become familiar with some of the public, or vernacular, origins of these fragments.

In many ways, we need to be critical of the traditional linear judicial narratives that assume that progress is incrementally being made as we have more and more Holocaust trials. Perhaps it is time that we admit that the selective knowledge from these trials—which comes to us through filters filled with contradictory mounds of archival, documentary, and testimonial evidence—can never provide us with any accurate picture of the Judeocide. The politics and ideologies associated with these trials will always mean that "court proceedings" are matters of both "deformation and reformation," as participants "render data legally cognizable."[77]

As a rhetorician working within the field of communication, I am fascinated by the tension that exists between what Gerry Simpson has called the "didactic" and "dissident" histories of various war crimes trials, where various rhetors and their audiences are offered a "series of complex and deeply ambiguous stories."[78] Didactic histories are provided by some lawyers and juries of courts who believe that such forums are pedagogical vehicles for the transmissions of messages to the "wider society."[79] These authorized versions of the trial have the advantage of being presumptively legitimate renditions of history, but they are always in competition with the voices of "dissidence," those losers or critics who try to leave us traces of their "discordant notes."[80] The "judiciary," notes Curran, "mirrors the process of memory Aristotle discussed as *anamnesis*, or willed recollection, but excludes *mneme*," those memories that come unbidden to the surface.[81]

It is therefore imperative that critics pay attention to the rhetorical origins and processes that are involved in the creation of these authoritative didactic histories and their shadowy dissident competitors. When we are trying to evaluate Holocaust memories, we need to do more than simply presuppose the existence of some unitary "history," Archimedean "rule of law," or mythically "neutral" judicial procedure. This is the time to acknowledge that the very tools and standards that we use for evaluative measurement are themselves coproductions that are based on temporary societal negotiations. The brightest of jurists are only providing us with small parts of a complex "palimpsest" that "underlies and colors layer after layer of superimposed texts."[82] Even the clearest and most convincing of witness testimonials, or the most authentic of Nuremberg documents, or the most aesthetic wartime photos, can only "stabilize" or "rupture" some audiences' memories.[83]

Given the fragile nature of both memories and amnesias, what role should the state play in the preservation of these didactic or dissident legal memories of the Judeocide? As a descriptive matter, Douglas may be right that "the law" provides "imaginative solutions to the problems of judgment posed by the crimes of the Holocaust,"[84] but this sidesteps the question of whether these are the best solutions or the most legitimate societal judgments. The valorization of the words of great jurists—or the preserved edicts of "great Holocaust trials"—can deflect attention away from the ways that these ideas are themselves often reflections of larger cultural formations. How are participants in these courtroom show trials uniquely qualified to teach the pedagogical "lessons" that will help deter future genocides? Are there psychic as well as social costs involved in these proceedings?[85]

As I argue throughout this book, Holocaust trials become problematic when they close off rather than open up debate about the Judeocide. For example, what does it mean when a court is asked to take "judicial notice" of the facticity of the Holocaust? Alan Dershowitz once observed:

> I get bored by thinking about how five mediocrities in robes may ultimately resolve a given issue. I want to talk instead about freedom of expression in the broadest sense of that term. . . . I am categorically opposed to any court, any school board, any governmental agent taking judicial notice about any historical event, even one that I know to be the absolute core of my being occurred, like the Holocaust. I don't want the government to tell me that it occurred because I don't want any government ever to tell me that it *didn't* occur.[86]

This same analysis is equally applicable to all types of civil and criminal Holocaust trials, including the Nuremberg- and Eichmann-type proceedings. We need to be wary of any iconization of select Holocaust representations. Nadine Fresco, who covered the French "Faurisson Affair," openly acknowledged that she disagreed "with the referral of such a matter [Holocaust revisionism] to the judicial authorities."[87] David Bloxham did his best to be charitable when he intoned that "the collection and cataloguing of documentation" at Nuremberg provided a "uniquely valuable service to students of Nazism," but that the "overall analyses of the murder of the Jews by the American courts" were "nowhere near as helpful."[88]

Perhaps it is time that we begin questioning the heuristic value of holding any future Holocaust trials. Èric Conan and Henry Rousso, in *Vichy: An Ever-Present Past,* ask similar questions and make these statements about the role that courts should play in our deliberation over World War II histories:

> Should the duty to remember be shelved back away in school lockers? Not at all, but let us bring an end to the silly ritual that consists of being indignant every six months because a new scoop reveals that some French people collaborated or that Vichy was an accomplice to the "Final Solution": this is known, it is said, it is taught, and now it is commemorated. What is important now is no longer to denounce nor to unveil secrets, but to understand and even more, to accept. . . . [T]ribute must be paid to those who lit the wick or threw the stones. But today, does the duty to remember give the right to put the war generation constantly on trial?[89]

Legal Rhetoric, Memory, and Historical Remembrances

While there are a number of heuristic approaches that could be taken in looking at these questions by scholars who are interested in retributive justice or reconciliation, a critical legal approach could help shed light on the question of Holocaust trials. As Shoshana Felman explains, the study of "critical legal events" means that the critic pays attention to the legal and cultural issues that become a part of the "veritable theaters of justice," as well as the "judicial blindness" of individual consciousness and cultural traumas.[90] This type of pragmatic approach would build on the interdisciplinary work that comes from many related areas, including historical, memory, trauma, and Holocaust studies. By employing what communication scholars call an "ideographic" approach to legal discourse,[91] I hope to show how various characterizations, topoi, icons, narratives, myths, and other figurations have influenced the ways that various publics and elites think about the Holocaust. I therefore combine material that comes from judicial and extrajudicial sources, and I look at how particular texts and arguments become a part of some complex reservoirs of memory. This type of longitudinal approach also asks scholars to think about the rhetorical origins of many of our didactic and dissident histories.

Since at least the early 1970s, a host of interdisciplinary scholars have followed James Boyd White's[92] lead in calling for analyses that look at the interrelationship that exists between rhetoric and law, and there is no reason that these critical legal analyses can't take advantage of the work that is being done on history and memory as well. For example, Culpepper Clark and Raymie McKerrow have recently invited researchers to think of the ways that a historical account may at times be a "narrative construction of memory" that is "by its very nature an argument—a selective remembering to validate thought and action."[93] This argumentative way of thinking about historiography is relatively controversial, because there are still those who "continue to confide in a 'documentary' or 'objectivist' model of knowledge that is typically blind to its own rhetoric."[94]

Yet a growing number of scholars are adopting academic perspectives that treat the study of rhetoric as a intricate part of many social scientific and humanistic investigations. In recent years, researchers from the fields of communication,[95] history,[96] Holocaust studies, law, literary studies,[97] political science,[98] psychology,[99] and sociology[100] have taken an interest in exploring the persuasive dimensions of individual and communal remembering and forgetting. Moreover, some investigators are willing to consider the possibility that histories and/or memories are crafted by interested social agents who have conflicting ideological agendas.[101] As Pierre Nora insightfully observed, any symbolic representation "proceeds by strategic highlighting, selecting samples and multiplying examples."[102] James Young has echoed these sentiments, claiming that "[memory] is never shaped in a vacuum; the motives of memory are never pure."[103]

If this is the case, then we need to rethink our traditional judicial views that separate the "rule of law" from "rhetoric," opinions from facticity. No individual or collective opinion—no matter how logical or persuasive—can avoid such issues as polysemy, partiality, power, and legitimacy. Although many lawyers and judges like to think of their "rules of law" as a collection of logical rules and principles that exist apart from the vagaries of politics and the mundaneness of the everyday world, our jurisprudential principles are in fact simply the accretions of popular collective memories. Regardless of whether we are talking about the laws that are written down or the informal rules of justice that influence the way we think about equity, we are in the domain where the "practice of law as rhetoric may make a humanizing difference" in the world.[104] For Robert Weisberg, critics are constantly having to discover "the hidden narratives underlying legal pronouncements that purport to have no history, or a different history."[105]

When one argues that the "rule of law" and equitable principles are rhetorical in nature, that does not imply that jurisprudential elements are complete fabrications or without substantive meaning. The existence of multiple legal interpretations of an event does not mean the end of "truth" or substantive knowledge. My own brand of postmodern thinking acknowledges that there are differences between physical, material realities, and social, interpretive realities. Because of the selective nature of individuals, collectives, and even disciplines, we often treat our discussions of licenses, rights, and obligations as if they were a part of a physiological system that has no history or social origins. Treating laws in this manner has the advantage of creating the appearance of coherence, simplicity, and settlement, but it comes at the price of forgetting that these maxims are often the truncated shards of much more complex narratives that surround any particular "rule of law."[106] For example, the existence of "massive resistance" in many parts of the South after the announcement of the *Brown v. Board of Education* decision in 1954[107] illustrates how the enforcement of formalist laws depends on their acceptance or rejection within broader rhetorical cultures.

No matter how logically or internally consistent the laws on the books might be, if they are not persuasive or ideologically potent, they lose their salience and resonance and are left in the dustbins of history. In choosing between various legal storylines, audiences have at their disposal various interpretations of facts and "emplotments"[108] that influence the strategic appropriation of legal precedents, theories, and narratives. If Marita Sturken is correct when she argues that memory is "a field of cultural negotiation,"[109] then academicians should be attentive to the ways that prior legal prefigurations influence our discussions of "liberty," "fairness," "freedom," and "evil." These symbolic terms are not just crafted by empowered judges and legislators, but by ordinary human beings who use vernacular arguments in everyday conversations about the law.

While many memory studies point out that there are a number of important functions involved in individual and collective remembering and forgetting, one of the key dimensions of such cognitive and affective activities involves the process of commemoration and veneration of the past.[110] Sociologist Barry Schwartz, who has recently attacked many of the postmodernists who apparently trivialize the importance of traditional memories, argues that our "commemorative" activities are more than just nostalgic feelings for an inauthentic past.[111] Schwartz elaborates by noting that as "residual patterns of belief often reflect deliberate efforts to renew ties to a past that emergent patterns challenge, it is no surprise to witness thousands of amateur oral historians seeking to recover the ethnic communities of their parents and grandparents, hundreds of thousands of Americans undertaking genealogical inquiries to identify their forebears."[112] Given this varied interest in extrajudicial memory work, we clearly have a wealth of sources that can preserve our social, public, and other collective memories.

Because of the rhetorical nature of these commemorative sites, visitors who go to such hallowed grounds are able to bring together their prior preconceptions of the past and tie them to the symbolic meanings that are evoked by the presence of various monuments and memorials. For example, visitors to the Vietnam memorial sometimes come to such sacred places in order to "imbue" them with "a diversity of meaning."[113] The individuals involved in these commemorative events lavish a large amount of money on these museums, educational institutions, advertising billboards, and other sites of "public rhetoric."[114] Stephen Browne has recently shown that the "politics of commemoration" and "nationhood" sometimes involved a discursive "battle over Crispus Attucks and the memorial that took his name."[115] Browne goes on to observe that these disputes were influenced by "post-Reconstruction politics, immigration dynamics, and shifting class alignments."[116]

Yet museums and monuments are not the only enduring *les lieux de mémoire* (sites of memory). Youth movement ceremonials, scrapbooks, textbooks, photos, calendars, videos, holidays, and festivals are just some of the influences that shape the contours of elite and vernacular memories. Through the use of multiple examples and narratives, we craft our commemorative strategies and think of what we are willing to forget. These events, writings, and occasions provide performative opportunities, and even if we have not actually lived through an event, we can nevertheless vicariously believe in the need for the celebration or veneration of key evocative symbols.[117] Commemoration thus becomes an act of cultural practice that reaffirms our allegiance to particular values and value systems. This does not mean that just any rhetorical artifact can have persuasive potency—the crafting of some collective memories may depend on how these resonate with various traditions and value systems.[118]

At the same time that we selectively choose which people, events, or places we would like to commemorate (or cast into oblivion), we are simultaneously framing the way that we think about ourselves and others. Dickinson averred that visiting these discursive and nondiscursive sites of memory helps to "authenticate the identities of those who visit them."[119] "Our memories are naturally exposed to dissolution and mutilation," Bodei opined, "and no form of identity can be indefinitely preserved in time without being transformed."[120] Consciously or unconsciously, our memories help us to find our own subjective positions, social boundaries, and, of course, power relationships.[121] For example, our own national identities—self-created or forced upon us—involve questions of narration and memory.[122]

Yet as Nietzsche observed in the epigraph at the beginning of this chapter, there are times when memories are too painful to remember, and forgetting may provide individuals and communities with coping mechanisms that allow them to deal with traumatic events. Many of the ancient Greeks, who understood the importance of *memoria*, also left us some cautionary tales about the problems of having too much noise, too many memories. For example, in the ancient Greek play *Metamorphoses*, Ovid introduces audiences to a character by the name of Echo, a nymph who has lost her ability to initiate speech as punishment for her ceaseless chatter.[123] Echo occasionally tried to engage the goddess Juno in conversations while the god Jupiter was off philandering with other nymphs, and when Juno discovered this interloping she decreed that "Echo can mime no more than the concluding sounds of any words she's heard."[124] These allegories admonish us to remember the ambiguities and subtleties of memory and oblivion, fabrication and authenticity, existential and vicarious remembrances.

In more recent times, both empiricists[125] and humanists have also looked at the ways that individuals and communities write and talk about their remembrances and amnesias. As Greenberg once explained, the recent "attention to witnessing, representing, and narrating of traumatic events has fostered dialogue among various academic and professional disciplines."[126] The merger of theory and practice allows scholars to look for the psychic diagnoses and therapies that will help participants cope with the material and symbolic scars of various traumatic experiences.[127] Such approaches attempt to broaden our understanding of "trauma," so that we begin to think of it as more than simply another word for a single disaster.

These trauma investigations illustrate the importance of memory studies for legal analyses because they show the importance of applying the insights that come from novel theoretical paradigms. The local, regional, national, and international discussions of memory, history, and rhetoric have not taken place within a political vacuum—many of these inquiries have been involved in the debates over the modern "crises of representation," especially in the area of Holocaust studies. The advent of poststructural and postmodern interpretations of history and memory has complicated matters even further, because now there was concern that the decentering of subjects and the fragmentation of communal memories meant that there was no solid ground for comparing any "echoes" with any solid historical or personal foundations. From a postmodern perspective, what prevented entire nations from legitimately leaving behind some of the painful memories of the past in order to feel the pleasures of a less complicated present?[128]

Other key dimensions of memory work that are closely tied to the problematics of traumatic memories and contested histories involve issues of testimonial authenticity, individual recollection, and "working through" components of remembrance.[129] One psychoanalyst, Doris Laub, argues that scholars should attend to three distinct levels of witnessing—being a witness oneself to the Holocaust experience; being a witness to the "testimony of others"; and being a "witness to the process of witnessing itself."[130]

Finally, the polyphonic nature of remembrance means that rhetorical investigations can help provide voices for "the Other," the silent sojourners in history who have shared Echo's fate. By looking at key legal cases and discussions of these decisions, we can help to create the countermemories that question the taken-for-granteds of traditional narratives and texts. Sarat argued in 1999 that each legal transcript gave "potent evidence of the perspectivism and polyvocality of human experiences of point-counterpoint in which competing renditions of events, motives, possibilities sit side-by-side. . . . [T]he trial transcript . . . is at once an assertion of history against memory and a particular kind of memorialization."[131]

By constantly interrogating this "memorializing," and demystifying the role of elites, we can gain some understanding of the histories and memories that have been left behind. Comparative national and international analyses of a broad range of rhetorical artifacts—speeches, newspaper accounts, Internet sites, law reviews, legal cases, transcripts, and so forth—provide scholars and laypersons with a richer appreciation of some of the complexities that are involved in seminal Holocaust trials.

The Trajectory of This Book

I begin my diachronic and synchronic account of Holocaust trials in chapter 2 by looking at how national and international audiences dealt with Europe's "catastrophe" both during and shortly after World War II.[132] While there were purges and trials that involved thousands of defendants, there came a time when European governments were being asked to forgive and forget, where acts like the passage of statute of limitations signaled the institutional (and temporary) "end" of some war crimes trials.

Many of these trials are remembered only by the participants in these proceedings or academicians, but this is not the case with high-profile trials like the Nuremberg (chapter 2) and Eichmann proceedings (chapter 4). Some observers have been left with bittersweet memories of the postwar Nuremberg tribunals, because singling out the individual actions of some twenty-two defendants—and the focus on the "aggression" of the Nazis[133]—inadvertently reduced both the scope and nature of the Judeocide. This segment of the book also provides a synchronic analysis that compares the ways that various communities in Canada, England, and the United States discussed the liberation of the victims who survived the concentration camps and death camps. Unfortunately, the relative paucity of discussions of the Holocaust during this period would provide some argumentative ammunition for revisionists and deniers who would later take this as "proof" that the Holocaust was a political invention. The lines between the acts of discovering the ontological existence of the Holocaust and the epistemic performances involved in the reconstructing, understanding, and interpreting the Judeocide have often been blurred.

In the third chapter of the book, I highlight how various German and Allied communities wrote about the Auschwitz trials. In 1954, West Germans incorporated the crime of genocide into their criminal codes, but they also decided that their laws would contain constitutional provisions that excluded *ex post facto* prosecutions. This created a situation where the trial of Nazi functionaries by Federal Republic officials would involve frameworks where perpetrators would be prosecuted under conventional murder or manslaughter statutes.[134] Many German citizens knew about these trials, but the "lessons" that came out of them resonated with these audiences in unanticipated ways.

The fourth chapter of the book shifts our gaze toward the Middle East, where we look at some of the rhetorical arguments that circled in Israel between 1948 and 1993. By providing an analysis of the Kastner, Eichmann, and Demjanjuk trials, I illustrate how a host of contradictory ideological considerations influenced the changing Israeli characterizations of Holocaust victims, perpetrators, and bystanders. For example, during the Kastner trial, the majority of Jews living in the diaspora were treated as if they were "lambs" going to the slaughter, communities who had forsaken the options of revolt, rebellion, and Zionist steadfastness. When we place some of the arguments that appeared in the Kastner trial alongside the commentaries that surrounded the Eichmann trial, we can see how these proceedings brought both didactic and dissident contextualizations of Europe's "catastrophe." Eichmann had been a high-ranking official in charge of the Nazi transportation schemes for the movement of many Jews to the East during the war, and Israeli prime minister David Ben-Gurion wanted him put on trial in Israel for his crimes. Critics of some of these Israeli legal activities, like Telford Taylor, have argued that this type of action hurt the Nuremberg principles that had treated genocide as an international problem,[135] but Ben-Gurion's defenders responded that the Allies had underestimated the extent of the Judeocide. In theory, televising the Eichmann trial helped move such discussions into the national and international spheres. The final section of that chapter extends this analysis by looking at the rhetorics that framed the Demjanjuk trials, and here we get a detailed discussion of how Israeli decision makers had to make key decisions about the veracity of witness testimony, the authenticity of documentation coming from Communist countries, and the procedures that were deployed in these types of Holocaust proceedings.

In the fifth chapter of the book, I look at Canada's experiences with Holocaust denial trials and war crimes proceedings. Many Canadians believe in the importance of balancing ethnic tolerance with rights of freedom of expression, and sometimes Canadian communities have passed laws that outlaw hate speech. For example, Ernst Zündel, a German citizen who had immigrated to Canada. He was in court for more than a decade because of his dissemination of some of his revisionist materials. In the 1890s he distributed and published a number of documents that critics believed to be anti-Semitic and pernicious. Zündel would be characterized as "the country's most prolific distributor of Holocaust denial and neo-Nazi publications,"[136] and during his first trials under "false news" statutes he received a massive amount of publicity. Some observers complained that these trials just exacerbated the situation by giving unwarranted media attention to fringe groups that enjoyed going to court. By looking at the Keegstra, Zündel, and Finta trials, I hope to show how Canadians have had some very ambivalent feelings about the ways that they want to remember the Holocaust and the postwar years.

The sixth chapter of the book provides some rhetorical histories of British involvement with Holocaust memories. This portion of the book analyzes how English courts have dealt with both war crimes and Holocaust denial. It begins with the Allied liberation of some of the camps and takes us up to the recent debates over legality of the *Irving v. Penguin Books and Lipstadt* trial. This chapter shows us how some Holocaust revisionists are now beginning to take the offensive, and how their critics hope that Holocaust trials can provide defense measures that counter these offensives. In the name of freedom of expression, "dissident" historians, like David Irving, are using libel laws in an effort to promote what they consider to be more open debates about issues like Hitler's knowledge of the "Final Solution," the existence of gas chambers at Auschwitz, and the number of Jews who were killed during World War II. The clash of memories that took place during the *Irving v. Penguin Books and Lipstadt* trial reminds us of the difficulties that attend the establishment of any judicial historical "record."

In chapter seven, I conclude my investigation by providing a summary overview of some of the costs and benefits that are associated with these Holocaust trials. There I contend that the focus on collective guilt and the privileging of victims' testimonials in courtrooms have eroded many of our liberal ideas regarding the preservation of defendants' rights and procedural due process. Moreover, I argue that while some national communities talk about the importance of balancing individual rights and collective needs, or freedom of expression with multicultural sensitivity, in the end many of them support the passage of restrictive and counterproductive legislation.

If decision makers around the world are still enamored with the purported pedagogical benefits of Holocaust trials, and if they truly believe in the importance of community involvement in remembrances of the Judeocide, then we need to move these debates out of nationalistic forums and into the broader international sphere. Was Arendt right when she claimed that Eichmann's "banality of evil" helps us understand these "administrative massacres"?[137] What happens when jurists make unpopular decisions that are based on libertarian notions of free speech or free press rights? Who has the right to speak "for" survivors, and whose memories of the Holocaust should be prioritized? What will future remembrances look like in the narrative advanced by the bystanders, perpetrators, and victims involved in the Holocaust? At the end of this last chapter, I advocate that we move toward replacing nationalistic Holocaust trials with international "truth and reconciliation" commissions or international tribunals that are better able to deal with the ambiguities and coproductive elements of legal and popular memories.

Conan and Rousso were right when they commented on how collectives couldn't resist the "temptation" of putting "the course of history in parentheses."[138] As I noted earlier, when we applaud the arrival of Holocaust trials that temporarily preserve select academic histories or popular memories, we run the risk of closing off debate or meaningful discussions of the nature, scope, or magnitude of the Judeocide. I hope that in some small way this book will help us critically evaluate the public and legal arguments that are used in nationalistic defenses of select show trials. There has to be a time when communities can forgive and engage in acts of forgiveness and reconciliation - and Holocaust memories don't need the imprimatur of any judicial forums.

2

The Nuremberg Trial of the Major War Criminals and Early Legal Remembrances of the Holocaust

The judgments at Nuremberg have not increased the security of the world against wars by one jot.

—Otto Kranzbühler, "Nuremberg Eighteen Years Afterwards"

As I noted in chapter 1, it is crucial that scholars begin their analyses of Holocaust trials by looking at a wide range of representations of the Judeocide, so it is fitting that I start my own narration of these events by taking us back to some of the contested World War II legal and public memories. Today, the growing popularity of "memory" studies in many academic cultures has paralleled the political interest that various publics have in the preservation of Holocaust remembrances,[1] but this has not always been the case. Earlier generations have often recalled the feelings of relief and sorrow following the "liberation" of the camps,[2] and for some two decades after World War II there were few scholarly works that "criticized the actions of the Allies or suggested that much more could have been done which was not done."[3] Yet today, Deborah Lipstadt speaks for many observers when she notes that between 1933 and 1945, the reporting of the Holocaust was "literally beyond belief, and the press either missed or dismissed this news story, burying specific news of gas chambers, death camps, and mass killings in tiny articles deep inside the papers."[4] Lipstadt perhaps assumes too much when she talks about the existence of a single "news story," and she may underestimate the amount of coverage that was given to the systematic annihilation of Nazi enemies during these war years.[5] Moreover, the existence of multiple communal memories and the holding of diverse political views militate against the possibility that any one totalizing interpretation of the Holocaust can adequately explain the rhetorical complexities of these wartime acts.

Yet in spite of the existence of these contingent polysemic and polyvalent rhetorics, there are times when key legal cases are said to provide us with "vectors" that help convey the performative aspects of "commemorations, historical narratives, political debates, and other cultural forms."[6] For example, the trial of the major war criminals at Nuremberg,[7] argues Michael Marrus, was a "spectacular media event" that presented the "first comprehensive definition and documentation to a non-Jewish audience of the persecution and massacre of European Jewry during World War II."[8] Some 800 Nazi documents that were used at the Nuremberg trials commented on the Judeocide, and dozens of witnesses touched on various aspects of the Nazi master plans.[9] Gary Bass, who would have liked to have seen even more specific commentary on the Jewish Holocaust at these proceedings, has noted that "Nuremberg remains legalism's greatest moment of glory. . . . [I]t has been so exalted by advocates of war crimes trials that almost any noncongratulatory account of it will seem critical."[10] For many decades and for many reasons, it would be remembered as the shining example of liberal pragmatism, the exemplar of how staying the hand of vengeance could deter future aggression, militarism, or imperialism.[11] Yes, as a practical matter this was a trial that was governed by the four major victors in the war—the United States, Great Britain, France, and the Soviet Union—but in theory they were representing more than thirty members of the United Nations. As one of the first sites of memory for commentary on the Holocaust, the Nuremberg trial would naturally become a contested arena that dealt with a host of controversial issues, but this should be expected when tackling massive events that involved "not just" "Nazi "anti-Semitism but alliance with "other racisms—pre-eminently anti-Slavism," "anti-Bolshevism," and "perhaps amoral utilitarianism in a context of extreme wartime radicalization and barbarization."[12] I contend that many of the judicial choices that were made at this time—the selection of relevant facts, the interpretative frameworks that organized these facts, and the bracketing out of alternative "Nazi" viewpoints[13]—helped with the formation of a very unique and popular Holocaust trial.

There are obviously many rhetorical vectors that have aided with the temporal transportation of these influential judicial memories and didactic histories—books that chronicle the actions of both the Allied participants and the Nazi defendants,[14] law review articles that separate out the "legal" from the "political" dimensions of the proceedings, popular journals and magazines that explain the implementation of the Allied trial plans, newspaper articles that praise the magnanimous attitude of the victors, and films that document the horrors of the concentration camps and death camps.[15]

Yet our hasty embrace of some of the idealism associated with these proceedings needs to be tempered with a rhetorical appreciation of some of the critical commentary that has shadowed the Nuremberg trial throughout these same decades. As Gary Bass has insightfully observed, the "trials are incorrectly recalled as more selfless than they actually were."[16] Advocates of these proceedings have often successfully belittled, truncated, or answered these critiques in a variety of legal and public forums, and many audiences now view many of these negative critiques as misinformed or erroneous apologies. However, the vanquished, as well as the victors, supply us with some of the key shards of memory that have their own echoes.

When the Allies publicly circulated their indictment of the major German war criminals in October 1945, they framed this trial as one that pitted the prosecutorial International Military Tribunal (IMT) against defendants Wilhelm Göring, Rudolf Hoess, Joachim von Ribbentrop, Robert Ley, Wilhelm Keitel, Ernst Kaltenbrunner, Alfred Rosenberg, Hans Frank, Wilhelm Frick, Julius Streicher, Walter Funk, Hjalmar Schacht, Gustav Krupp von Bohlen und Halbach, Karl Dönitz, Erich Raeder, Baldur von Schirach, Fritz Sauckel, Alfred Jodl, Martin Bormann, Franz von Papen, Arthur Seyss-Inquart, Albert Speer, Constantin von Neurath, and Hans Fritzsche, "individually and as members" of several disreputable organizations.[17] As Raul Hilberg once explained, the "selection of the defendants betrayed a definite emphasis upon the charge of aggression," and yet "the bulk of them had been heavily implicated in actions against the Jews."[18]

Many contemporary and modern observers have defended the legitimacy and efficacy of these proceedings, but some skeptics have openly espoused their view that legal, positivistic trappings could not hide the underlying political dimensions of this judicial theater. Note, for purposes of illustration, the dissenting tale of the Nuremberg trial that was told in

1979 by a German historian, Werner Maser.[19] Maser, who met with several of the key defendants and collected some of his own archival materials, cobbled together an alternative narrative that highlights many of the forgotten dimensions of the proceeding. He argued that the Allied judges and prosecutors assiduously avoided talking about the Red Army invasion of Poland, and he implied that the Allies unfairly placed the burden of proof on the defendants when they used legal theories that focused on collective involvement with the "Nazi master plan" and "not individual barbarities."[20] Moreover, he argued that the prisoners were "aggressively" interrogated within the Palace of Justice,[21] that key exculpatory evidence mysteriously disappeared,[22] and that "no one in Nuremberg succeeded in proving the German Wehrmacht" had "prepared for a war of aggression in 1939."[23] Maser was convinced that the judgments of the IMT might ultimately prove to be "mere theorizing," and that this "light in the darkness" had not "succeeded in giving mankind an assurance of peace."[24]

One wonders if Maser's collection of arguments—that focused on the problematic nature of the Nuremberg trial of the major war criminals—provides us with residual legacies of some countermemories, some fragmentary and yet representative vectors of memory that may have been parts of larger resonant narratives and myths. Given the fact that the Nuremberg judges and prosecutors often ruled out the possible use of the "superior orders"[25] or "necessity" defenses, or treated defense commentaries of Allied violations of international law as "irrelevant,"[26] we can understand how military leaders would be some of the leading critics of these proceedings.[27] Were these isolated voices crying in the wilderness?

In this chapter, I provide a critical rhetorical analysis that assesses the arguments presented by both the defenders and the critics of the Nuremberg proceedings, and I juxtapose the didactic and dissenting histories that surround various judicial memories of these trials. Nancy Wood once explained how some trials have symbolic anchors that tie together "consensual representations" of common pasts with "affective" investments in "a specific set of *lieux de mémoire*,"[28] and Maser may be partially right when he noted that the "World War II generation in the United States" looked "upon the IMT almost as an immutable law of nature."[29] One of the obvious issues, of course, is whether these emotive attachments have been constructive, and whether the costs of this particular Holocaust trial was worth the investment. Did the collection of historical evidence about Europe's "catastrophe" create a situation where we can live comfortably with Nuremberg's "complex and deeply ambiguous" stories?[30]

Before I begin my critique, I need to point out that I believe that many of the social actors who were some of the leading actors in the Nuremberg morality plays were well-intentioned human beings who were sometimes caught within their own contradictory webs of signification. Many of the Allied lawyers and judges wanted to defend the positivist frameworks that separated the "rule of law" from politics, and yet they also wanted to make sure that the "German people" learned about the dangers of organized Nazism and nationalist aggrandizement. Mounds of documents were used in narratives that detailed the pervasive influence of propaganda, and yet defendants were supposed to have exercised their own powers of judgment and disobeyed illegal or immoral orders.[31] The mixing and matching of American and Continental procedural and substantive rules of law has left us with many Nuremberg legacies, and we forget too much when we try to abstract out key legal principles from the rhetorical contexts that infused them with meaning. As I noted in chapter 1, we have to have scholarly recontextualizations that look at both judicial and extrajudicial remarks if we truly want to understand how various generations have remembered Nuremberg and the Holocaust.

With this in mind, I have divided this chapter into several key sections. The first portion provides an overview of some of the key arguments and other rhetorical vectors that circulated in the years preceding the 1945-1946 Nuremberg trial of the major war criminals, while the second focuses on major legal characters who helped with the formation of dominant, didactic Nuremberg judicial memories. The third section complements these court performances with a survey of extrajudicial commentaries, as we follow the public and official reactions that circulated outside of the Palace of Justice. This is followed by a fourth portion of the analysis that presents some of the dissenting histories and countermemories that shadowed the dominant didactic tales. Finally, in the concluding segment of the chapter, I comment on the costs and benefits of our inherited Nuremberg legacies.

Allied Decision Making and Europe's Catastrophe in the Pre-Nuremberg Years

Many scholars have looked at how the Nuremberg trial of the major war criminals has influenced the ways we think about war crimes in general, genocide,[32] the defense of superior orders, or international law, but we also need to study the prefigurations that were circulated in the pre-Nuremberg years.[33] The vectors that served as ideological vehicles during this period often focused on the problematic nature of Allied responses to the Holocaust. For many observers, Hitler's plans for the extermination of Europe's Jewry were self-evident or transparent, and critics argued that the Allies knew or should have known about these horrors. Moreover, they should have been more actively involved in the rescuing of refugees between 1933 and 1945. As an editorial writer for the *Jewish Chronicle* would ask in December 1942:

> Are we, while the process of slaughtering a few more million Jews goes on, to rest content with a solemn indictment of the murder-gangs and a promise of punishment? . . . When questioned as to whether any who could escape from the occupied countries would be welcomed and assisted by the United Nations, the Foreign Secretary repeated that "certainly we should like to do all we possibly can" but added that "there were certain security formalities to be considered. . . ." The various details are accepted by everyone, the necessity for security measures and the geographic difficulties. But to place them on the same level of importance as the extermination of a whole people is to suggest a limited ability to appreciate the magnitude of the disaster.[34]

This type of commentary is notable for several reasons. First, it provides us with an example of how some contemporary writers were talking about what would later be called "genocide" years before we knew about the particularities of the Auschwitz, Treblinka, and Chelmo horrors. Second, it shows us that there were critics of the Allied policies who were willing to argue publicly for less restrictive immigration policies. Third, it indicates that some of these same critics were aware of the existence of competing wartime priorities, even in situations where they disagreed with the allocation of Allied resources. Finally, it provides us with some of the evidence and arguments that would supplement a few of the claims and narratives that would be deployed during the Nuremberg proceedings.

Critics argued that some of the Allied leaders or members of the public were provided with sufficient warnings and information, but that ignorance, apathy, or anti-Semitism framed the reception or interpretation of this information. In one of the most quoted memos that appears in many of these postwar critiques, Assistant Secretary of State Breckinridge Long opined that American consuls could stem the tide of unwanted immigration "by simply advising our consuls . . . to postpone and postpone and postpone the granting of the visas."[35] In theory, Allied refugee policies during the late 1930s and 1940s were inextricably tied to the decisions that were being made by Hitler and other leaders of totalitarian states.[36]

In many ways, some of the modern defenses of the earlier Allied decisions are themselves rhetorical fragments that recirculate the prefigurations that appeared in World War II press accounts of Holocaust responses. For example, on December 18, 1942, an editorial writer for the *New York Times* claimed that "the most tragic aspect of the situation is the world's helplessness to stop the horror while the war is going on. The most it can do is denounce the perpetrators and promise them individual and separate retribution."[37]

There were obviously some Anglo-American writers and thinkers who were willing to flesh out just how the "rule of law" would be reintroduced after the end of hostilities. In 1941, a politically ambitious Jackson would tell an Indianapolis meeting of the American Bar Association about the existence of the "bedrock belief of a system of higher law" that existed "under today's political and economic chaos."[38] Prefiguring his Nuremberg addresses, he explained that "new concepts" were being developed that would help observers discriminate between those who engaged in acts of "self-defense" and those who were "aggressors," "lawbreakers and outlaws."[39] Furthermore, the "fact that Germany went to war in breach of its treaty discharged our country from what might otherwise be regarded as a legal obligation of impartial treatment toward the belligerents."[40] Building on the work of Oliver Wendell Holmes Jr., Jackson wanted to ensure that the "bad man" theory of law would be applied to teach the Germans of the "advisability of keeping the peace."[41]

Both during and after the war, literally thousands of essays and articles had been written about ex post facto law, superior orders, the flexibility of international law, aggressive warfare, and slave labor. These commentaries were not just dry defenses of select legal rules and principles—they were also the shards of histories and memories that would be reconfigured in many legal and public discussions of Axis war crimes. For example, note the mixture of legal and extrajudicial commentary in one of Raphael Lemkin's public pronouncements:

> When any unprecedented situation in international relations occurs, a parallel necessity for enlarging the scope of international law is presented. . . . Hitler acted with premeditation and deliberation in every one of the crimes that he instigated. . . . The Jews were put in the same category as work animals. . . . The greatest, most atrocious crimes . . . have been committed by the S.S. and the Gestapo.[42]

As far as Lemkin was concerned, these genocidal acts were clear violations of international law.

During the first several years of the war, the Allies were on the defensive, but U.S. entry into the conflict significantly altered the balance of power. Both sides funded massive industrialization, waged intensive propaganda wars, and escalated the bombing of military targets. If this war was going to end, then pressure was going to have to be brought to bear on both combatants and noncombatants, and someone had to be blamed for starting this conflict. In the summer of 1942, Air Marshall Arthur Harris broadcast this message to "the people of the Reich":

> Now you send only a few aircraft against us, and we are bombing Germany heavily. Why are we doing so? It is not revenge—though we do not forget Warsaw, Belgrade, Rotterdam, London, Plymouth, and Coventry. We are bombing Germany, city by city, and ever more terribly, in order to make it impossible for you to go with the war. That is our object. We shall pursue it remorselessly. . . . Therefore, we hit your houses and you. We regret the necessity for this. . . . [W]e shall certainly make it impossible for any German Government to start a total war again.[43]

In these popular didactic tales, the Allies were acting defensively, on the basis of "necessity," while the Axis powers were imperialistic, militaristic, and aggressive. During this same period of time, Polish sources began circulating atrocity stories that detailed the activities of death squads and labor abuses, and President Roosevelt announced that the perpetrators of these crimes would be held to "strict accountability."[44]

Throughout 1942 and 1943, the defenders of postwar Allied legal tribunals tried to anticipate and answer their critics by focusing attention on the failures of the Treaty of Versailles and the infamous Leipzig trials.[45] At Yalta, Roosevelt, Churchill, and Stalin announced to the world that the Axis leaders would be "punished," but it was unclear if the "joint decision of the governments" was going to involve any criminal trials.[46] Franz von Papen, one of the defendants who would be acquitted at Nuremberg, was convinced that at one time the Allies were seriously considering "summary proceedings" for some "fifty thousand" of the "leading personalities" in Hitler's Germany.[47]

Yet the fine line between offensive and defensive warfare often depends on the eye of the beholder, and each side accused the other of having violated international rules of engagement. As more and more Allied writers and audiences learned about the magnitude of the Holocaust, there would be vociferous calls for summary executions, quick military trials, and the dismantling of the Nazi political and economic machinery. The term "legalism" was used to describe the position of those who wanted tempered Allied justice—pedagogy but not coercion. Simpson explains that the defenders of the Nuremberg trials wanted to make sure that the right "messages" were "being transmitted to the wider society."[48] Would the Allies carry out their promises of retribution, and would these trials of war criminals really provide an "accurate historical record" of the nature and responsibilities associated with genocidal crimes?[49] A cynic might even argue that prosecuting Nazi war criminals helped shift the focus of attention away from misguided Allied refugee or military policies and toward the aggressive wartime policies of the Axis powers.

Rejecting the "Poisoned Chalice": Jackson's Didactic Tales and the Fairness of the Nuremberg Trials

In the aftermath of the devastation of World War II, where more than 50,000,000 soldiers and civilians may have lost their lives, one can readily understand why Brigadier General Telford Taylor, the chief counsel for the second wave of Nuremberg trials, used the word "holocaust" in his 1955 characterization of the end of this particular bloodbath.[50] In an essay entitled "The Nuremberg Trials," he defended his own participation in what he called the "vehicle of salubrious enlightenment in Germany," where audiences learned about the victims of Nazism:

> Never have there been more powerful witnesses than those who spoke at Nuremberg—whether from the witness box or by the written word, from the grave or in the flesh—to expose the disaster and disgrace of a citizenry that abjures its civic responsibilities, or to extol the democratic way. . . . For it is Nuremberg's continued function to prick the memory and conscience of governments and peoples, and it is precisely where the pain is sharpest that the loudest protests are evoked.[51]

In reality, only a few dozen witnesses were invited to present any oral testimony, and most of the evidence that was used in the prosecution of twenty-two leading war criminals came from interpretation of German documentary texts. For several years, a great deal of time and money (more than $4 million) were expended in the collection of trainloads of evidence for the purposes of creating what Lawrence Douglas has called "a didactic paradigm organized around documentary proof."[52]

To establish this Nuremberg record, the Allies began collecting hundreds of thousands of German letters, reports, diary entries, and even visual materials in order to display the magnitude and the maliciousness of their Axis foes. As early as February 1943, Viscount Simon, England's lord chancellor, explained how the Allied governments were amassing a wealth of material, and the military tribunals would probably investigate war crimes that would "by no means be confined to eyewitness reports but in some cases would consist of documents."[53] Several years later, Robert Jackson proudly reported to President Truman that this "gigantic trial" had involved the collection of over 100,000 enemy documents, millions of "feet of captured moving picture films," and tens of thousands of "still photographs" that were used as exhibits in the Nuremberg proceedings.[54] The combination of this visual and nonvisual evidence was meant to "translate shocking images of genocide into an idiom consonant with, and supportive of the prosecution of functionaries responsible for a campaign of renegade militarism."[55]

Obviously it was going to take a long time before all of the "war crimes" were going to be discovered, but there had to be a beginning, and the winning participants in the war were sure that the losers needed to be taught some moral and legal lessons. Ideally, in the future, all members of the "United Nations" (including the four Great Powers) would be bound by the rules of war instantiated by the London Charter and the Nuremberg trials, but for the time being the victors were going to judge the vanquished. In his famous opening statement for the U.S. prosecutorial team, Jackson confidently proclaimed that there was a difference between "vengeance" and "a just and measured retribution," and he assured listeners that he wanted to avoid passing "these defendants a poisoned chalice" that might eventually be "put" to "our own lips as well."[56]

The symbolic imagery of the "chalice"—which appeared in many American and British judicial narratives—may have resonated with some of the participants or viewers at the time for a number of reasons. It gave the impression that evil was something that could be contained and domesticated, controlled by the righteous power of Allied "crusaders" who performed the virtues associated with democratic liberalism. For example, Jackson's opening statement discussed the importance of having an "inquest" that would look into the "sinister influences that will lurk in the world long after" the "bodies of the prisoners have returned to dust."[57] Lord Justice Lawrence would therefore be recognized as the chivalrous chief judge in the Palace of Justice, the corporeal embodiment of the neutral scales that represented Anglo-Saxon justice.[58]

When these principles were put into practice, however, the Nuremberg proceedings often became a one-sided affair, because in Jackson's dichotomous world, there would be no indictment of any Allied soldiers, politicians, diplomats, or leaders. For nine months, the victors would trace the activities of those who in "daily practice followed its [the Axis] leaders with an idolatry and self-surrender more Oriental than Western."[59] In one key portion of his opening statement, Jackson claimed that the "Nazi Party was not put in power by a majority of the German vote."[60] Herman Goering and the other defendants were said to have engaged in war crimes, crimes against humanity, and crimes against peace.

Robert Jackson's opening statement was the type of vector that was filled with moral and historical certainties, where the Nazis played the major role of instigators and aggressors. In the chief counsel's rendition of affairs, the "twenty-two broken" men in the prisoners' dock were simply the relics of the "social forces" of nationalism and militarism that had ravaged Europe for generations. Jackson proclaimed that he was speaking in the name of "Civilization" when he cataloged the pathological crimes of the Nazi leaders.[61] Their "National Socialist despotism" had been built on the scapegoating of "Jews, Catholics, and free labor," and this modern evil was something that was "equaled only by the dynasties of the ancient East."[62]

In order to help legitimate this trial, Jackson crafted a legal narrative that emphasized the conservative nature of this "novel and experimental" tribunal. By taking his audience back to the time of "early Christian and International Law scholars like Grotius," viewers were supposed to see how "common sense" demanded the "re-establishment of the principle that there are unjust and unjust wars."[63] When Hans Ehard, the minister-president of Bavaria, recalled these "memorable words," he complained that perhaps it was "no coincidence that the prosecutors developed the noblest eloquence," particularly at times when "substantive law no longer offers any conclusive arguments."[64]

Jackson's presentation was a carefully prepared document that wove together many threads that came from a plethora of Anglo-American prefigurations, but America's chief prosecutor must have ruffled some Allied feathers when he averred that some who lived during "the age of imperialist expansion during the eighteenth and nineteenth centuries" had forgotten these ancient lessons when they "added the foul doctrine" that "all wars are to be regarded as legitimate wars." As far as Jackson was concerned, all nations needed to avoid doctrines that "give war making a complete immunity from accountability to law."[65] Furthermore, the chief prosecutor promised his listeners that the defendants would be given a "fair opportunity to defend themselves"—a "favor" that the Nazis had "rarely extended to their fellow countrymen."[66]

The American prosecutors had been assigned the task of showing some of the aggressions and conspiracies that were associated with the Nazi crimes against peace and humanity, so a section of Jackson's presentation was entitled "The Lawless Road to Power." His tale of origins began with Adolph Hitler's assumption of leadership of the Nazis in 1921, and it ended with the September 1939 crossing of the German armies into Poland. The prisoners in the dock were accused of having been a part of an "evil combination" that helped Hitler become chancellor of the German Republic in January 1933.[67]

Jackson worked hard to create a picture of a "German people" who were overwhelmed by Nazi power, and he talked about the battles that had been fought against the working class, the churches, and the Jews. He mentioned how the defendants' own documents and films would be used against them to prove these charges, and he gave the defense many clues of what they would be facing when he made this famous synthetic statement:

> Of the 9,600,000 Jews who lived in Nazi dominated Europe, sixty percent are authoritatively estimated to have perished. 5,700,000 Jews are missing from the countries in which they formerly lived, and over 4,500,000 cannot be accounted for by the normal death rate nor by immigration; nor are they included among displaced persons. History does not record a crime ever perpetuated against so many victims or one ever carried out with such calculated cruelty.[68]

Jackson was sure the magnitude of these crimes could only mean that there had to have been "an official plan rather than a capricious policy of some individual commander," and he indicated that he was going to show his audience the "knowledge" that was "common to all" of the defendants.[69]

By now Jackson was in the middle of his four-hour-long presentation, and he used a series of extensive quotations from a variety of German sources to show Germany's rearmament, invasion plans, the creation of the concentration camps, and the proposals for the extermination of the defenseless. In the chief prosecutor's chronicling of these events, by June

1941 the Nazis were ready to hurl "troops into Soviet territory without any declaration of war," and the "entire Europe world was aflame."[70]

At this point in the address, listeners may have wondered why an American was presenting this summary of European affairs, so Jackson needed to relate these events to the U.S. entry into the war.[71] After having just indicted the Germans for their own racial policies, the chief prosecutor decided to make these ethnic comments:

> The Nazi plans of aggression called for the use of Asiatic allies. . . . They were brothers, under the skin. . . . On April 5, 1941, Ribbentrop urged Matsuoka [the Japanese foreign minister] that entry of Japan into the war would "hasten the victory" and would be more in the interest of Japan than of Germany since it would give Japan a unique chance to fulfill her national aims and to play a leading part in Eastern Asia. . . . The proofs in this case will also show that the leaders of Germany were planning war against the United States from its Atlantic as well as instigating it from its Pacific approaches.[72]

Some of the readers who circulate defensive accounts of these Nuremberg trials conveniently avoid commenting on some of this Orientalist stereotyping,[73] and scholars forget that this was just once possible chronicling of these historical events. Many German officers would later contend that they thought that Japan would enter the war by attacking Russia, not the United States, but this was obviously not the type of argument that would fit within Jackson's rendition of events. Not surprisingly, not a great deal of time was spent discussing America's lend-lease policies while it was a "neutral" observer, nor were there any detailed legal commentaries on any Allied violations of international norms.

Jackson's speech obviously provided just one "primary vector of memory,"[74] and it was clear that the Allied prosecutors were intent on showing the multifaceted nature of the Nazi aggressions. Scholars today often complain that the Nuremberg tribunals focused too much attention on crimes of "aggression" and avoided tackling the issue of the "uniqueness" of the Judeocide. These scholars have a point, but they may underestimate the number of times that the Allied prosecutors talked or wrote about the "extermination" of Europe's Jews in the establishment of their case against ranking Nazis. Note, for example, some of the evidence that Telford Taylor has left us when he recalled the testimony of Otto Ohlendorf, one of the field commanders of the SS *Einsatzgruppen* (killer squad) units that worked with the German army. In an interview with James Podgers, Taylor recalled how "Ohlendorf was a very, very able and highly educated man.

He was handsome, small, couldn't have appeared more like a nice young man, and there had been no forewarning to the audience about him, or to the judges, either. Ohlendorf was asked 'How many did your *einsatzgruppe* kill during the war?' . . . 'According to our records, approximately 300,000.' A chill ran around the courthouse."[75]

After hearing this type of evidence, we can readily understand how the court could finally decide that eighteen of the defendants were guilty of various crimes, and by the time the judgment was read (September 30–October 1, 1946), the perpetration of the Holocaust was an established judicial fact:

> The persecution of the Jews at the hands of the Nazi Government has been proved in the greatest detail before the Tribunal. It is record of consistent and systematic inhumanity on the greatest scale. . . . The Nazi persecution of Jews in Germany before the war, severe and repressive as it was, cannot compare, however, with the policy pursued during the war in the occupied territories. . . . In the summer of 1941 . . . plans were made for the "final solution" of the Jewish question in Europe. This "final solution" meant the extermination of the Jews.[76]

The survival and recirculation of these types of fragments clearly supports the claims of those who view the Nuremberg trial as one of the first of the Holocaust trials.

For several years, reporters, interpreters, and prosecutors tried to make sense out of the Nazi drive for European domination, and formalistic rationales were used to explain that many of the atrocities occurred because of alleged breakdowns in national and international "rules of law." Occasionally, one of the participants in the trial might talk about economic or political causation, but the primary focus of the proceedings was on the dominant personalities who coerced the German nation into taking some unwise courses of action. Teleological views of history clearly helped frame World War II as a battle between the forces of civilization and tyranny. Edward Morgan, in an essay entitled "Retributory Theater," averred that

> the tribunal's self-concept was that of an international authority sitting in judgment over acts that somehow differed from "ordinary" domestic crime. . . . The notion of community that the Nuremberg tribunal presents, therefore, is all-encompassing, embracing the human race in its personalized demeanor as well as in its pose as distinct national groups. The decision speaks as the normative mouthpiece of this world community. . . . As a piece of legal theater with a world-wide audience, the symbolic point of the punishment is to reassure people everywhere in the rational basis of autonomous

personal existence and the emotional connectedness of peoples in their collective existence as nations.[77]

When some of the Nuremberg defendants were finally acquitted (Schacht, von Papen, and Fritzsche), this helped the Allies counter claims that these were just show trials with preordained endings.

Did these types of prosecutorial arguments resonate with Anglo-American or German audiences? Were there readers and listeners who shared this symbolic world, filled with crusading Allies and malevolent Nazis? Had legalism triumphed over summary execution?

Extrajudicial Commentaries and the Didactic Legacies Associated with Nuremberg

During the Nuremberg proceedings, hundreds of reporters came from "more than twenty nations," and most of the members of the American press "considered the fate of individual defendants to be of secondary importance."[78] Some of the earlier newspaper commentators defended the novel creation of some of the Nuremberg precedents by noting that "never before have 4,000,000 been deliberately and systematically massacred."[79] An essayist for the *Manchester Guardian* surmised that "behind the documents lie the outraged feelings of whole peoples, whose memories carry a far heavier load than ours, and no one can go through the long catalogue of evil caused by Nazi rule and Nazi war without feeling it entirely right that now at last the Nazi leaders should have to answer for their actions."[80]

While some writers commented on the efficacy or the fairness of the proceedings, others still wanted to talk about the trial's pedagogical possibilities. For example, in 1945 one British journalist proclaimed that "no question can ever be raised concerning the fairness of the rules of evidence and procedure administered by the Nuremberg Tribunal."[81] Russell Hill, writing for the *New York Herald Tribune,* told readers even the *Berliner Zeltung* was calling Jackson's statement a "great speech and significant document." One German interviewee was said to have represented the feelings of many of his compatriots when he espoused the belief that the defendants "should be put into concentration camps or made to clean up the rubble."[82] In England, a contributor to the *New Statesman and Nation* averred that a "precedent in international law and morality has now been set which extends far beyond this particular instance of the Nazi war criminals."[83]

With the passage of years, there would be many other observers who defended the nobility of the goals of the Nuremberg proceedings, while simultaneously admitting the difficulties of reeducating or denazifying Germany. Many of the former participants in the trial of the major war criminals would also become some of the leading defenders of these proceedings. An unidentified writer for the *New York Times* would note on March 7, 1947, that Telford Taylor was convinced that trying "to impress the Germans with the idea of collective guilt or with what they did to the rest of the world is pretty hopeless."[84]

In spite of these types of suasory problems, the Nuremberg trials gained their "legacy,"[85] and even writers who had ambivalent feelings about some possible procedural irregularities understood the symbolic importance of these judicial performances. Eugene Davidson had this to say about the consequences of the proceedings:

> The trial of these Germans was a collective trial, but it is through the life stories of each individual that many hidden springs of the National Socialist State may be detected. . . . Even if the trial was imperfect and the representatives of the Soviet Union charged the Germans with crimes the Russians had committed, the trial had to be held in some form. A catharsis of the pent-up emotions of millions of people had to be provided and a record of what had taken place duly preserved for whatever use later generations would make of it.[86]

As Brian Feltman has recently observed, these types of remarks "provided the public with a deeper understanding of the tribunal's purpose and contributed to widespread approval of its findings."[87]

The Nuremberg evidence provided foundational records for many writers, and those who used this information were convinced that the trials had chronicled the steps that were taken in the Nazi formation of the "Final Solution." Gerald Reitlinger used some of Otto Ohlendorf's testimony in his description of the *Einsatzgruppen* activities, and in an appendix he tried to update the statistical information on the magnitude of the Judeocide that was available at that time.[88] Raul Hilberg used material from both the Nuremberg major trial of the war criminals and the subsequent American trials in putting together *The Destruction of the European Jews,* and Whitney Harris could write an entire chapter in 1954 that outlined the Nuremberg revelations about the "Final Solution."[89] Slowly but surely, readers were now being afforded material that supplemented the Allied focus on Nazi "aggression."

Judith Shklar thought that, over time, the revelations about crimes against humanity were productive, but that the great trial failed when it tried to educate spectators or provide "rigorous attribution of guilt for specific acts."[90] The Nuremberg prosecutors may have claimed that they were not talking about the collective guilt of the German people, but one scholar intoned that the guilt of these leaders was not "unlike that of the individual German," the millions who served in the armed forces, on the farms, and in the factories. "The trial," in Davidson's words, "was the trial of the Germans."[91] Admirers drafted both the Genocide Convention and proposals for a more permanent international criminal court.[92]

Given this cultural milieu, we can understand why in June 1946 Robert Jackson could proclaim that Americans "may disregard the few sympathizers who would have set the prisoners free" and that "the only real criticism" of President Truman's "decision to hold the trials comes from the 'shoot 'em at sight' school."[93] This type of reductionist thinking dismisses a whole range of possible objections,[94] and it of course ignores the fact that "many people, outside as well as inside the government opposed trials." Jonathan Bush elaborates by noting that diplomats had to worry about rebuilding war-torn Germany; that prominent jurists such as George A. Finch, Hans Kelsen, and Max Radin questioned certain features of the trial; and that Senator Robert Taft was a vocal Nuremberg critic.[95] One of Jackson's colleagues on the U.S. Supreme Court, Chief Justice Harlan Stone, would claim that this trial was simply a "high class lynching party."[96] Even the *Chicago Tribune* had a leading editorial (October 2, 1946) that argued that the "truth of the matter is that no one of the victors was free from the guilt which its judges attributed to the vanquished."[97]

Justice Jackson may have believed that he had put together a Nuremberg record that would be beyond dispute, but many observers could accept the facticity of the Judeocide or the reality of war crimes without having to accept the Allied apportionment of blame, historical representations, or interpretations of international law. As Vivian Curran has recently observed, the "law's interaction" with the Holocaust has involved matters that "stray far from the traditionally legal," and this in turn means that many social agents and their audiences must deal with a welter of conflicting histories and memories.[98]

Of Dissident Histories and Countermemories: Contemplating the Possibility That Nuremberg Represented Victors' Justice

When scholars try to decode and reorganize some of the key arguments that have been advanced by critics of the Nuremberg trial of the major war criminals, they will find that these observers were complaining about disparate power relations, jurisdictional oversights, historical omissions, procedural irregularities, and idealist positions on warfare and deterrence. One German politician remembered how Jackson had talked about a "poisoned chalice" that would be "put to our own lips," but he wondered why the Nuremberg Charter did not bind all members of the "community of nations."[99] Even Francis Biddle—a jurist at Nuremberg—had to acknowledge that a balancing of "practical" and ideal values—and not necessarily "logic or consistency" alone—explained how he could object to the punishing of Germans for breaches of international law that both British and Americans had committed (submarine warfare), and yet approve the condemnation of Germans "for acts of which the Russians had also been guilty" (aggressive war against Finland and Poland).[100] One reviewer, Lord Hankey, went so far as to argue that if the focal point of penal responsibility was going to rest on the crime of aggression, then perhaps all of the Nazi war criminals deserved amnesty.[101] Ironically, during the cold war, some of the thousands of prisoners who were still being held by the Allies were given some type of clemency, but it would take many months before victorious decision makers could think in those terms.

Some of the most scathing criticisms of the Nuremberg trials came from detractors who worried about jurisdictional issues and the original composition of the Allied courts. Given that fact that some thirty members of the "United Nations" were said to be a part of the winning coalition, why were the Americans and the three other powers dominating the legal conversation? When critics asked for the international legal sources that would confer the tribunal judicial authority, they were often told that the Nuremberg Charter was the United Nations' confirmation of that power. As F. A. Voigt noted in 1946, it appeared as though the court itself was being conceived as precedent, and the Allies were automatically accepting the "Coalition of Powers'" argument that the Allies had criminal jurisdiction. The very vagueness of the term "aggression," and the fact that this seemed to be a "revolutionary" rupture of "judicial continuity," did not sit well with those who believed in the principle *nulla poena sine lege* (no penalty without a law).[102] Their argument was based on the fact that the indictments included allegations about crimes against peace and humanity, which were new international law violations. How, they asked, could anyone receive a fair trial when Allied judges took the seats that could have been occupied by "neutral" parties?[103] Montgomery Belgion, for example, averred that the verdict of the trial was tied up with postwar policy making, where decisions were "pre-determined" and "self-conferred."[104]

Even if one granted that the victors could try the vanquished, critics could then argue that the tribunals' lawyers and judges were chaotically mixing and matching American and Continental rules. Many observers who were interested in more dissident vectors of memory reminded readers that, for nine months, these defendants had to deal with a plethora of procedural irregularities—the automatic dismissal or marginalization of certain defenses, the prohibiting of defense team visits to Allied archives, the one-sided rules that demanded that the prosecutors oversee defense requests for documents (this was modified during the proceedings), the selective handling of international law maxims or customs, and the dismissal of applicable German laws.[105]

Many of the prosecutors and jurists who participated in the Nuremberg trial of the major war criminals prided themselves on having amassed mounds of German documentary evidence as they established what they called "the record," but in many ways they glossed over many of the historiographic erasures that came from the collection, selection, translation, and interpretation of these shards of history and memory. Jess Joseph Silverglate once noted that time and power limitations created situations where untrained personnel were sometimes screening matters that came from all parts of Europe. Many members of the Allied legal staff were not competent in German, and one analyst even admitted that he "felt" the import of key documents as he remembered how his own mother had died in one of the German gas vans operating in Czechoslovakia.[106]

Let me be clear—these were not necessarily problems that stemmed from ill intentions or from prosecutorial misconduct—I am arguing that the very creation of these historical records was itself an inherently rhetorical exercise, necessarily selective, partial, and interested. One skeptical writer has remarked that part of the reason that historians "tended to be more critical of these materials" is that when these researchers "look at most wars, they think of them not as events that are planned, but as things that happen."[107] Prosecutors at Nuremberg were sometimes dealing with extant records that were not verbatim transcripts, and sometimes the documents revealed "plans" that were not always followed.[108]

In a typical critique of the dominant histories that were presented by Jackson and some of his colleagues at Nuremberg, a writer for England's *Economist* claimed that the judgment included a "curious oblivion"—the Allies appeared to be assiduously avoiding the topic of the German-Soviet Non-Aggression Pact of August 1939. This insightful critic went on to argue that perhaps this "inhibition" came from the fact that these types of details threatened to "interrupt the flow" of the prosecutory "narrative" and that the defendant Ribbentrop was said to have traveled to Moscow with the intent of negotiating a "non-aggression pact with the Soviet Union."[109] This type of prosecutorial framing provided the Allies with a tale that let them acknowledge the existence of the pact, but now they could tailor their arguments in ways that deflected attention away from the active involvement of the Soviets.

In other renditions of the histories associated with these trials, none of the victorious countries could claim that they were "free from the guilt which its prosecutors ascribed to the vanquished,"[110] and the defense was prohibited from focusing exclusive attention on Hitler's edicts. Even more controversial was the claim that Allied histories were forgetting about the eviction of persons from Poland, Czechoslovakia, Hungary, and parts of Russia.[111]

In the end, some of the strongest critiques of the Nuremberg proceedings came from observers who thought that the Allies were simply being too idealistic when they talked about laws deterring wars or state acts of aggression. In many of their opening and closing statements, the chief prosecutors often provided a welter of natural law or legal realist rationales for why international communities needed to regulate war, but they were still making distinctions between "just" and "unjust" wars, or "aggressive" and "defensive" conflicts. Given the fact that the IMT was not trying to ban all wars, why were the Allied judges refusing to hear evidence about possible Allied aggression? The Germans claimed that in the prewar months, they worried about Soviet troop movements on the Russian west border.[112]

Some perhaps believed that the Allied judges and prosecutors were simply asking too much—how could any exemplary legal definitions of norms, violations, punishment, or guilt deal with disparate power bases and conflicting human motivations? The tribunals' idealism seemed to be ignoring the fact that "the IMT's didactic prescription of standards of behaviour" seemed to be "basically unattainable by future mankind."[113]

If Robert Jackson's words represented some of the thinking of the Allies, perhaps Otto Kranzbühler provided some of the most interesting dissident commentaries that sutured together many of the procedural and substantive problems that shadowed the Nuremberg crusaders. Ann Tusa and John Tusa observed how Kranzbühler "was reckoned to be the most brilliant of the defence lawyers,"[114] and this former chief counsel for Grand Admiral Karl Dönitz has left us with an intriguing 1965 critique that detailed some of the reasons for the alleged unfairness of these postwar trials. In his analysis of both the "so called international trial" and the dozen smaller trials of the IMT, the former fleet judge-advocate brought together many of the complaints that had been circulated in legal and public circles for dozens of years: the trial was "political" and "legal"; it was a "revolutionary event in the development of international law"; the defendants did not have the same access to the German archives that were collected; the defense could not use Allied documents; and the London Charter took away many defenses that existed under international law. Furthermore, Kranzbühler asserted that the Allied mandate "was merely intended to bring certain defendants to prosecution and conviction"; that the prosecutors crafted a "ghost-like apparition" called the "duty to resist"; and that the Americans wanted to find "that Germany conducted in an illegal war" so that they could justify the U.S. delivery of fifty destroyers to the British before America's entry into the conflict.[115]

Kranzbühler argued that a truly international tribunal would try to prevent war through the use of both judicial and nonjudicial means. This meant acknowledging the need for an organization that was powerful enough to "render" judgment "without bias and with historical truth."[116] The lack of any discussion of the aggression in Korea, Laos, Vietnam, Egypt, or Cuba showed how many nations were selectively applying the Nuremberg standards. Even more objectionable were the ways that the Nuremberg judges tried to differentiate between the supposed "total war" of the Nazis and the "development of warfare itself." These types of political constraints were said to stand in the way of international justice. However, Kranzbühler believed that in spite of these problems, the "obvious crimes committed under Hitler's leadership"—particularly "the annihilation process against the Jews"—meant that some "expiation" had been needed to "discharge the victors and the vanquished."[117]

For many decades, writers around the world would read and quote from Robert Jackson's speeches and essays, while Kranzbühler would be remembered as one of the minor figures in an epoch democratic morality play. Modern commentators might abstract out and use some permutation of these marginalized claims, but the context that infused them with meaning would be lost when most experts and laypersons looked back on the Nuremberg legacies.

Selective Remembrances, Nuremberg Legacies, and Holocaust Historiographies

In 1955, Telford Taylor was convinced that "the Nuremberg monument" came from "time's chisel," where in spite of criticisms, it would emerge "not as the tombstone of a black era," but as a cornerstone of "justice under the law among men and nations."[118] He would be partially right. Many of the legal and political decisions that were made during the Nuremberg trial of the major war criminals clearly resonated with a host of diverse national and international audiences, but the temporal needs of various generations have often changed the interpretations or valences that we associate with this trial. Future generations were not always enamored with the idea of "conspiracy,"[119] and restrictive interpretations of "superior order" defenses continue to be matters of debate. They also had differing views on the didactic importance of the trial, the historical framing that may have marginalized the Judeocide, and the deterrent value of the Nuremberg proceedings.

In most traditional narratives that celebrate the Nuremberg trials, the judges and prosecutors who were major players in this judicial theater are still configured as dispassionate participants who did their best to provide justice in an imperfect world. Defenders of these trials might admit that there may have been occasional problems with translations, some quibbling between American and Continental lawyers, and a few instances where the defense did not receive the same treatment as their opponents, but all in all the defendants got better than they deserved.

For many observers, the Nuremberg tribunals had established the precedents, principles, and frameworks that would be needed by future generations that were going to have to handle other "war crimes" and "crimes against humanity." One of the assistant editors for the *American Bar Association Journal* remarked in October 1993 that "in such places as Korea, Vietnam, Afghanistan, Iraq and, most recently, the Balkans, Nuremberg is the reference point for measuring when war becomes criminal in the eyes of the world."[120]

With the passage of time, the popularity of various war crimes trials at both the national and international levels has also brought growing criticism of these proceedings, and the interrogation of the Allied choices has meant that a variety of interdisciplinary critiques are now willing to reassess many of the arguments that were used in the Nuremberg trial of the major war criminals. In the 1960s and 1970s, interest in the Eichmann trial[121] or the legal conundrums associated with the Vietnam War helped keep alive some of the earlier debates that had taken place about the documentation of the Holocaust, the legitimacy of state war crimes trials, or the superior orders defense. Moreover, some scholars were calling for studies of the "social and political advisability of continuation of the Nuremberg policy," as a way of augmenting the repetitive "probing of technical legal issues."[122]

Bradley F. Smith was one of the harshest critics of these proceedings, and in *Reaching Judgment at Nuremberg* he explained that the German people as a whole had not learned the lessons that were being taught by the Allies. He was sure that "most of them acted like spectators, paying only fleeting attention to the trial when it was in process," and aside from the grumbling about individual verdicts, forgetting "it as soon as possible when it had run its course." Bradley acknowledged that the Nuremberg trials appeared to be some type of "ritual performance," but that perhaps this was tailored "for the gratification of the victors."[123]

By the 1980s and 1990s, temporal distance allowed for more interrogation of historical and legal taken-for-granteds, as observers realized that Nuremberg-type trials were here to stay. Now writers were taking up the question of how politics, power, and rhetoric were involved in the communal production of Holocaust trials and Holocaust remembrances. Changing legal paradigms and the flowering of key studies (Holocaust studies, memory studies, critical historical investigations, law and literature studies, and so forth) helped create what Bloxham has called a "Nuremberg Historiography of the Holocaust."[124] Other modernists had written about positivistic legacies, formalistic reasoning, or the organic growth of international law, but now reviewers could talk about the discursive power of Nuremberg's "nomenclature"[125] or "explicit interpretive bequests of the trials."[126]

These rhetorically sensitive analyses help us appreciate the polysemic nature and the artifice behind the construction of any "record" or any legal "history." American and British audiences may have congratulated themselves that they were putting together a historical record that was dismantling the Nazi ideological frameworks, but they perhaps failed to acknowledge that they themselves were acting ideologically as they talked and wrote about civilization, fair trials, denazification, Axis aggression, and so forth. Consciously and unconsciously, the vectors that they brought together—films, German documents, testimony, and so forth—became parts of other rhetorical layers—the "blue" and "green" series and other artifacts that would serve as "archival" material for half a century. We forget that tons of captured materials were never kept or sorted, that the defense exhibits were "not given the status of Nuremberg documents, and were not supplied with symbol of number,"[127] and that behind the scenes the Allies themselves had countless disagreements about key procedures and decisions.

This all goes by the wayside in totalizing legal commentaries that eulogize Jackson's words or ossify the Nuremberg legacy. In sum, by carefully crafting what Osiel has called a "founding myth" or "monumental didactic,"[128] the Allied prosecutors could punctuate time in rhetorical frameworks that deflected attention away from any postwar debates about colonialism, domestic lynchings, Dresden, Hiroshima, and the treatment of Polish prisoners. Critics and scholars have not spent a great deal of their time writing about the Katyn massacre,[129] the heroics of Stalingrad, or the role that the "Soviet Union" played in ending the Holocaust. Nor have they focused a lot of attention on the immigration policies of non-Western nations during the World War II years.[130] In "their own diverse ways," argues Bloxham, the Allied prosecutors "intentionally and inadvertently," by "omission and commission," contributed "to the creation of some of the most influential paradigms of Nazi criminality."[131]

Did Jackson and the other Allies really avoid leaving us with a poisoned chalice? Perhaps it is time that we reconsider entire Nuremberg frameworks. One of the most devastating dissident critiques that has ever been written about these proceedings comes from the pen of István Deák, in an essay entitled "Misjudgment at Nuremberg."[132] Deák argued that the defense was "gravely handicapped throughout the trial," that the German lawyers were not shown secret British documents on the invasion of Norway, that the defense was forbidden to talk about the millions of Soviet and German prisoners of war who died in camps, and that "anti-Nazi" partisans also "robbed and terrorized the rural" populations.[133] Deák was sure that the best way to "avoid the sorry spectacle of a country or countries equally guilty of war crimes sitting in judgment over the defeated country" was to make sure that in the future there were "no other trials following the model of the Nuremberg trials."[134]

In an era filled with talk of revenge, where policy makers were considering alternatives such as Morgenthau's dismantling of Germany or summary executions,[135] holding even an imperfect trial may appear prudential. However, if we truly want international standards and norms, we need to do more than simply recirculate the same victors' tales over and over again, with little renegotiation or rehabilitation. If justice truly involves the coproduction of knowledge and morality, we need to admit openly that some of these Allied legal fragments were selectively created at a time when retributive justice was in the air. Deák thinks that the solution lies in trying "to encourage the newly constituted authorities in the defeated country to deal with their own war criminals."[136] I deal with that suggestion in some of my other chapters, but for now I offer a better solution—no more Holocaust trials, or at least publicly acknowledge the limitations of these trials.

3

The Difficulties of "Mastering the Past": Contemporary and Modern Vectors of Memories and the Auschwitz Trial

At the very least, the experience of the Auschwitz trial problematizes any easy supposition that trials can serve an unmediated public pedagogical function.

—Devin Pendas, "'I Didn't Know What Auschwitz Was': The Frankfurter Auschwitz Trial and the German Press, 1963–1965"

"Since the 1960s," argued Nancy Wood, the confusion between "the politics of *Aufarbeitung* ('coming to terms with the past')" and *Vergangenheitsbewältigung* ('mastering' or 'overcoming' the past) have been a constant feature in the German political and cultural landscape."[1] In the minds of many observers who hold this view, a society may indeed share some type of exculpatory consensus that allows members of a community to go on with their lives in spite of some troubled past, but the strategic use of the rhetorical vectors that carry markers of evasions, denials, moral equivalencies, or minimalizations are not good indicators that some collective has actually come to terms with that past.

Until the mid-1990s, there were worries that future German generations would forget about the Judeocide, and as many of the victims passed away, a host of officials, companies, organizations, and individuals worked frantically to make sure that our depositories of memories had adequate amounts of information on the Holocaust. While many of these communities had disagreements about the universalist framing of key Holocaust narratives,[2] there was general international acknowledgment that Holocaust consciousness-raising needed to be a part of our politics and curriculums.

Since at least the end of the 1940s, the ideograph "Auschwitz" has become a key symbol in many of the contested struggles that have taken place over the nature and scope of our Holocaust histories and memories. Over time, many of us have learned about the fact that millions of victims were deported by trains to a Polish area that would be designated as a major death camp, and researchers today know that the vast majority of these victims were Jews. Recognizing and understanding the horrors of Auschwitz have taken on performative importance for those observers who are interested in the uniqueness of the Holocaust, and many plaques and museums have changed the signification on their vectors as tourists visit the massive complex that we call "Auschwitz."[3]

Today we sometimes hear assertions that claim that earlier generations of jurists, prosecutors, and legal experts should have known about the extent of these Auschwitz horrors (Aleksander Lasik has complained that less than 15 percent of the SS garrison who worked at this concentration camp were ever brought to trial),[4] but we need to bear in mind that during the 1950s and 1960s, many audiences were being presented with conflicting and competing Holocaust frameworks. For example, recent material from Russian archives reveals how Soviet war crimes trials were events that "revealed the active participation of the German civil administration, the Order Police, and rear army units in the Holocaust,"[5] but the victims were characterized as the "Soviet people," Polish Jews, soldiers, civilians, people from "the Motherland," fascist targets, and so forth. We can readily understand why some leaders were asking for summary executions, and Stalin once suggested at the Tehran Conference that the Allies needed to shoot some 50,000 members of the German military without any legal trials.[6] The existence of these competing (and sometimes contradictory) World War II genres has meant that those who are interested in the dispensation of blame have had to make choices regarding the appropriate framework, and "Auschwitz" has become a key figurative marker in our symbolic representations of the Holocaust.

A rhetorical analysis of many of the discursive and nondiscursive shards that circulated in the Anglo-American presses during the 1940s, 1950s, and 1960s shows the polysemic and polyvalent nature of these Auschwitz histories and memories. Many writers covered what would be called the "Auschwitz trial" (1963–1965)—"the longest trial in German legal history."[7] During these proceedings, participants and observers recirculated judicial fragments that contained both intentionalist and functionalist arguments about the Holocaust, and by this time we see many observers who were commenting on the specificity or uniqueness of the Holocaust. Gerd Wilcke, who wrote many articles on this trial for the *New York Times,* informed readers in December 1963 that most of the people killed at Auschwitz were Jews, and that the estimated number of victims was believed to be somewhere between 1,000,000 and 3,000,000.[8]

However, documenting the extent of what Osiel has called "administrative murder" did not always mean that jurists or audiences shared the same "collective conscience," and they were often operating from different types of "legal storytelling" or "competing theatrical genres.[9] Various social agents disagreed about the causes of the war, the culpability of the ordinary German soldier or citizen, the sentencing of guilty parties, and the jurisdiction of national court systems. In many of the German trials of alleged war criminals, it seemed as though the Auschwitz death camp was just one of many horrible places, and the Allied authorities seemed to know more about Bergen-Belsen and Dachau.

As I noted in chapter 2, the Allied victors spent several years preparing for their war crimes trials, and in theory many international communities were going to be involved in the postwar dispensation of justice. International Military Tribunals (IMTs) would sit in Nuremberg from October 1945 to October 1946, but there would be other military commissions that would try former Nazis in Germany, France, Italy, North Africa, and the Soviet Union. Many of the German trials were supposed to follow at least the spirit of Control Council Law No. 10, where the Allies dealt with crimes against peace and crimes against humanity (*Humanitätsverbrechen*).[10] Many observers realized that a mastering of the past was going to be viewed as a precondition for lasting judicial reform.

This was easier said then done because of the postwar circulation of what Robert Moeller has called the "selective remembering" of persuasive war "stories" in Germany, where audiences heard stories about the bombings at Dresden,[11] the capture of 3,000,000 soldiers by the Soviets, and the expulsion of some 12,000,000 people from Eastern Europe.[12] The Allies may have wanted them to remember the roles that perpetrators or bystanders played in the Jewish "catastrophe" and the perpetration of other Nazi war crimes, but the ideological battles of the times included fragmentary arguments about moral equivalence and relative blame.[13] This meant that members of the new postwar German judiciary had to accomplish two sometimes contradictory tasks—they needed to illustrate the existence of stable and continuous German laws that dated back to the time of the Weimar Republic, and they had to document Nazi deviations from those same foundations. All of this needed to take place at a time when the "Western [*sic*] German administration [at] all levels" was "shot through with former Nazis."[14]

Ironically, many of the ideological impediments that hindered these prosecutions came from the Allied military tribunals. Gerald Reitlinger noted in 1956 that "the [tribunal] prosecutors accepted a hypothesis which had been created before the war by German refugees, their press and their writings. According to this hypothesis the SS was a state within a state, responsible only to itself, the terror of German bureaucrats and the force that impelled them to tyranny and cruelty. Ten years of Allied war trials have not killed this view; on the contrary, they have encouraged it."[15] Even though there was a great deal of Holocaust evidence that tended to show the involvement of the "entire German bureaucracy," the first Nuremberg tribunal had avoided judging the "German nation as a whole."[16]

Yet in spite of the fact that the Konrad Adenauer government tried to keep "political or judicial action against Nazi criminals to a minimum" in the "building of a new democratic West German identity,"[17] some victims and citizens refused to believe that the Germans had mastered their past. At the same time that Israeli authorities were planning the capture and trial of Adolf Eichmann (chapter 4), former Auschwitz prisoners were demanding that Robert Mulka, Wilhelm Boger, and other prison guards at some of the major concentration camps be tried by German authorities. Critics argued that West Germany's fifteen-year statute of limitations on the crime of murder needed to be extended, or otherwise tens of thousands of alleged war criminals "would escape indictment, trial, and punishment merely by virtue of the passage of time."[18]

German officials set up the Central Office of the National Judiciary Authority for the Investigation of Nazi Crimes, and this rhetorical gesture in the late 1950s seemed to provide concrete proof that there were many members of the judiciary who understood the importance of investigating unsolved Nazi crimes. Hermann Langbein[19] helped convince the Central Office that some of the former guards could be successfully prosecuted in German courtrooms. Yet given the political and legal difficulties associated with the collection of this type of wartime material, it would take some five years before the main proceedings would begin against Mulka and twenty-one other defendants.[20] Many of these defendants were leading "normal lives under their own names for many years before they were indicted," and few of them were treated as "outcasts" by their communities.[21] Moreover, some of these Frankfurt defendants had been sentenced and pardoned by other tribunals.

Many West Germans had convinced the Allies that Nazi criminals could be convicted under ordinary German criminal codes, and eventually the use of the Allies' Law No. 10 was prohibited in German courts. This proved to be a mixed blessing for potential defendants. They were not having to hear about international crimes against humanity or peace, but they would be tried as "killers, rapists and thieves."[22] The Nazi defendants might want to talk about "political victimization," but now the Federal Republic had officials who willingly looked into cases involving deportations, medical crimes, killings by the *Einsatzgruppen,* and other types of mass murder.[23] During these early years, officials had to deal with crimes on an "unknown scale," a "chronic shortage of personnel," the loss of registry records, the lack of coordination between public prosecutorial offices, and the existence of a police force "that was not yet large enough to conduct thorough supra-regional investigations."[24]

Many Germans had ambivalent feelings about these proceedings. Some called for amnesties, while others expressed the sentiment that Justice Minister Ewald Bucher needed to halt the war crimes investigations.[25] Contemporaries often commented on the various public pronouncements of approval, hostility, resentment, or resignation that greeted these trials. Arthur Olsen gave this assessment of West German public opinion:

> The testimony of a seemingly endless line of witnesses adds only a grim degree of detail to a twice-told tale. . . . [T]he trials are not popular. They were initiated not by a political decision in Bonn nor by the pressure of public opinion, but by local law enforcement agencies. . . . Independent observers, relying on impressions obtained from public discussions, letters to newspapers and conversations, tend to agree that the West Germans' consensus is reluctant support for the distasteful prosecutions. They are accepted as an unavoidable, painful step toward "mastering the past."[26]

Public opinion polls taken in the aftermath of World War II showed that perhaps 80 percent of the German public had read newspaper accounts of the Nuremberg trials, but many scholars today would perhaps agree with Mark Osiel's claim that "only when the first postwar generation reached adulthood in the mid-1960s was the Holocaust reexamined and discussed in great depth."[27] The supposed vehicles that helped with this reexamination of the past in West Germany were the trials of the "Auschwitz guards" that purportedly "captured the imagination of millions of young Germans."[28]

By the summer of 1941, the Führer had informed Heinrich Himmler that Auschwitz was going to become a key part of the "*Endlösung* of the Jewish question,"[29] and since that time scholars, jurists, and laypersons have deliberated over the question of how to segregate out the bystanders, victims, and perpetrators of the Holocaust. Attorney General Fritz Bauer, one of the principal organizers of these proceedings, had his own views on the matter,[30] and in the fall of 1963 he would note that "Germany was not made up only of the Nazi Hitler and the Nazi Himmler. There were hundreds of thousands, millions of others, who not only carried out the 'Final Solution' because they had orders, but because it was their world view as well, which they willingly admit."[31]

Ian Buruma once observed that the "scale" of the Nuremberg trials was bigger, and the "defendants were grander," but that the "impact on most Germans of the *Auschwitz* and *Majdanek* trials" was "far greater."[32] Between 1963 and 1965, hundreds of journalists from many different nations watched as the focus of attention in these German proceedings shifted away from the Nazi leaders and toward the culpability of the aberrant Nazi soldier. More than 900 articles about the proceedings appeared in four of the major newspapers—*Die Welt, Frankfurter Allgemeine Zeitung, Frankfurter Rundschau,* and *Suddeutsche Zeitung*—and "almost every newspaper in the Federal Republic of Germany carried at least sporadic coverage of the 183 sessions."[33] Unlike some of the earlier trials that had focused attention on the social agency of the key leaders of the Nazi state, this would be a judicial forum that would look into the culpability of "small fish"—several former camp adjutants, members of the camp Gestapo, some of the medical staff, and even one "Kapo" (Emil Bednarek). One courtroom visitor who was trying to take the pulse of her compatriots astutely observed how the "entire press" seemed to be providing daily reporting of "what no one really wants to hear" and what those "who need it the most" will "not read."[34] Observers noticed that none of the defendants "had committed criminal offenses after the war," and "most had established a 'respectable middle-class' existence since then."[35] As with other Holocaust trials, there would be some audiences who refused to believe some of the evidence that would be presented in these judicial vectors of memory. Given these conflicting views, German officials had to make some key political decisions during the pretrial periods.

Germany Penal Codes, Pretrial Activities, and Key Historical Contextualizations for the Auschwitz Proceedings

In postwar Germany, many government officials realized that they had to construct a denazified jurisprudential system, and German decision makers reintroduced the pre-1939 system that included the Penal Code of 1871. Since the portions of the Penal Code that dealt with "genocide" would not be incorporated until "after the experience of the Third Reich," the only avenue for prosecution in the case of Nazi state-ordered mass murder" was through the codes that "were originally developed for the individual perpetrator."[36] The advent of new postwar prosecutions would therefore entail some complex planning, for thousands of SS troops had served at Auschwitz, and officials would question some 1,300 witnesses.[37]

Statutory penal codes were now going to be deployed that defined murder (*Mord*) as an act that could be characterized as "particularly reprehensible" (Article 211), while manslaughter (*Totschlag*) was defined in Article 212 as an intentional killing that didn't fit the definition of murder. As Friedlander explains, this meant that Nazi criminals could face murder charges in situations where there were killings for racial reasons and base motives (*niedrige Beweggründe*), where there were "cruel" killings by mass executions or gas (*Grausamkeit*), or where the use of subterfuge lured victims to their deaths in cunning ways (*Heimtücke*).[38] For example, a perpetrator who personally shared Nazi racial hatred, or who capitalized on that hatred for ulterior motives like career advancement, could be considered to be a person who "acted out of base motives."[39] At the same time, if someone knew that certain deportations were going to lead to gassing or annihilation, and they engaged in acts that facilitated those deportations, then these activities could be viewed as murderous acts.[40]

These categories get even more complicated when we realize that these 1960s German courts could even make distinctions between a murderer who might be characterized as a mere accomplice (*Gehilfe*) and a more culpable perpetrator (*Täter*). As a practical matter, as long as the defendants were conscientiously fulfilling their duty under German law, they could only be considered as accomplices and not perpetrators of crimes—regardless of the numbers of victims that might be involved.[41] To convict an accomplice, authorities had to show that a person had knowledge (by word or deed) that his or her participation was a part of the extermination process.[42] Helge Grabitz notes the importance of these subtle differences when she outlines the following scenario:

> It is true that in politically motivated and state-organized crimes, anybody who received an *Einzelbefehl* (direct personal order), such as to participate in a particular mass shooting, could not personally influence the commission of the crime in any way. Therefore, such a person will usually be convicted as an accessory. Members of police companies which were assigned to executions or to cordoning off ghettos whose inmates were to be deported for extermination may serve as an example of this.[43]

Under the new modifications that were made in the postwar penal codes, manslaughter carried a penalty of not less than five years, while a murder conviction carried more severe penalties. These distinctions, argues Friedlander, "proved particularly problematic in cases of mass killings organized and directed by the highest authorities of the state."[44]

For those observers who were interested in using the trial as a pedagogical forum for discussing both the scope and magnitude of the Holocaust, this was an infuriating way to talk about action and inaction during the Judeocide, because it meant that only those who had illustrated a high degree of personal initiative or illegal cruelty could be charged as murdering perpetrators. At the same time, these types of evidentiary requirements created situations where documents alone rarely brought convictions.[45]

By the end of the pretrial planning phase, German authorities had determined that although the official and civilian prosecutors in the Auschwitz trial could use a host of materials as they put together their cases, they would still need the eyewitness testimony. At various times during these proceedings, some 250 witnesses were invited to testify,[46] and at least one of these prosecutorial witnesses would be arrested.[47]

Some of these prosecutorial witnesses were former department chiefs who were in charge of the SS Head Office for Reich Security, and one can readily imagine how the defendants must have felt as they watched these generals and colonels enter and then exit the Frankfurt courtroom. Bernd Naumann perhaps captured some of the problematics associated with this particular narrative frame when he mentioned how these "exalted" and heroic gentlemen, who had "resided in the SS Olympus," could now leave the "courtroom head held high" as they returned to "today's bourgeois respectability."[48]

Prosecutorial Arguments Presented in the Auschwitz Trial

When these cases eventually reached the trial stage, the prosecutors—including State's Attorneys Hanns Grossmann, Joachim Kügler, Georg Vogel, and Gerhard Wiese—tried to retrace the individual culpability of each defendant. The district court would be guided by presiding judge Hans Hofmeyer, who was often characterized as a knowledgeable and stern jurist. Unlike other jurisdictions, the German court system allowed for a prosecutorial system that includes both official and civilian prosecutors. In the case of the Auschwitz trial, the civilian prosecutor, or *Nebenkläger*, is supposed to represent the interests of any injured civilian party, and that person enjoys the rights and privileges of the governmental prosecutors. At Frankfurt, there would be three different interests that would be represented by these civilian prosecutors: one representing the interests and survivors living in the German Federal Republic; another who represented those living in the German Democratic Republic;[49] and a third who represented those living abroad.[50] These trials would usually begin with the defendants taking the stand, and some of the judges would then ask them questions about their whereabouts during the selection process, the shootings, and other camp activities. The vast majority denied having any knowledge of any systematic mass murder of Jews.

Initially, prosecutors had hoped that they could charge all of the defendants as perpetrators, but by the time of the trial officials had reduced the charges against half of the defendants from *Mord* to accessory to *Mord*.[51] Given the legal challenges that were posed by the uniqueness of these German laws, the prosecutors in this case needed to show that these defendants had willingly imbibed the ideologies associated with Nazism—racism, militarism, genocidal tendencies, and so forth—and that they had internalized many of the motivations that could be defined as criminal behavior under ordinary German criminal law. For example, some of the doctors in the camps, like Franz Lucas and Willi Schatz, were said to have supervised the selection process that followed the arrival of transports. They, after all, were the ones who made the final decisions regarding who would be sent to the gas chambers, and they were the ones who supervised the introduction of Zyklon-B into these facilities.[52] Other defendants were accused of having committed random acts of brutality, violence, sadism, theft, torture, or murder. Herbert Kurz, for example, was able to talk about how Wilhelm Boger had shot at least fifty inmates near the infamous "Black Wall."[53]

From a historical or pedagogical standpoint, it is important to note that the defendants were willing to admit that there were many daily and total deaths in Auschwitz, but they vehemently defended their individual treatment of these prisoners as acts that were tied to the war effort—they were guarding soldiers, would-be terrorists, political troublemakers, and antisocial types who threatened the health of the German nation. The defendants crafted dissident narratives that underscored the shortages of food, medicine, and adequately trained personnel, and several claimed that the constant arrival of prisoner transports simply overwhelmed what could have been an orderly camp system. With the advent of war, a witness like Karl Höcker could explain that this area was really three camps—Auschwitz I, Auschwitz II (Birkenau), and Auschwitz III (Monowitz and other labor camps), and that "the prisoner compound was closed to the camp staff except members of its guard unit."[54]

During this early questioning period, many defendants denied any involvement in the selection process at the railroad ramps, and there was little mention of any executions at the Black Wall. Karl Höcker perhaps expressed the mood of many of his companions at this stage when he admitted that he was horrified by the smell of the gas chambers, and that "many SS officers tried to think of ways to help. But we did not have the means."[55] Pery Broad, who had been assigned to the Political Section of the camp, observed through a window how SS men with gas masks opened some containers and poured the contents through the roof of the Old Crematory.[56] These types of admissions helped establish the facticity of the Holocaust, but the bureaucratic nature of the Auschwitz system also created an atmosphere where functionaries could advance a host of arguments that deflected blame.

Given the legal importance of proving the pernicious impact of Nazi ideology on the human will, we can see why prosecutors asked so many questions about this topic, and the defendants provided the court with mixed messages about their party allegiances and their beliefs regarding military or legal duty. When Judge Hofmeyer reminded Pery Broad that the evidence tended to show that only 10 percent of the Auschwitz I prisoners escaped the gassings, the defendant admitted that under these circumstances the detentions in the camp were not legal.[57] Klaus Dylewski, a relatively young interrogation officer, opined that the orders that he received were legal, and that other officers like Grabner had told him that they were going to take responsibility for some of the shootings.[58] During one of these early courtroom question-and-answer sessions, Robert Mulka was asked why he thought that the Jews were brought to Auschwitz, and he replied that camp officers "wanted to rid the German Reich of Jews."[59] Few of the defendants showed any sign of contrition.

After these initial introductions of the defendants, the Auschwitz trial moved to a second phase, where the experts of the Munich Institute for Contemporary History provided the court with their historical findings. This group was asked to comment on the composition and structure of the Nazi bureaucracy.[60] Four German historians—Helmut Krausnick, Hans Buchheim, Martin Broszat, and Hans-Adolph Jacobsen—put together what they believed to be a dispassionate "statement" that chronicled the historical events that led to the Judeocide.[61] All of them wrote their own sections—Krausnick would write on social Darwinism and the early years of the prosecution of the Jews, Buchheim focused on the power of Nazi ideology and structure of the SS, and Martin Broszat provided illuminating commentary on life in the concentration camps between 1933 and 1945. Jacobsen's contributions recorded how some Nazis carried out mass executions of Soviet prisoners of war. These four historians defended an introduction that explained that sober work, common sense, and the "rationalism of the historian" could take the place of "moralistic emotional theorizing."[62] This jibe was perhaps aimed at more theological or metaphysical explanations for the Holocaust.

These types of logistical and philosophical assumptions apparently influenced the pretrial chronological planning of the German authorities as they prepared for the Auschwitz trial. Many officials must have agreed with the historians' argument that "contrary to normal Court procedure," those attending the Frankfurt forum needed to "hear experts *before* the witnesses," because that would provide "a better factual background" to the court when it measured the "witnesses' statements."[63] While they understood the importance of determining individual guilt or innocence, they shared the views of those who wanted more out of this trial:

> Actual violations of the law must not be allowed to become lost in general philosophizing about being caught in the toils of fate and carried into a crime. No right-thinking person whose sense of right and wrong has not been warped can declare a man innocent if he has murdered thousands of defenceless human beings, no matter whether or not he can cite an order bidding him to do so. In other words we are concerned not so much with the details of what the SS did but with the question of how an instrument of power such as that formed by the combination of the SS and the police could arise, and how it functioned.[64]

George Mosse later explained that the work of these four historians shows that "the Nazi prosecution of the Jews started slowly and took time to accelerate," but he worried that these authors were slighting the role that the German history of anti-Semitism played in the Holocaust.[65]

This type of functionalist approach could help contextualize some of the events that had taken place in the recent past, but the events created dilemmas for prosecutors who were trying to delineate the intentionalist motivations of individual defendants. Moreover, these historians perhaps realized that the notion of collective guilt could become a two-edged sword—it could be used to extend lists of possible perpetrators who needed to be tried in German courtrooms, but it could also be used as a way of avoiding responsibility—if millions were guilty, then why pick on the "small fish"?

Given the magnitude of the Holocaust, and the intentionalist requirements that were built into the German code, we can see how moving toward the third phase of the trial—where hundreds of witnesses took center stage—complicated matters for all of the parties. While the defendants had talked about the ravages of typhus epidemics and the occasional abuse of Nazi power, the former detainees talked about the daily commission of hundreds of war crimes. Dr. Otto Wolken, a sixty-year-old physician, was the first survivor who testified, and he explained how the Auschwitz death reports covered up the real causes of "departures" and illnesses. Early on in his oral commentary, he indicated that the atmosphere in the camps was constantly changing, but that there were some "SS men who could not sleep well unless they had beaten some men during the day."[66] Wolken was perhaps chosen as the first witness because of his exceptional memory, and he could document how hundreds of men, women, and children arrived on the seemingly endless transports. Yet when Wolken was asked to identify some of the almost two-dozen defendants, he only remembered one name—Stefan Baretzki.

Other defendants had different experiences, and some of them could walk across the courtroom and reel off the names of many of the defendants and their alleged crimes. Erwin Olszówka, for example, walked by the defendants, and correctly identified Oswald Kaduk, Herbert Scherpe, Josef Klehr, Hans Stark, Klaus Dylewski, Franz Johann Hofmann, and Boger. This particular witness provided some potential damaging testimony when he argued that some of Boger's acts were arbitrary, in that they took place without any order from Berlin. Olszówka was willing to say under oath that Boger shot dozens of prisoners on a daily basis.[67]

The act of witnessing often became a performative activity for these former detainees, who could now confront their former tormenters. Paul Leo Scheidel, a business executive working in Munich, testified that he saw the defendant Boger actually shoot three prisoners at the Black Wall. This witness showed the court a replica of the devilish "Boger swing," a torture instrument that was used to physically break hundreds of prisoners. Brieden, a fifty-year-old witness from Stuttgart, testified that he had been tortured by the former SS Oberscharführer, and he recalled how Boger had once pointed at the chimney of the crematory and said: "That's the only way you will get your freedom again."[68]

Several of these former Auschwitz inmates could also name names when it came to the question of who actually was involved in the gassing and cremation process. Walter Petzold told the court that Arthur Breitwieser was one of the SS soldiers who actually put the Zyklon-B pellets into the basement windows of Block 11,[69] and this particular defendant swore that he witnessed the first mass killing of 1,000 individuals in Auschwitz I.[70] Erich Kulka remembered that on March 7, 1944, a transport carrying more than 5,000 people arrived from Therensienstadt, and that only 14 had survived the gassings. Even more incredible was the fact that he had obtained a photograph album filled with pictures of Auschwitz. He testified that he personally knew Boger and Baretzki, and that they—along with Dr. Victor Capesius, Broad, Kaduk, and Mulka—were involved in the ramp selections.[71]

Yet this third stage of the proceeding was also filled with a series of prosecutorial mishaps that might have helped the defense's cause. Some of the witnesses misidentified the defendants, admitted lapses of memory, presented contradictory testimony, and magnified the numbers of atrocities that were supposedly perpetrated by some of the defendants. For example, when Dr. Czeslaw Glowacki accused Klehr of killing more than 10,000 people, Klehr asked Judge Hofmeyer how he could have "injected 16,000 people when in all of Auschwitz I had only 16,000 prisoners. That would have left only the band."[72] When some of the defendants heard these types of remarks, they were allegedly "laughing, smiling, smirking impertinence."[73]

These types of sarcastic remarks didn't help the defense positions, but the defendants did get modest help from some of the SS witnesses who testified for the various sides. Former doctors could talk about wartime conditions, and former soldiers couldn't identify individual culprits. For example, Albert Stenzel, who worked in Auschwitz as a guard and then as an instructor, claimed that he knew nothing about any crematory. When

State's Attorney Kügler intimated that he might need to start proceedings for false testimony, Stenzel admitted that although these things happened "pretty long ago," it was "possibly" true that people were gassed in the Old Crematory. This witness claimed that he never heard about anyone named "Boger." Otto Vollrath testified that Rudolf Hoess, and not Mulka, signed motor pool transportation orders.[74]

In June 1964, heated exchanges took place between the prosecutorial and defense staffs when one of the civilian prosecutors, Henry Ormond, requested that the Frankfurt court actually inspect the surviving Auschwitz site. Six months later many of the court participants journeyed to Poland, and some 200 journalists followed the participants as they tried to historically reconstruct these Nazi pasts.[75] Franz Lucas would be the only defendant who willingly took part in this trip to Auschwitz.

Naumann would record that on this trip, the visitors could see the wooden lids on the roofs of the Old Crematory, and that the whitewashed room appeared to be "barely fifteen feet wide and sixty feet long." Court participants could then take the path to the Political Section building and go past the gallows "on which Camp Commander" Hoess was "hanged on April 16, 1947." Some two decades after these events, the tall chimney towers were still standing, although there was no "lorry squeaking over the iron thresholds with its sorry load."[76] In the name of objectivity, the Ministry of Justice had officers who measured distances, used hearing tests, and surveyed the corridors and buildings. In January 1965, the court read into the record the inspection report of Judge Walter Hotz, and now audiences could see some of the thirty-seven photographs that provided visual evidence of the Block 11 prison cells.[77] At this stage in the proceedings, few questioned the ontological existence of the Holocaust or the magnitude of the Judeocide—the issues here were centered around the apportionment of blame.

The judges now had to take into account conflicting views on the causes of the horrific conditions at Auschwitz, and they had to make decisions about the credibility of key witnesses. The prosecutors buttressed their claims with evidence that came from footprints, postmortem reports, and pretrial testimony, but they soon discovered that many of the defense arguments attacked the credibility of many of the prosecutorial witnesses. For example, the defense claimed that some of the testimony that came from Polish witnesses had been doctored by governmental agencies in Warsaw, and that the former Kapo or Ukrainian witnesses were trying to save their own necks. At other times the defense argued that some of the

Jewish witnesses were being coached by members of the International Auschwitz Committee in Vienna.[78]

Court observers were therefore left with a number of alternative wartime scenarios. Pendas contends that this latter phase of the trial was

> marked by a series of ongoing conflicts which reflected the dual struggle at work in the trial to determine both the juridical outcome and its representational meaning. The most important of these conflicts were: first, the incongruity of interspersing SS and survivor testimony; second, the conflict between what the witnesses wanted to say and what the court needed them to say; and third, the political tension surrounding the testimony of East Bloc witnesses.[79]

At the same time, we need to remember that even reliable witnesses may have suffered some traumatic experiences when they were asked to reflect on their own Auschwitz experiences. As Hannah Arendt explained, the survivors fell into "two very different groups—those who survived by sheer luck, which in effect meant holding an inside job in [an] office, hospital, or kitchen, and those who, in the words of one of them, had understood immediately that 'only a few could be saved and I was going to be among them.'"[80]

In many ways, the combined efforts of the pretrial investigators and the prosecutorial staffs helped with the establishment of prima facie cases against specific defendants, but this focus on microcosmic individual acts didn't always paint a complete picture of the complexities of life in the Auschwitz camps. This particular trial, which focused on the agency of individual prison guards, obfuscated the roles that visiting doctors, truck drivers, chemical manufacturers, higher echelon SS officers, Wehrmacht soldiers, or ordinary citizens played in various Auschwitz dramas. Moreover, as we shall see in the next section, this focus on individual culpability meant that the defense teams could offer their own restrictive frameworks for analyzing the Holocaust.

A Rhetorical Analysis of Some of the Defense Positions Presented during the Auschwitz Trial

The twenty defendants who took center stage in this Auschwitz drama were represented by thirteen lawyers,[81] who for more than a year and a half filled the Frankfurt courtroom with commentary on this German court's lack of jurisdiction, the fallibility of twenty-year-old memories, the alleged prejudice that came from Communist witnesses, and the fragmentary nature of experiential evidence. Given the horrific nature of the Holocaust, and the emotional baggage associated with these atrocities, the defense attorneys in this case—led by Hans Laternser—tried to present themselves as objective officers of the court who wanted to focus exclusive attention on the personal guilt of each of the defendants. In many ways, they tried to take advantage of some of the rhetorical tensions that were circulating within the broader public sphere, where outside observers differentiated between Nazi adherents and German citizens. In the words of Robert Woetzel, the Federal Republic of Germany needed "to repudiate not only the individual murderers but any continuity between itself and the regime which represented what Karl Jaspers called the 'criminal state' (*Verbrecherstaat*)."[82] Yet the very existence of this extrajudicial goal—collective repudiation—threatened the procedural safeguards that were supposed to be respected in objective German courtrooms. Dr. Rainer Eggert, one of the defense attorneys, told audiences that in this trial, "the scope of the crimes threatens to overwhelm the question of individual guilt."[83]

Besides the usual jurisdictional arguments and claims that were made about the insufficiency of prosecutorial evidence, there were basically three major defense contentions that were advanced throughout these proceedings: the defendants lacked the requisite knowledge about the Holocaust that would have turned them into murderous perpetrators; if the defendants did engage in any reprehensible acts, it was because they were following "superiors' orders"; and if any of the defendants had been involved in the "selection" process, this *saved* at least some lives that would have been lost anyway.

Given the importance of individual motivations in these proceedings, it should come as no surprise that many of the defendants argued that they knew very little about the daily Auschwitz operations. Pendas reports that at one time during the proceedings, the lead defendant, Robert Mulka, averred that he "didn't know what Auschwitz was."[84] Mulka argued that he never heard shots during any executions and that he never set foot inside the gates surrounding the gas chambers. Pery Broad similarly argued that he new nothing about the gassings, that he knew nothing about the selections that were made in the camps, and that he hadn't heard about the lethal injections administered by members of the Political Section of the camp.[85] As these denials piled up, presiding judge Hofmeyer couldn't help leaving us this incredulous interjection—"No one did anything [at Auschwitz]. . . . The commandant was not there, the officer in charge only happened to be present, the representative of the Political Section only carried lists, and still another one came with the keys."[86] Naumann, who provided one of the most detailed discussions of the trial, would later aver that "if one listens" to some of the defendants' claims, "a mere four men—apart from Hitler and the top leadership—were responsible for the murder machinery of Auschwitz—Ho[e]ss, Aumeier, Schwarz, and Grabner."[87]

After hearing the prosecutorial evidence, German audiences appeared to have been left with many different characterizations of these SS functionaries. Broad, for example, had once provided British occupation forces with a very detailed description of the Auschwitz camp, and during his pretrial examination he was described as "communicative" when he admitted that he had shot at least one person and felt "relieved" by his arrest. Later on, witnesses at the trial characterized him as "death in kid gloves," a "clever, intelligent, and cunning" guard who took pleasure in his work.[88] He could therefore be configured as a tragic figure in the prosecutorial narratives, a bright German twisted by Nazi ideologies. The defense tried to counter these impressions by humanizing the defendants, and several witnesses did testify that some guards performed acts of human kindness. The very arbitrariness of the system created unusual situations and unpredictable twists. Denial of the larger macroscopic aspects of the Judeocide existed alongside some acknowledgment of smaller microscopic deeds.

Yet the lack of knowledge about the Holocaust was not the only, or even primary, defense that would be presented at the Auschwitz trial. The most popular arguments of the defense appeared in rhetorical narratives that underscored the importance of martial hierarchies and soldierly obedience. SS officers took pride in performing their duty, and some of the defendants appeared to be bewildered when their civilian audiences didn't recognize the importance of maintaining order in Hitler's Germany.

Hans Buchheim, one of the historians who prepared statements for the German prosecutors, would write that in "the Third Reich sovereignty and political power rested with" the "Reichsführer, not the state."[89] "Hitler's word had been law," noted Mark Osiel, "not merely in the realistic sense that his orders were followed as if they were law, but in that the Führer principle made his word the formal foundation of all legal authority."[90] Given the fact that none of the defendants could claim any special knowledge of German law or international diplomacy, they could advance the argument that they did not know that illegal orders didn't have to be carried out. Moreover, they could argue that they didn't know that they could have transferred out of Auschwitz with relative impunity. The problem with this "little-man theory," of course, is that it brought together two smaller and yet potentially inconsistent subclaims—that the defendants had been forced to do what they did, and that they didn't always think that it was wrong to do what they did.[91]

Many of the defendants tried to characterize themselves as luckless individuals who just happened to have ended up at Auschwitz.[92] Franz Hofmann told the court that he had joined the SS in mid-1932 for "business reasons," while Robert Mulka volunteered for the Waffen SS because he was denied entry into the Wehrmacht officer corps. Hans Stark talked about the influence of a stern Prussian father who taught him the importance of firm guidance, and he told his listeners in this Frankfurt courtroom that the SS was one of the few organizations that would take sixteen-year-old recruits.[93] Several other defendants told tragic tales about medical infirmities that made them unfit for front-line duty.

Within these narratives of the defense, camps that had once housed political prisoners had been turned into chaotic detention centers, where many soldiers became casualties of war. One of these defendants, Dr. Franz Lucas, tried to claim that when he heard about the gas chambers, he contacted his superior officer about a possible transfer and was told that "orders were orders." Lucas was informed that during this "fifth year of the war," his old unit was being disbanded.[94] One former inmate, Zygmunt Gawlowski, actually sent a telegram asking the court to believe that Dr. Lucas had saved his life when he was imprisoned at the camp in 1942.[95]

Some of these defendants obviously hoped that they could minimize their own social agency. Josef Klehr, who admitted that he had helped administer some lethal injections, had this to say in his defense: "Your Honor, let me describe the general situation to you. I was in a straitjacket. Who were we to say anything? We were ciphers, just like the prisoners. In his [the medical officer's] eyes a man without a higher education was nothing. We couldn't possibly dare to ask such questions, or else we too would have been put against the Black Wall."[96]

These types of class-based or hierarchal arguments may have resonated with some contemporary audiences, but they did not help at Nuremberg, and they were still considered to be problematic among reformers in the mid-1960s. "In general," notes Grabitz, "necessity to obey orders" was not an effective defense in many of the Nazi trial cases, because "assisting in the commission of murder" was not viewed as an "appropriate means of averting danger."[97] Defendants may have wanted to talk about inflexible superiors or a force majeure situation, but the binding effects of these military orders were supposed to be limited to matters of police or military activities. The defendants were caught in a situation where their camp behaviors could be configured as nonmilitary activities—here they were hurting defenseless citizens.[98] The prosecutors noted that even if the defendants had received some types of orders from above, these didn't include written orders about the "rabbit chase," the use of the infamous "Boger swing," the punishments administered with "standing cells," or the random shootings that were a part of everyday life at Auschwitz.[99]

In theory, a person who unknowingly walked into a murderous situation, and believed that disobedience would bring death, might try to use this type of defense, but prosecutors and other observers frequently noted that individuals could often transfer (and occasionally did transfer) to other units with minimal consequences. The existence of a chain of command did not obviate the need for personal choice and responsibility. Ormond, for example, commented on the potential usage of some of these hierarchal defenses when he characterized this as the "myth of having acted on superior orders."[100]

These court commentaries on Nazi command and compliance must have provided some of the most embarrassing moments in these proceedings for the German jurists, because the defense could imply that many of the civil servants in the courtroom had also followed the edicts of the Nazi regime. Laternser, for example, pointed out that if German law demanded that soldiers and citizens not follow unlawful Nazi edicts, then why didn't the prosecutors in earlier periods take action "against flagrant violations of the law, like the destruction of Jewish businesses and dwellings in November, 1938, the murder of [the] mentally retarded, and finally the murder of Jews? Hadn't the prosecution known at the time that these were crimes? Which judge or state's attorney at the time had protested, let alone resigned?"[101]

This defensive posture at least had some plausibility, especially when we take into account some of the defense's weaker arguments.

Defense Arguments Claiming That the Selection Process Saved Lives

Given the fact that multiple prosecutorial witnesses could testify to the fact that many of the defendants were involved in at least part of the "selection" process at Auschwitz ramps, the defense had to try and find some legal arguments that might help explain or justify these decisions. Some defendants argued that they suffered nervous illnesses or drank excessively, and many claimed that they were ashamed. Mulka, for example, openly proclaimed that "special treatment was murder," and that "he was deeply incensed" when he found out about these activities.[102] Willi Frank similarly remarked that he considered "what was happening to be monstrous."[103] Yet few of them did anything to slow down or stop the extermination process.

Given these types of arguments, and the legal difficulties associated with proving *Mord,* one might think that the defendants might have put together coherent narratives that deflected attention away from themselves, but perhaps given the circumstances, this was too much to ask. At both the pretrial and trial stages, many of the defendants sabotaged their own cases when they started attacking each other's defenses. For example, when Kaduk found out that Mulka had been released on bail while undergoing interrogation, he told his listeners that the other officers had been on those selection ramps, and that they looked ridiculous when they denied that fact.[104] He also claimed that Boger, Frank, and Broad had gone to the Black Wall with pistols. These types of arguments resembled some of the earlier claims that appeared in texts written by Rudolf Hoess, who blamed both the *Reichsführer SS* (Himmler) and his poorly trained guards for the creation of conditions that made him unhappy.[105]

On the 182nd day of the proceedings, Judge Hofmeyer finally announced the opinion of the court. He and the other two judges stood as he read out the sentences. They announced that three of the Auschwitz trial defendants deserved to be acquitted (Breitwieser, Dr. Schatz, and Schobert), that twelve defendants were accessories to *Mord* (Baretzki, Boger, Broad, Dr. Capesius, Dylewski, Dr. Frank, Hantl, Höcker, Klehr, Dr. Lucas, Mulka, Schlage), and that six had committed *Mord* (Baratzki, Boger, Hofmann, Kaduk, Klehr, and Stark). Six of the defendants—including a former Kapo—were sentenced to life in prison, while eleven others received sentences ranging from three to twenty years.[106]

Some critics would later point out that many of these sentences appeared to have been tied to legal frameworks that privileged atrocity tales over genocidal stories in the narration of Auschwitz pasts. Hofmann, for example, would be the only defendant who would be convicted as a perpetrator for his role in the selections at the ramp, and the court seemed to have accepted at least some of Laternser's arguments that had focused on the limited social agency of the defendants once the *Reichssicherheitshauptamt* (RSHA) transports arrived at the Auschwitz facilities.[107] Those who received the harshest sentences were characterized as weak, brutal, sadistic, and politically motivated individuals who disobeyed the German laws that governed camp behavior. These distinctions meant that the "government did the work of *Vergangenheitsbewaltigung* (mastering the past) for its citizens."[108]

As I note below, there would be observers who categorically defended or attacked many aspects of the Frankfurt decisions, but a more nuanced rhetorical approach would see these decisions as negotiated legal compromises that melded together some of the intentionalist and functionalist arguments of both the prosecutors and the defense attorneys. On the one hand, the court accepted the prosecutorial and civil counsels' positions on the defendants' knowledge of the illegality of their acts and the excessiveness of many of their personal acts. On the other hand, Hofmeyer and the other judges seemed to have also been persuaded that either wartime conditions or superior orders helped create determinist conditions that undermined the potential social agency of individual defendants. The prosecutorial witnesses may have helped prove that a particular person was present at the Black Wall or at the Auschwitz ramp, but without sufficient evidence of any base motive, he would be considered an accomplice, and not a perpetrator, of *Mord*. In many ways, the Frankfurt court seemed to have shared the defense's skepticism regarding the testimony of former victims—a stance that resembled the earlier Nuremberg tribunals' privileging of documentary[109] over testimonial evidence. In the end, as Pendas so insightfully points out, the same bad act that might be tied to the killing of thousands could be interpreted in two ways—depending on whether a person was constructed as a "good German" who simply followed orders (an accomplice) or a "bad Nazi" who went overboard and became a perpetrator.[110] These legal ambivalences clearly mirrored the truncated and selective memories of German complicity during the Judeocide, where German citizens would recognize both the victimage of the camp detainees and the psychological and physical scarring of the guards and the other Germans who were caught up in the Nazi maelstrom.

Regardless of how one felt about the causes of the war or the conditions in the camps, there is little question that participation in these court proceedings must have been a traumatic affair. One witness recalled that Judge Hofmeyer's voice grew "louder and louder" as he read his summation, and "that the audience swelled to thousands upon thousands" as they heard these words: "And now, beyond these judgments so pronounced, I sentence all those here who were of age in 1933—and I include myself—to be confined for life in moral prison; for each of us has helped, be it by blindness or inadequate resistance, to bring about conditions such as have made criminals of all of these weaklings."[111] Perhaps the jurists sensed that even their protracted trial was only providing them a small sliver of a much larger and totalizing picture of mayhem and destruction. Would contemporary and future generations share Hofmeyer's views on the importance of this "moral prison"?

National and International Remembrances of the "Lessons" of the Auschwitz Trial

While some contemporary members of the German press trumpeted the pedagogical and social significance of these trials, many other observers believed that "the trials by the German courts merely represented a continuation of denazification under another name."[112] As noted above, many German audiences had been opposed to these proceedings when they first began,[113] and few changed their minds when they heard about the decisions of the district court. This did not sit well with intellectuals who worried about the rhetorical status of German "public opinion." An obviously exasperated Arendt averred:

> Exposure for twenty months to the monstrous deeds and the grotesquely unrepentant, aggressive behavior of the defendants, who more than once almost succeeded in turning the trial into a farce, had no impact on this climate of public opinion, although the proceedings were well covered by German newspapers and radio stations. . . . This came to light during the heated debates in the first months of 1965—in the midst of the *Auschwitz* proceedings— . . . when even Bonn's Minister of Justice, Mr. Bucher, pleaded that the murderers among us "be left in peace."[114]

The use of the German penal code of 1871 may have provided the appearance of jurisprudential continuity, but it couldn't provide all of the symbolic tools that were needed for dealing with administrative massacres. Naumann had to admit that "neither the judges nor the jury found the truth—in any event, not the whole truth."[115]

The hundreds of witnesses who testified at the Auschwitz trial received a warmer reception when their arguments were recycled in countless national and international press outlets. They became social agents who performed their pedagogical roles both inside and outside the courtrooms, and hundreds of newspapers quoted their accounts of life in concentration, labor, and extermination camps. While the liberals in West Germany (especially the German Social Democratic Party) adopted a "didactic" moralistic critical framework that focused on how the suffering of the witnesses supported anti-Nazism, their more conservative counterparts underscored the "inviolability of the *Rechtsstaat*."[116] Ordinary citizens could therefore choose from a number of different postwar frameworks. In a letter to one of her friends written in May 1964, Emmi Bonhoeffer observed:

> [W]e have been entertaining the witnesses only after the hearings are over. When weather permits we go on walks with them, show them the town or whatever may interest them. . . . What the friendliness, trust, and gratitude on the part of the witnesses toward us really means is something one can grasp only if one realizes over and over again what they lived through in Auschwitz. There, at least two and a half million people were gassed, shot, or killed by injection; or they starved to death in stand-up cells, or died of typhus. Some sixty thousand have survived, a chance which was given primarily to doctors, medics, and linguists, who were useful as interpreters and scribes, or to indoor craftsmen, who were essential to the maintenance of the camp and its personnel. These were the "privileged."[117]

Scholars and news writers who lived through this period have also left us the tracings of their memories of these controversial proceedings. For those who ruminated about the legal and historical importance of the Auschwitz trials, this seemed to be a time when the Federal Republic had indeed mastered the past, and when at least some Germans had totally rejected the tenets of the German state.[118] Naumann, who covered the trial for the *Frankfurter Allgemeine Zeitung*, was convinced that the Frankfurt court was "not an assembly of angels of vengeance." In his mind, it should have been viewed as "a legally constituted body charged with searching out the facts and meting out punishment within the limits prescribed by the law."[119] Helmut Krausnick, Hans Buchheim, Martin Broszat, and Hans-Adolf Jacobsen provided an alternative perspective in their *Anatomy of the SS State*, where they reminded critics of these proceedings that these trials involved both the "task of meting out justice for wrong committed" and the "connection between political tyranny and ideological crime."[120] Yes, it might be true that the historians who were involved in the case were not necessarily concerned with the "guilt or innocence" of any particular individual, but the fact that the court had heard the "experts before the witnesses" helped provide a "better factual background" for the measurement of the "witness' statements."[121]

Yet as Ian Buruma has observed, this mastering of the past had to be handled with "a certain amount of discretion":

> The problem was how to turn millions of former Nazi supporters into loyal citizens in a liberal democracy. . . . [T]he Bogers, the Mulkas, and the Dr. Capesiuses were accused, albeit twenty years after the war, and their reaction was often one of indignation. "Why me?" they would say. "I just did my duty. I just followed orders like every decent German. Why must I be punished?" . . . A trial can only be concerned with individual crimes. . . . History is reduced to criminal pathology and legal argument. . . . Which is not to say that the trials were wrong. But they will not do as history lessons, nor do they bring us closer to that elusive thing . . . a German identity.[122]

Even Krausnick, Buchheim, Broszat, and Jacobsen had to admit that some segments of the German public would continue to believe that "these crimes were the work of a misguided body of men who had no place in the main stream of Germany history of the period."[123]

From a rhetorical vantage point, observers could admit that genocidal acts had taken place, but the blame could be placed on the "desk" murderers who transferred Hitler's orders and sent them down the chain of command to the unfortunate "small fry," represented by the Auschwitz defendants. Leon Poliakov explained that "thanks to the methods used at Auschwitz as well as in the other extermination camps, only a few dozen officials actually saw and lent a hand to the extermination process proper. The *Sonderkommandos,* composed of prisoners, served the crematories; a handful of SS men and a few doctors constituted the German personnel. It was a factory working with great efficiency on the assembly line principle. 'I have never personally killed or struck anybody,' [Rudolf] Hoess could state."[124]

Citizens and scholars who read the press accounts of the trial could not help but notice that in some of these cases, one's class and court demeanor influenced the ways that critics wrote about the blameworthiness of certain individuals. For example, Dr. Lucas, one of the defendants, apparently showed the Frankfurt court some deference, didn't insult witnesses, and was praised by several witnesses for his kindness and help. Arendt even claimed that she didn't "quite understand why" he was "there at all."[125] Yet even she acknowledged that the evidence tended to show that he may have been on the selection ramps that separated the able-bodied personnel from the doomed.

The passage of time has not reduced the intensity of the debates that have taken place over the pedagogical importance of the Frankfurt trials, but it has altered the trajectory of the arguments that are used in more modern commentaries on these proceedings. Fewer commentators would remember the names of the witnesses or the defendants, but there were still many debates about the formalistic rules that governed the standards of criminality in the case. Some critics recalled the judicial difficulties associated with proving individual culpability, the low conviction rates, the social costs of these affairs, and the reductionist framing of the Holocaust. Helga Grabitz, who was convinced that these trials were needed so that the "grandchildren's generation" could confront the Holocaust, responded to these lamentations by noting that "such arguments deliberately ignore the punitive purpose of a conviction."[126] At a time when Holocaust denial was in the air, and German citizens were watching the rise of neo-Nazi parties, these trials represented "at least attempts not to let the horrible German past fade into oblivion."[127] Trying to conduct these types of proceedings at this late date might even bring the risk that some of the witnesses might feel traumatized as they recalled these horrific events, but these participants needed to realize the transcendent pedagogical importance of ensuring that the "German people" didn't file "the Holocaust away in history books as a regrettable industrial accident and [move] on to business as usual."[128] In theory, moving away from even a flawed intentionalist framework would mean that too many perpetrators would slip through the legal nets.

By the time that international scholars began studying the public celebrations associated with the fiftieth anniversary of the Allied liberation of Auschwitz, pundits were once again taking the pulse of the German people and recorded some of the enduring pedagogical lessons that were associated with those earlier 1960s trials. In many ways, supporters of modern trials and tribunals of war criminals could look back with nostalgic longing for a time when another generation seemed to understand the symbolic and legal significance of holding the Nuremberg and the Auschwitz trials. Gordon Craig, writing in 1994, was sure that the earlier effect of these types of proceedings "upon the public consciousness was devastating" and had "not diminished."[129] Six years later, Gary Jonathan Bass asserted that "many" former West Germans saw the Auschwitz trial as a "necessary way of focusing attention on the Holocaust in a way Nuremberg had not."[130] Bass goes on to explain that

> according to sophisticated polling by the American occupation authorities, about two-thirds of Germans in the American zone supported Nuremberg, and half thought that all the defendants were guilty.[131] But many Germans

> were distracted by the ruin of their country and the shock of defeat. As time went on, German distaste for war crimes trials grew. Four years after Nuremberg, only 38 percent of German respondents in the American zone thought well of subsequent trials. By 1949, many Germans disapproved of American trials of industrialists and senior military men.[132] . . . West Germany's own trials for Auschwitz . . . helped drive home German guilt, but only after a new postwar West German generation had come to the fore.[133]

Other modern observers who have looked back through the mists of time have not been so charitable when they studied the ideological impact of the Frankfurt trials. Lawrence Langer, who personally visited some of these courtrooms in the summer of 1964, opined:

> Readers of the proceedings of the so-called Auschwitz trial of former camp guards that ran for 20 months . . . will discover not a narrative leading to insight and understanding but a futile dispute between the accusers and accused. The prisoners in the dock denied virtually everything. Mulka was not there when the prosecution says he was; Kaduk never shot anyone; Boger only used his infamous torture instrument, the "Boger swing," on rare occasions; Klehr was on leave during Christmas 1942, when he was charged with murdering inmates by injecting phenol into their hearts. Guilt exists, but the agent is always someone else. Little in this bizarre courtroom drama leads to a unified vision of the place we call Auschwitz. Scenes remain episodic and anecdotal; scenarios never coalesce; characters stay vague, so protagonists dissolve into helpless victims . . . while antagonists collapse into mistaken identities or innocent puppets maneuvered from afar.[134]

Langer was perhaps highlighting what some critics were missing—that there is a difference between establishing the facticity of the Holocaust and controlling the master narratives that are told about the nature and scope of these facts. Those observers who saw the complementary nature of the Auschwitz and Nuremberg trials may have gotten some satisfaction that both big and small fish had been put on trial, but the fragmentary and individualist frameworks that had to be used in these trials may have inadvertently contributed to the trivialization of the Holocaust.

The Politics of Pedagogical Lessons

In sum, I argue that the rhetorical nature of the Auschwitz proceedings may indeed have taught some pedagogical lessons, but that scholars and other audiences won't always be pleased with the political framing of those lessons. In many ways, those observers interested in any critical assessments of the Auschwitz trial would have to admit that it brought mixed results. On the one hand, the very idea that German authorities were willing to try dozens of German citizens for ordinary crimes that were committed during the Nazi era provided the Allies with some solace that their denazification efforts were not a total failure, and that at least some members of the West German judiciary understood the importance of contrition. Some of the defendants had received life sentences for their treatment of Jews and other "inferiors," and there were indications that these types of trials would be conducted for at least another decade.

Yet Allied satisfaction with these trials has to be tempered with the realization that the inherent polysemic nature of legal proceedings facilitated selective remembrance of Auschwitz, and that audiences could acknowledge that gassings took place without acknowledging either the uniqueness of the Judeocide or the functional nature of this catastrophe. Dr. Otto Wolken, one of the first witnesses for the prosecutors, told the Frankfurt court that before he gave his testimony, he wanted to correct the mistaken notion that "Auschwitz" was only "a Jewish affair." He wanted to highlight the fact that non-Jews—members of other religions and nationalities—were also "brutally mistreated and gassed."[135] As noted above, the demonization of guards like Mulka or Boger meant the dissociation of Germans from Nazis, or humane Nazis from brutal Nazis. Within some of the dominant narratives that circulated in the 1950s and 1960s, a rational and normal person—who may have been involved in the killing of tens of thousands of individuals—was not automatically viewed as a perpetrator or murderer.

Some modern critics have argued that the inadequacy of the legal definitions in the German criminal code helps us understand the reasons for the leniency of these decisions, but even the strictest of formalistic rules had to be applied in a cultural atmosphere that was filled with political tensions and conflicting wartime memories. The German judiciary was having to negotiate a treacherous terrain—they had to display their objectivity and diligence to the Allied audiences, and at the same time they needed to avoid narrations that implicated the ordinary soldier or civilian caught up in the fog of war.

Given the polysemic nature of all legal trials, there are many different didactic lessons that can come from the presses or publics that visit these proceedings, and in this particular situation the Auschwitz trial could be characterized as just another political or show trial, another act that illustrated the continuing victimage of Germans who had now survived both a world war and an occupation. As Arendt once observed, "the majority of the German people" had no "enthusiasm" for these proceedings—the very "big fish" got away, the defendants hadn't volunteered for duty in Auschwitz, and there were other "desk" murderers who were the real parties "responsible for the main crime committed in the camp, the extermination of millions of people through gas."[136] Hans Buchheim similarly observed:

> For the extermination of the Jews, for instance, the substantive order was issued by Hitler and Himmler passed it on through non-official channels to certain selected SS commanders, involving ideological considerations as the basis of their duty to obey; the deportation of the condemned Jews, however, necessitated certain auxiliary measures which had to be taken by official state institutions, such as finance offices, the railways, etc.[137]

Yet any trial of these "desk" murderers or other civil servants may have opened up a Pandora's box filled with politically explosive questions. Even Bernd Naumann thought that he needed to remark that "the attempt at expiation" was "not commensurable" with the "criminal facts." "Neither the planners, the assistants, the murders, nor the victims" could "hope to find ultimate justice in a regular court of a legal state."[138] Those criminals who received the harshest punishments were those individuals who were characterized as irrational violators of many German laws—including the Nazi regulations of the 1940s—and this provided the Adenauer generations with the legal tools, and the pedagogical lessons, that they needed to go on with business as usual. Characterizing the defendants as "warped" (the four historians) or as "parasites and profiteers" (Arendt) may have inadvertently contributed to this legal amnesia.[139]

Is Grabitz right when she argues that the "purpose of these trials is not only to convict but to remind and to serve as warning" for future generations?[140] Should that be the avowed goal of any legal system, and should we react when a court becomes a part of a narrative vision that we don't share? One of the difficulties, of course, is that we can't always anticipate or control the rhetorical directions of these lessons. Grabitz may want to have punitive proceedings, but even she concedes that "the collective guilt of an entire generation or of the whole German people cannot exist morally or legally."[141] If this is the case, and if some critics don't like the fact that only a few "small fish" were the defendants at Auschwitz, then perhaps we need to conclude that we may be asking too much from these legal forums—historically and contemporaneously.

4

Israeli Judicial Proceedings and Changing Remembrances of the Holocaust

A remarkable monster of a Kastner returns to Budapest. . . . His silence in Kluj was a death sentence for twenty thousand, minus three hundred.

—Ben Hecht, *Perfidy*

In this chapter, I study the circulation of Holocaust remembrances in Israeli judicial proceedings. By reviewing some of the rhetorical dimensions of the Kastner, Eichmann, and Demjanjuk cases, I hope to provide a rhetorical analysis that explicates some of the legal complications that attend the politics of nationalistic remembering and forgetting. As I noted in chapter 1, many observers are convinced that governmental authorities have to be active agents in the preservation of genocidal memories, and they are bothered when certain vectors of memory tell tales that exclude their versions of the truth. As Shoshana Felman observed in *The Juridical Unconscious*, prior "to the *Eichmann* trial, what we call the Holocaust did not exist as a collective story. It did not exist as a semantically authoritative story."[1] I would slightly modify this analysis and argue that perhaps it did exist as a possible dissident tale within some American and Israeli communities, and the Eichmann trial helped turn this same constellation of arguments into a more didactic tale.

Perhaps this condensation of arguments into a more didactic story is because there are many different types of vectors, and it takes time for accretive texts to become a part of what scholars now call collective memories or didactic histories. For Rousso, the diverse types of nationalistic memories were circulated in the vectors that were configured in official, organizational, cultural, and scholarly artifacts.[2] As I argue below, in the case of Israeli Holocaust histories and memories, the Eichmann case provided a type of judicial theater that resonated in polyvalent ways. Critics might complain that this was just another show trial,[3] but supporters liked to think that this trial was helpful: it filled in some of the gaps that existed in the historical "record"; it provided a safe forum where victims were allowed to tell their traumatizing tales; and it showed how nation-states could hold their own legitimate war crimes trials.

In many ways, the Eichmann trial, like the Nuremberg proceedings, has its own judicial legacy. George Will, for example, viewed it as precedent for an Iraqi trial of Saddam Hussein, reminding us that over time "there was no nonsense about Eichmann being tried by 'the international community' for crimes against 'humanity.'"[4] Daphne Eviatar, after reviewing the work of Lawrence Douglas and Mark Osiel, noted how this trial provided key touchstones for those legal theorists who were defending war crimes show trials.[5] In theory, effective war crimes trials can be "carefully orchestrated" so that they can "teach history to a world audience."[6] However, there are those of us who share the views of Marie-Bénédicte Dembour and Emily Haslam, who argued in the spring of 2004 that the "privileging of law" should not "suppress or unnecessarily delay the development of other nonlegal narratives."[7]

In the case of Israeli legal rhetorics, many of the discursive origins of the vectors that make their appearance in many post–World War II judicial narratives can be traced back to the mid–1930s, when tens of thousands of Jews fled Nazi Germany. Because of these challenges, "Jewish legal immigration reached unprecedented numbers after the Nazis came to power: 30,000 in 1934, 42,000 in 1935, 62,000 in 1936. . . . The Jewish population in Palestine doubled to about 470,000."[8]

For many members of the Mapai Party, or labor party, the beginning of the "annihilation" could be traced back to prewar activities. Even though the Nazi plans for the systematic annihilation of Jews did not begin before 1941, the Mapai speakers were "looking for the appropriate words to describe the mass arrests, sporadic killings, humiliations, and abuse that culminated in the events of the *Kristallnacht*."[9] Long before the formal construction of the state of Israel in the late 1940s, organizations had gathered information about wartime atrocities.[10] Moreover, members of the Yishuv—the Jewish community in Palestine in the prestate 1940s—worried about Rommel's troops in North Africa,[11] and they constantly demanded that the Allied powers support the creation of Jewish battalions. Tales of patriotic paratroopers landing behind enemy lines were popular storylines, and these communal narratives served the rhetorical function of removing some of the spatial and relational distance that existed between Palestine and the embattled Allies.

Yet not everyone would have these same memories of British Palestine's participation in Allied war efforts. Just as the French have had their "Vichy Syndrome" (Rousso), some Israelis worried about domestic and international perceptions of Zionist noninvolvement in ending the "catastrophe." Dina Porat explains that ever "since the end of the Second World War, the Israeli public has been traumatized by feelings of guilt concerning the Holocaust. The prevailing opinion has been that the Yishuv failed to do what could have been done to rescue Jews in Nazi-occupied countries."[12] Many of the participants in these Israeli courtrooms tried to answer their critics, and they provided their own historical reconstruction of wartime events.

Israeli Politics, the "Catastrophe," and the Kastner Trials

The United Nations sanctioning of the formation of the state of Israel in 1948 helped open many immigration doors, and now thousands of former "displaced persons" could move to Palestine.[13] The survivors, rescuers, and former collaborators came to Israel with diverse experiences, and there were many debates about the causes of the Holocaust or the ethics of particular survival techniques.

Take, for example, the trials and tribulations of one of the Zionist Hungarian leaders, Rudolph (Israel) Kastner.[14] In August 1944, a train carrying more than 1,000 Hungarian Jews made its way across Germany into Switzerland. Kastner—who participated in negotiations with Adolph Eichmann and other Nazi functionaries—was credited with having helped save more than 1,600 Jews.[15] What made this escape so unusual was the fact that it was taking place at a time when 12,000 of their compatriots were arriving daily at Auschwitz.[16]

Were these 1,600 survivors just lucky individuals who happened to escape the Judeocide? Or had opportunists like Kastner paid a heavy price for the escapees on the "Bergen-Belsen" transport? As one might imagine, not all Israelis were enamored with the idea that negotiating with the enemy was the best way of dealing with the Nazis. As David Morrison explained in 1997:

> What has come to be known as the "*Kastner* Affair" was one of the most painful chapters in the history of the state of Israel. The American fascination with the recent O. J. Simpson trials pales in comparison to the degree to which the Israeli public and government were preoccupied with the progress of this nine-month trial in 1954–55. In the wake of the verdict of the trial, the Israeli government fell. . . . Despite the sensational nature of the *Kastner* Affair, it is little known today. Its painful revelations, many feel, are best forgotten.[17]

Some of the rhetorical reasons for this forgetfulness have to do with the divisive nature of this particular Holocaust proceeding. The Kastner trial would become the first case in which "the actions of a Jewish leader under Nazi rule . . . were subjected to legal investigation."[18]

In 1950, Israel's parliament, the Knesset, passed the Nazi and Nazi Collaborators Law, which punished defendants who had committed crimes against the Jewish people, crimes against humanity, and war crimes.[19] As Trunk pointed out in 1972, this law meant that "the courts in Israel from 1951 to 1964 tried a number of Kapos and ghetto policemen who had entered the country with the wave of mass immigration to Israel."[20]

Interestingly enough, these rules and regulations weren't always interpreted by the Israeli courts in ways that led to the indictment of former Council members of the European "Judenrate," and even when lower courts found against the defendants, the Israel Supreme Court often quashed the sentences. These were clearly controversial interpretations, and their judicial logics resonated with Israeli audiences in diverse ways. Yitzhak Olshan of the Israeli Supreme Court once remarked that many opponents of the Jewish Councils thought that it was "impossible to talk about good or bad Councils," because "the very existence of this institution and of the Jewish police" meant that "they themselves and their remembrance" needed to be "punished with the pillory."[21]

Convictions rarely brought large penalties or lengthy jail sentences, because many members of the Israeli appellate system clearly thought that they understood many of the moral dilemmas that confronted the Jewish leaders who worked with the Nazis during the war. Judge Olshan explained that

> facing a horrible, tragic situation, the Jewish leaders . . . on whom the terrible burden had been imposed were forced to become obedient to the Nazis while maneuvering, calculating, and hoping to weaken orders to rescue or to postpone executions. They could not but appear cruel, or perhaps traitors, in the eyes of the unfortunates who themselves or members of their families had been shipped to the camps—and this despite the fact that the majority of Councilmen and policemen were murdered too.[22]

As an anonymous writer for the *New York Times* would report from Tel Aviv in January 1958, many "refugees living in Israel" believed that these Council leaders saved "their lives."[23]

With this in mind, we can now turn our attention back to the role that Kastner would play in some of these early Israeli Holocaust trials. Yehuda Bauer once characterized him as an ordinary hero with his share of human foibles.[24] Other Israelis contextualized his decisions in a very different light—he was labeled a "perjurer"[25] or "Quisling."[26] This Hungarian activist once worked as a journalist in a provincial town, but his critics claimed that he had bragged about his Nazi connections. For example, he was labeled a "cynical opportunist" who had "misled, and ultimately sacrificed the multitude in order to save himself and his family."[27] In the minds of many Israelis, Kastner became a symbol of the failure of Europe's leadership, where delusional or misguided Jews living in the diaspora were wasting time in the old world.

It is debatable whether this was the dominant view of Kastner in Israeli circles during the 1950s, but he certainly had no shortage of critics. Kastner's legal troubles with authorities began just after the end of World War II, when he was asked by the Zionist Congress in Basel to provide evidence that justified some of his more questionable activities.[28] In his report to the Jewish Agency, Kastner made these provocative claims:

> It was a slippery slope that almost always led to destruction. Everywhere the Jew was faced with the same problem: Should I be the traitor so that here and there I'll be able to help or even be the savior, the rescuer, or should I abandon the community to its fate and let others decide its fate? Is not the flight from responsibility merely another kind of betrayal? And if I do take this upon myself, what is the line that I should never cross? Should I release myself from responsibility at the cost of destroying myself through suicide or being executed? Common sense is almost incapable of drawing the line between self-sacrifice and betrayal.[29]

Devin Pendas has recently reminded us that many of our memories of Auschwitz or the Holocaust are "mediated by *post hoc* interpretations,"[30] but this was obviously not the view of the survivors and families who were willing to comment on the culpability of the members of the Judenrate.

Like many other survivors, Kastner walked into a prefigured world that was filled with frustration, suspicion, and ridicule. Before leaving for Israel, Kastner complicated matters when he provided evidence at one of the Nuremberg trials that "saved a Nazi war criminal, Kurt Becher, from punishment."[31] In the early 1950s, Malkiel Greenwald (Gruenvald) openly accused Kastner of having collaborated with the Nazis in Hungary during 1944–1945.[32] Greenwald belonged to the Ha-mizrahi, the religious wing of the Zionist party, and he saw himself as an educator who used his pamphlets as a weapon in the war against government corruption. In one of his publications, Greenwald made the following claims:

> Dear Friends: The smell of a corpse scratches my nostrils! This will be a most excellent funeral! Dr. Rudolf Kasztner should be eliminated! For three years I have been awaiting this moment to bring to trial and pour the contempt of the law upon this careerist, who enjoys Hitler's acts of robbery and murder. . . . I see him as a vicarious murder of my dear brothers.[33]

Ben Hecht, one of Greenwald's biggest fans, remarked that the elderly Israeli was now "confronted by this topsy-turvy denouement of lambkins crowned as lions," so he "bought a walking stick" and decided to "become a journalist again."[34] Eventually, he would allege that Kastner, in collusion with some Nazis, had stolen Jews' money and helped some of the Germans with their Nuremberg trials defenses.[35]

Greenwald's attack on Kastner was considered to be an attack on the Ben-Gurion government itself,[36] and so Kastner was given the choice of either resigning his post or becoming a witness in a government case of libel. Kastner decided not to resign, and what began as a minor personal squabble turned into a major political struggle. With only slight exaggeration, Pnina Lahav called the Kastner judicial opinions some of the "most explosive material in Jewish history since the destruction of the Second Temple."[37] Lawrence Douglas would argue that these trials tested the Israeli "court's capacity to situate itself with sensitivity in an impossible history."[38]

Part of the reason that Kastner faced such hostility is that the Hungarian Jews were considered to be living in relative safety prior to 1944, and therefore were candidates for possible rescue missions. All of this changed with the entrance of the German army into Hungary. Levin contends that while "Hungarian Jewry" was the last to be attacked, they "suffered the most concentrated and methodical deportation and extermination of any in Europe."[39] In May and June 1944, "the Nazi machine of death worked ceaselessly and wiped out almost 400,000 Jews."[40] During the same year, Eichmann and his ilk decided to reactivate some of the Auschwitz crematoria, and the ghettos were being emptied of Jews.[41]

Not everyone went along with these Nazi plans for the Judeocide. One of the first historians of the "Final Solution," Gerald Reitlinger, would write that from the "symbolic angle," the events in the Warsaw ghetto represented "the first national military struggle of the Jews since the rebellion of Bar Kochba in the reign of Hadrian," and "the ghetto rebellion has become a Jewish epic in its own right and must forever remain so."[42]

Kastner was among the group of Jewish Hungarian leaders who had not followed the lead of the Jewish resistance fighters. Reitlinger has argued that Kastner's work was crucial because the "fate of these 1,684 Jews now became of prime importance to the 250,000 Jews remaining in Hungary. Once the group was accepted in an Allied or neutral country, a revival of the deportations would become unlikely."[43] This hope was short-lived. In Hungary, the Germans decided to depose Prime Minister Miklos Kallay, and a new wave of anti-Jewish decrees were passed—including the requirement that all Jews had to wear the yellow Star of David.[44]

Some optimistic Hungarians still viewed rescue as a viable option, and they wrote about massive parachute drops and the bombing of the Auschwitz railways. One of the most intriguing—and complicated—attempts at negotiation came from the work of Joel Brand, a member of the Relief and Rescue Committee of Budapest (Va'ada).[45] Brand's famous "blood for goods" proposition involved an arrangement where 10,000 trucks and other equipment would be traded to the Nazis in exchange for 1,000,000 Jews. This plan supposedly received the endorsement of both Adolf Eichmann and Heinrich Himmler, but it eventually failed because of several complications.[46] Brand himself was detained by the British in Cairo, so one of the key negotiators of this plot was physically unable to continue his bartering.[47]

From the point of view of many Israelis, these misguided efforts had hurt the cause of more radical interventionists, and the elderly Greenwald seemed to be a critic who understood the importance of Jewish resolve. As Lahav recently explained, Greenwald may have been the type of character who represented the Old World Jewry—he mistrusted the government, he refused to recognize the achievement of Israeli officials, and he was constantly complaining about conditions in Palestine. The prosecution's case for libel thus became a vehicle that would "purge such calumny from the new society."[48]

The Mapai Party that backed Kastner soon found that they were getting much more than they bargained for. Greenwald may not have had all that many options, but he secured the help of Shmuel Tamir—a young, bright, and gifted orator. Tamir's very name meant "tall" in Hebrew, and his presence reminded observers of the "sabra," the homegrown warrior who despised the weakness of those who lived in the diaspora. Israeli conservatives could empathize with this valiant defender of a Holocaust survivor who was unwilling to forgive or forget.

For several months, Tamir was able to put his cross-examination skills and his legal acumen to good use. He turned a libel trial that was supposed to be about Greenwald's newspaper into a political proceeding that put Kastner on the hot seat for his alleged World War II transgressions. Tamir's defensive strategy was as simple as it was transparent—he would argue that no real victim who really cared about his or her fellow Jews would have even considered negotiating with Nazi criminals. Tamir asserted that if Hungary's "Jews had been informed of the Nazi extermination plan, many of them could perhaps have escaped to Romania, revolted against the Germans, or sent calls for help to the outside world."[49]

In many ways, Tamir's legal narratives were populist in nature, perfect examples of what Osiel has called "monumental" spectacles, those dramaturgical proceedings that try to "maximize their pedagogic impact."[50] Greenwald's supporters tried to create the impression that all Jews had to work together in stopping the Nazi oppression.[51] When a few elite leaders saved themselves, or when the Judenrate protected only the remnants of the larger Jewish "people," then these acts could be interpreted as immoral appeasements. Tamir used his own choice of vectors in the crafting of a fascinating narrative of lost opportunities, treachery, and moral failure, and the past became the present as observers now had to question some of their own leaders and their Zionist principles. Was Israel's present leadership simply a continuation of European collaboration?

Tamir's defensive strategy resonated with those audiences who were willing to indict both Kastner and his modern supporters, and his narrative frameworks allowed witnesses to make explicit connections between the spirit of the Jewish resisters during World War II and the fighters for Israeli independence in the 1950s. Tom Segev noted that "the *Kastner* trial" had "become the trial of Mapai."[52]

In many ways, the Kastner trial was unique, because this was one of the first public gatherings of individuals who testified about their activities during the Judeocide. The Nuremberg hearings, with their focus on international law and Nazi acts of "aggression," had provided extensive documentation of the annihilation of Europe's Jewry, but there was little commentary on the role of the Jewish leadership or the uniqueness of the Holocaust. In the Kastner case, the Holocaust became the center of attention, and reporters were hearing testimonials from key Israeli officials, Shoah survivors, and international Zionists.

Yet even in this case, one wonders about the "lessons" that were being taught. What advantages would come from a messy affair that divided many of the communities that had members who thought that they had left behind the traumas and scars of the Old World? Is this really a constructive example of Osiel's "social solidarity"?[53]

In June 1955, after months of heated testimony, Judge Benjamin Halevy ruled in favor of Greenwald, the defendant. In a key portion of his 234-page opinion, Halevy argued:

> The temptation was great. K [Kastner] . . . was dazzled by the chance to save prominent figures, from provincial towns and even from Budapest. To rescue them would be both a personal achievement and a Zionist victory. . . . K was extremely pessimistic about the odds that Jews could escape on their own from the Nazi extermination machine, which had already liquidated almost all the Jews of Europe and he saw the main hope for rescue in an agreement with the Nazis. . . . In accepting the offer, K sold his soul to the devil.[54]

Halevy found Greenwald to be innocent on three of the four counts.

From a rhetorical vantage point, Halevy's use of the anonymous "K" was a brilliant political maneuver, because now Kastner's actions could be tied to the activities of the World War II Judenrate.[55] Within a matter of weeks following Halevy's decision, the Mapai-dominated government was toppled, in part by the circulation of charges that the older government was plagued by what contemporaries called "Kastnerism."[56]

Many members of the Mapai Party realized that Justice Halevy's lower court decision had to be appealed. Tamir's attacks on the leadership of the Yishuv, and Judge Halevy's apparent validation of many of these claims, had touched many raw nerves and tapped into some collective Israeli anxieties. Were the nation's rulers really as weak as the lambs in the diaspora? Mapai leaders, like Cohn, hoped that appealing Greenwald's case might end these verbal interrogations, and between 1956 and 1958 a panel of five judges began hearing all of the evidence all over again. In March 1957, just a few months before the Israeli Supreme Court announced its decision, Rudolph Kastner was assassinated. At this stage in the proceedings, Shmuel Tamir celebrated the acts of the new Jewish heroes (modern Maccabees) as he vilified the more passive "galut" leaders.[57]

Obviously, many of Israel's ruling elite did not share Tamir's narrative emplotment that criticized the activities of the Jewish Agency during the perpetration of the Holocaust. The presence of the five appellate justices symbolized the importance of the Kastner decision, and Yitzhak Olshan asked Justice Simon Agranat to write the majority opinion. Agranat produced a 194-page document that was endorsed by Deputy Chief Justice Shneur Cheshin and Justice David Goitein. The Israeli Supreme Court spent almost half a year reviewing all of the evidence, and most justices eventually decided that Tamir had presented Israeli audiences with an unfair rendition of Kastner's role in the Hungarian deportations.

Agranat's complex opinion perhaps provides us with an example of what Simpson has called a "dissident" historical tale,[58] in that Agranat was willing to interrogate the popular Tamir/Halevy position. Lahav has recently argued that Agranat's "*Kasztner* opinion was ahead of its time," because his "history of the Holocaust" refused "to echo popular opinion."[59] After reviewing Halevy's synthesis of the four counts against Greenwald, Agranat concluded that the only one that could be sustained was the count that claimed that Kastner had helped Becher. The majority of the appellate court concluded that Greenwald had indeed libeled Kastner, when the appellee falsely accused the former Hungarian Zionist leader of collaboration, laying the groundwork for the mass murder of Jews, and embezzlement.

Agranat's opinion was considered to be pathbreaking for many different reasons, including the stance that he took regarding the role that Israeli courts could play in crafting or circulating Holocaust remembrances. Unlike many other jurists, Agranat argued that it was very difficult to draw a clear line between truth and ideology, libel and partisanship. Citing the work of G. M. Trevelyan and Isaiah Berlin, he pointed out that even the best of scholars "do not arrive at the truth, but only a particular version of it."[60]

This type of approach to law and ethics must have displeased many of the former victims of the Holocaust and their relatives, because it seemed to imply that courtrooms were not the best places for the discovery of universal truths about historical events. Moreover, Agranat claimed that Halevy's decision was itself filled with ideological assumptions. As one *New*

York Times correspondent would report, the five justices found that Kastner's actions were "reasonable under the conditions existing in Hungary at that time" because "the Jews of Hungary" were not "equipped for an uprising."[61]

The Agranat narrative framework tried to present an empathetic picture of the beleaguered European leaders who dealt with empowered Nazi officers. This Israeli appellate jurist claimed that a judge in such situations needed to "put himself in the shoes of the participants themselves" and understand life "as they understood it."[62] This would certainly not be the type of argument that would become popular in many future Holocaust trials.

Many of the argumentative vectors that were presented by both Halevy and Agranat were recirculated in the Israeli press, and millions of Israelis took up sides in this ideological struggle. The Kastner trial became a "dramatic *j'accuse*" that shook Israelis and "exposed a tortured, pained, divided and confused people."[63] "Between 1953 and 1958," noted Lahav, "Jewish activity during the Holocaust occupied the front pages of newspapers and the deliberations of the Knesset, the cabinet, and the courtroom."[64] Akiva Orr, who had been a student at the Hebrew University in Jerusalem in the mid–1950s, remembered some of the ambiguities and queries that shadowed these proceedings: "Like most other Israeli youths I was surprised and puzzled by this news. For me—and for many others—the questions raised were: who is this Greenwald, and who is this Kastner? . . . Why did the government find it necessary to sue an individual for libelling another individual? How was it possible for a Jewish collaborator with the Nazis to live in Israel for nine years without being publicly denounced?"[65]

Such debates continued into the 1960s, when several major newspaper columns, journal articles, and books were written that spotlighted the activities of Kastner. It did not help matters that Eichmann himself, in several interview sessions that were reported in *Life* magazine (November and December 1960), specifically mentioned Kastner as one of the "idealists" who shared Eichmann's views on life.[66]

Eichmann's commentaries in 1960 deflected blame away from Hitler, the Nazis, and the German citizenry and placed it squarely on the shoulders of the international communities who purportedly turned their backs on Europe's Jews. It would be one of many early postwar indictments of wartime decision making. Reitlinger, for example, argued in 1961 that if news of the annihilation of Hungarian Jewry had been publicized before July 1944, then "200,000 Jews or more might not have left Hungary."[67]

In sum, the rhetorics surrounding the Kastner trial, and the public commentaries filled with vectors about this case, provide us with interpretative prisms through which we can see many of the fissures that existed in the national and international memories of the European "catastrophe." Less than a decade after the end of World War II, many of the victims, bystanders, and perpetrators disagreed among themselves on just who helped facilitate the Nazi implementation of the "Final Solution." There simply was no single "rule of law" or Archimedean standard of justice that could be applied in these complex situations.

One of the best assessments of the moral and pragmatic dilemmas of these times came from Yehuda Bauer, who refused either to valorize or excoriate Kastner and the other Jewish negotiators. Bauer recognized that the "massive social trauma that overcame the Jewish people after the war" meant that it was not easy to accept the "realization that the Allies had not done much to save the Jews from the clutches of the Nazis."[68] Moreover, the very magnitude of the European catastrophe meant that "many Jews wallowed in self-pity and exaggerated anti-Allied or, generally, anti-Gentile accusations."[69] In his trenchant analysis of the Nazi-Jewish negotiations, Bauer concluded that

> during the war, with no realistic options for rescue by resistance or by flight, the only way out seemed to be negotiating with the murders. Himmler's concerns led him down a converging path. . . . The Jewish individuals who opened the door to negotiation took tremendous risks, personal and communal. In the end, our conclusion must be that they did the right thing, took the only possible way to save lives. Contrary to all logic, some lives were saved. . . . Katzner was an ambitious, overweening, and authoritarian personality, guilty of rescuing Nazis from postwar justice to satisfy his sense of honor and power.[70]

I hope that by now readers can appreciate why I have spent so much time on the Kastner case and the debates that circulated about this decision. Enraged commentators would later vilify Hannah Arendt for her commentaries on the Eichmann trial and the role of the Judenrate, but my critical analysis provides some examples of how these types of divisive fragments were already being circulated in many postwar debates about Europe's catastrophe. As I note below, when we juxtapose some of the arguments and narratives that appeared in the Kastner and the Eichmann cases, we can see how focusing attention on the social agency of key Nazi bureaucrats may have served several ideological functions—it shifted attention away from the role of Jewish leaders like Kastner, it reiterated the uniqueness of the Judeocide, and it allowed the Israelis to critique the shortcomings of Nuremberg and other Allied postwar tribunals. At the same time, the leaders of the Yishuv would no longer be blamed for their purportedly passive role during the Judeocide.

The millions who watched the Eichmann trial would soon forget about Kastner, and some of these debates would temporarily be elided from modern memory work. If scholars and laypersons are going to defend the claim that pedagogical trials serve didactic purposes, then we need to live with the memories of the Kastner as well as the Eichmann trials.

Holocaust Remembrances, the Eichmann Trial, and the Banality of Evil

In May 1960, Israeli prime minister David Ben-Gurion proudly told the Knesset that "one of the greatest of the Nazi war criminals" had been found by Israeli Security Services and would be tried in Israel under the Nazi and Nazi Collaborators Law.[71] Eichmann, the former Nazi "expert" on the "Jewish Question," was now being accused of personally bringing about the murder of hundreds of thousands of Jews "through murder squads that followed the German army into Poland and Russia," and he was said to be responsible for the "deportations to the death chambers of Auschwitz, Chelmno, Belsen, Sobibor, Treblinka, and Maidaneck [*sic*]."[72] Some 300,000 survivors were now living in Israel,[73] and in spite of the dangers that came from confronting a traumatic past, many appeared to have supported their nation's decision that Israel would try Eichmann for his transgressions. The Nuremberg spotlight that had been placed on violations of international law or crimes against humanity[74] bracketed out the uniqueness of the Holocaust.[75]

Many of the contemporary and modern commentators who have written about the Eichmann trial have advanced a variety of arguments that explain the pedagogical features of these proceedings.[76] Lawrence Douglas, for example, argued that this Israeli courtroom provided a forum for Ada Lichtmann, Leon Wells, Zivia Lubetkin-Zuckerman, Yehiel Dinur, and Rivka Yoselewska, and in the process these officials have left us some "testimonial" evidence that may be just as important as the documentary evidence that was collected at Nuremberg.[77] Some four decades earlier, one optimistic observer hoped that the trial would "provide a healing catharsis" that purged Israel and Germany "of a nightmare."[78]

Yet in our search for nationalistic precedents and redemptive legal tales, we sometimes forget that there were many other communities who worried about the desirability of legitimacy of the Eichmann proceedings. In Israel, many who had "suffered the most from the Nazis" appeared to be "the most inclined not to try."[79] Lawrence Fellows, who interviewed a host of Israelis, claimed in one of his vectors of memory that only a minority of the people living in that nation really saw any "advantage" in having this trial. He elaborated by explaining that the majority of people living in Israel were the "so-called Orientals [from Africa or Asia]," who on "the whole" felt "precious little association with Jews from Europe or their past troubles except on purely humane grounds."[80] Some of these attitudes may have changed when the trial began in April 1961, but we need to remember that this was a divisive topic in many national and international communities.

In the United States, it appears as though the most publicized attack on the legitimacy of the Israeli trial came from the pen of Telford Taylor, a former American prosecutor who participated in several Nuremberg proceedings. Taylor worried about the rationales that Ben-Gurion had openly defended in various presses, but he got nowhere when he remarked that this type of "absolute nationalism" was "irreconcilable with international law." Even before the trial began, Taylor tried to warn American readers that the trial was also going to be used to "portray some groups and individuals in the United States and Western Europe as insufficiently concerned with the fate of the Jews under Hitler, so that they ignored or let slip opportunities for Jewish emigration to safety."[81] These types of universalist sentiments were tied to a host of political judgments.

Defenders of the Eichmann trial could also argue that the Nuremberg trials were just the beginning—and not the end—of postwar judicial activities. For example, Lord Russell maintained that even the International Military Tribunal (IMT) had "assumed that other war-criminals would, in due course, be brought to trial in the countries where they had committed their crimes," and the "Jews were one of these peoples."[82] Gideon Hausner, the leading prosecutor in the case against Eichmann, had this to say about the higher purposes of these Israeli proceedings:

> This was the course adopted at the Nuremberg Trials—a few witnesses and films of concentration camp horrors, interspersed with piles of documents. It was all efficient and simple. But it also was one of the reasons that the proceedings there failed to reach the hearts of men. . . . [A] fraction of [the archives] would have sufficed to get Eichmann sentenced ten times over. But I knew that we needed more than a conviction; we needed a living

> record of a gigantic human and national disaster. . . . Our younger generation, absorbed as it was in the building and guarding of the new state, had far too little insight into the events which ought to be a pivotal point in its education.[83]

In order to get this needed education, various Israeli generations needed to feel and see that justice had been rendered.

In many symbolic ways, Eichmann seemed to be the perfect candidate for this pedagogical trial. After the annexation of Austria in 1938 (the Anschluss), he was one of the key Nazi leaders who was transferred to Vienna in the hopes that he would help convince the Jews of that city to emigrate. While we don't know all of the details of his activities at this time, we do know that in less than two years he was believed to have encouraged many of the 150,000 Austrian Jews to leave that country.[84] His Nazi superiors were astonished when they heard about his Austrian successes, so Eichmann was put in charge of the Office for Jewish Emigration. This promotion meant that he would now be arranging the emigration of the Jews who were living in Czechoslovakia and the older parts of Germany. After the invasion of Poland, Eichmann also became a part of Himmler's *Reichssicherheitshauptamt* (RSHA), an organization that was dedicated to ensuring the separation of the Jewish and German "races." In 2004, Hanna Yablonka would write that Eichmann's "talents for organization were expressed in the coordination and dispatch of some half million Jews to Auschwitz within less than two months," and that he was "cunning enough to deceive Jewish leaders in such a way as to allow him absolute freedom of movement in carrying out his enormous enterprise."[85]

Eichmann was therefore a highly visible Nazi who could be tied to many facets of the Holocaust, and his trial could provide an exemplary didactic forum. The trial lasted from April 11 to December 15, 1961, and it was televised in many parts of the world.[86] When Dr. Robert Servatius, the lead counsel for the defense, tried to argue that the three Israeli judges would be prejudiced by the fact that their relatives died during the "Final Solution," presiding judge Moshe Landau rejected these objections by noting:

> Counsel for the Defence says that he fears that the memory of the catastrophe and the holocaust [*sic*] which exterminated their people, which is the background of the various offences in the indictment, may influence the judgment and impair their ability to do justice. . . . We are professional judges, used and accustomed to weighing evidence brought before us and to doing our work in the public eye and subject to public criticism.[87]

This commentary on judicial constraint seemed to imply that Eichmann would be individually tried for his acts, and that some of the positivist ideals of the times would prevent this from turning into a show trial. One of the difficulties, of course, comes when we try to follow Landau's advice at the same time that we hear from Ben-Gurion and Hausner.

Many Israeli officials understood the controversial nature of these proceedings and the importance of defending this trial's legitimacy, and so they apparently tried to find ways of balancing the needs of individuated justice and collective remembrance. They helped pay for Eichmann's German lawyer, they made sure that he understood their questions, and they provided him with copies of his indictments. During the early stages of this process, Eichmann learned that he was also accused of having sent millions of laborers to transit and concentration camps, of helping with the sterilization of Jews and Gypsies, and of allowing civilians to starve.[88]

In order to support these allegations, the Israeli prosecutors brought together "twenty-eight Jewish witnesses under Eichmann's exclusive jurisdiction, in addition to witnesses from Germany, Austria, and the 'Protectorate' who had direct contact with Eichmann."[89] Yablonka's research indicates that Judge Landau would put "questions to ninety-six witnesses," and that he "conducted the trial high-handedly, expressing his dissatisfaction with every emotional or theatrical manifestation."[90] What modern observers sometimes fail to mention is that there were days when witnesses provided general testimony about World War II atrocities without ever mentioning Eichmann.

Many of the names of these witnesses came from Rachel Auerbach, a historian who worked at Yad Vashem, the Holocaust memorial. Investigators also brought Hausner truckloads of books and files that had been collected by the Israeli police and by researchers who reviewed the Nuremberg files.[91] Many Israelis thought that the chronology of the Eichmann trial needed to begin with only a brief discussion of the early stages of Nazi prosecutions, and then quickly move to the exterminations.[92] The Eichmann trial would then serve to unify the nation and to heal some of the traumatic wounds that had been opened during the Kastner proceedings.

In Hausner's opening statement (eight hours long), he created a picture of the world that had lost millions of potential Zionists, who had been "exterminated" while awaiting the arrival of the "Jewish state."[93] Israel's chief prosecutor averred that Eichmann's position gave him the power to continue massive deportations, even at a time near the end of the war when the "handwriting was on the wall." When he later reminisced about his trial remarks, Hausner claimed that "with defeat looming ahead, Eichmann spent most of his energies working for the destruction of every last Jew he could still lay his hands on."[94] At one dramatic point in his opening presentation, Hausner "waved a black-gowned arm at the defendant and cried: 'six-million prosecutors stand beside me to stab a finger of accusation and cry out, 'J'accuse!'"[95] Tom Segev has written that "from this point onward," the trial became the "central event in the lives of many Israelis."[96]

For several months, the prosecutors covered everything from the planning at the Wannsee Conference to the destruction of Hungary's Jews. Writers like Ka-Tzetnik appeared at trial, so that they could help survivors "unlock what had been sealed within their memories," to "redeem them and an entire generation of survivors."[97] Dr. Georges Wellers talked about the deportation of some 4,000 Jewish children who left France on their way to gassing installations.[98]

Oftentimes the judges intervened to query the witnesses, and sometimes they asked a very embarrassing question—why hadn't there been any more resistance during the perpetration of the Holocaust? On May 1, 1961, for example, Moshe Bejski was testifying that he had been one of between 15,000 and 20,000 Polish workers guarded by a few hundred Axis police officers. This witness was caught off guard when Hausner asked him point blank, "Why did you not revolt?" The forty-year-old Bejski tried to explain that the Jews were desperate, providing needed labor, and that even if they had succeeded in breaking out of the camp, where would they go?[99] An anonymous writer for the *New York Times* explained to readers that many "in the post-war generation here, proud of their victories over the Arabs, have been openly critical of the death camp victims who allowed themselves to be slaughtered like sheep instead of going down fighting."[100]

Initially, some of the witnesses had worried about the traumatic experiences that might come from the trial, but they were persuaded that their testimony would help with the prosecution of a war criminal. For example, Rivka Yoselewska told the audiences in the courtroom that the SS had shot the people of her village after ordering them to undress and stand at the edge of a pit, and more than two dozen witnesses talked about the abuse of children.[101] As Douglas insightfully observes, the accumulation of this information was meant to have "its effect not upon the accused, but upon the spectators at the trial."[102]

Some of the most damaging testimony came from witnesses who could and did link Eichmann to some very reprehensible acts. Pinchas Freudiger talked about meetings in Hungary between Jews and Germans, and he remembered "*Obersturmbannfurhrer* Eichmann in uniform, high boots and a pistol in his hand, shouting at me in a tone of voice so typical of the Master Race."[103] Freudiger testified that Eichmann made many key decisions about deportations, and he talked about the terrible conditions that the tens of thousands of deported Hungarians experienced. Other witnesses detailed what happened at Theresienstadt, where Eichmann had special authority.[104] Abraham Gordon, a Hungarian by birth who lived in Israel, had this exchange with Gabriel Bach, a member of the prosecutorial team:

> Bach: Do you remember 19 March 1944?
> Gordon: Yes, it was a Sunday, the day when the Germany Army occupied Hungary, and entered Budapest. . . .
> Bach: Were you, shortly after the German occupation, taken away from school with a lot of other young Jews and made to work?
> Gordon: Yes, we were arranged in groups for various types of work. . . .
> Bach: During your work did you ever see Adolf Eichmann?
> Gordon: Yes . . . after we had finished work on the tunnels we were taken to a villa which, I found out later, was Adolf Eichmann's. . . .
> Bach: Will you tell the Court in your own words what happened? . . .
> Gordon: I saw Slavic [Eichmann's bodyguard] and Eichmann enter the tool-shed and the door was closed behind them. Then I heard frightful screams and beatings, thuds and weeping.
> Bach: Could you identify the voice?
> Gordon: It was the voice of the boy Solomon. The screams lasted for about ten or fifteen minutes, and then for the first time they stopped. The door was opened and Eichmann came out of the tool-shed. He was rather dishevelled. . . . I saw stains which I thought were blood-stains.[105]

By the time that the defense team took center stage, they had an uphill battle. Audiences following the trial could understand why Hausner considered this former Nazi to be a "cunning, flinthearted [*sic*] plotter, with a demonic personality which certainly was completely indifferent to the suffering he inflicted, either collectively or individually, and which reveled in the exercise of personal power."[106]

During the trial, Eichmann and his defense lawyer used a variety of tactics to try and justify, explain, or mitigate the gravity of the situation, and when cornered they often fell back on the claim that Eichmann had been a transportation expert who "was merely following orders."[107] The defense tried to characterize Eichmann as a normal human being who had been caught in some abnormal circumstances. As Hausner explained five years after the trial: "When 'other ways and means'—actual physical extirpation—were ordered by higher authority later on, he felt himself bound by his oath of allegiance and his duty to his country to carry out such commands as he received; in his opinion these had nothing whatever to do with the actual extermination itself. The measures imposed were against his own good judgment, but he was seized at the time in the iron grasp of necessity."[108]

Within Eichmann's narration of events, his actions showed that he was trying to prevent murders, and interlopers had foiled his own plans. When some functionaries from Berlin visited him in the East, he explained:

> This is like an automatic factory, like a flour mill connected with some bakery. At one end you put a Jew who still has some property, a factory, or a shop, or a bank account, and he goes through the building from counter to counter, from office to office, and comes out at the other end without any money, without any rights, with only a passport on which it says: "You must leave the country within a fortnight. Otherwise you will go to a concentration camp."[109]

This account is fascinating from a rhetorical vantage point because it punctuates time so that the focus of legal culpability takes us back to the early war years, when Nazis were demanding that Jews obey German law and leave the country. This magnifies the social agency of the Jews, and makes it appear as if they were partly responsible for their own trials and tribulations. At the same time, this stance also meant that the defense could craft the type of subtext that might resonate with some Israeli observers—when the Nazis had tried to carry out their prewar emigration policies, they hadn't received the requisite Allied help.

As far as the Israeli judges in this case were concerned, none of these positions were persuasive. Ultimately, the three-member Jerusalem court found him guilty on many counts, and the Israeli Supreme Court decided that they would reject Eichmann's appeal. He was hanged on May 31, 1962.

Many have argued that the Eichmann trial provided a key moment in the incremental recognition of the Judeocide, but this would not be the only rhetorical function of these proceedings. The polysemic nature of this massive testimony could also be used to shift attention away from the political squabbling that had existed within Israeli political communities during the 1950s. Moreover, the case magnified the social agency of those participants who had signed memos, arranged train schedules, or kept meticulous records of the number of human beings who were put in ghettos, deported, or eventually exterminated. Like all rhetorical scenarios, these Israeli narratives were ideological and selective, in that they refused to give any credence to the possibility that wartime situations created circumstances that overwhelmed human agents. Agranat's commentaries on the reason for Kastner's actions were now overshadowed by Hausner's vilification of Eichmann.

In the early 1960s, the Eichmann trial served as a lightning rod for legal and public criticism, especially when observers reflected on how the Israeli judges in the case allowed in a great deal of evidence that seemed to have little to do with the defendant's personal culpability. The Israelis had piggybacked on the Nuremberg notions of "conspiracy," which meant that they could justify the casting of a wide net when it came to cataloging violations. Moreover, when it was learned that the defendant would have access to prosecution documents, but couldn't spend comparable amounts of money in his own defense investigations, observers complained that the deck was stacked against Eichmann to the point where this was a "political" trial rather than a search for justice.[110]

At the same time, what sometimes gets overlooked in some laudatory readings of these proceedings are the rhetorical fragments that tend to show how at least some Israelis seemed to be trying to turn the trial into a critique of Allied rescue policies during the war. This was at least how some Israelis viewed the proceedings. One writer for *Davar*, a Mapai Party outlet, explained that "world opinion" needed to know that "not only Nazi Germany was responsible for the destruction of six million Jews of Europe."[111] Ben-Gurion pulled no punches when he remarked that he believed that Britain's Ernest Bevin had "policies" toward "the refugees who sought asylum in Israel" that "cost the lives of hundreds of thousands of Jews."[112]

Some supporters of the Eichmann trial openly defended the more didactic dimensions of the trial. For example, Hausner told readers of the *Saturday Evening Post* that "while the purpose of the trial was to probe into charges preferred against one man," the government also wanted to "bring the enormity of Eichmann's and the Nazis' crimes down to the point where average people could comprehend it."[113] Ben-Gurion argued that the former SS lieutenant colonel did not need to be tried in either Germany or in an international tribunal because Eichmann was being "accused of murdering millions of Jews as Jews."[114] Israel's head of state explained why this was more than just a religious dispute:

> Jews in Hitler's Germany were murdered not because they were human beings but because they were Jews. It is foolish to claim, as some do, that these Jews were not part of our people but merely shared the same religious

> beliefs. In Eastern Europe, where many of Hitler's victims lived, Jews in the ghettos of Russia, Poland or Lithuania, for example, never considered themselves Russians, Poles, [or] Lithuanians, but Jews. Israel is the only inheritor of these Jews for two reasons. First, it is the only Jewish state. Second, if these Jews were alive, they would be here because most if not all of them wanted to come to live in a Jewish state.[115]

From within this framework, the Eichmann trial was simply another example of a legitimate forum that looked into criminal wrongdoing.

Such explanations were not always persuasive, and there were many critics who questioned both the desirability and the legality of these proceedings. In *Eichmann in Jerusalem,* Arendt claimed that Israeli prosecutors tried to provide us with "bad history and cheap rhetoric."[116] For example, she ridiculed Hausner's remarks because they appeared to be at "cross-purposes with putting Eichmann on trial," in that they framed the catastrophe as a part "of some mysteriously foreordained destiny."[117] Arendt also implied that at least some of the Israeli officials were purposely avoiding discussions of Jewish Councils and their complicity. In one of the key passages in *Eichmann in Jerusalem,* Arendt argued:

> True it was that the Jewish people as a whole had not been organized, that they had possessed no territory, no government, and no army, that, in the hour of their greatest need, they had no government-in-exile to represent them among the Allies (the Jewish Agency for Palestine, under Dr. Weizmann's presidency, was at best a miserable substitute), no caches of weapons, no youth with military training. . . . The whole truth was that if the Jewish people had really been unorganized and leaderless, there would have been chaos and plenty of misery but the total number of victims would hardly have been between four and a half and six million people.[118]

Arendt's previous work on the power of totalitarianism[119] provided her with an alternative explanation for the Holocaust that was radically different from the eschatological or anti-Semitic interpretations offered by Ben-Gurion, Hausner, and other defenders of the Jerusalem proceedings.

Arendt's account of the motivations of the perpetrators and the causes of the "Final Solution" were sophisticated, cynical, and provocative. She had the temerity to question the wisdom of the three Israeli judges who supervised the Jerusalem District Court proceedings. While she gave them credit for openly recognizing the importance of political self-restraint, she went on to argue that they hadn't controlled people like Hausner. In her (dissident) discussion of the "banality of evil," Eichmann was simply an ignorant, unreflective, and minor bureaucrat who spoke in clichés, a person who "had been raised and had lived all of his life as a law-abiding citizen."[120]

Arendt was just one of the many observers from all different parts of the political spectrum who were mesmerized by many of the issues that were raised by the trial. By the spring of 1961, the Eichmann proceedings were becoming an international jurisprudential event. In America, for example, Gallup polls showed that 87 percent of adult Americans had heard or read about the trial, and 75 percent of them expressed some interest in its outcome.[121] "The capture and trial of Eichmann, along with the publication of Hilberg's book," noted Christopher Browning, "initiated many studies of the middle-echelon perpetrators."[122] Browning considered this revival of interest in the so-called *Alltagsgeschichte* (history of the everyday life) as a mixed blessing. On the one hand, these types of functionalist approaches served the laudatory purpose of supplementing existing accounts of the Holocaust and reminded us that the leaders at the top were not the only perpetrators. On the other hand, these same functionalist approaches could also be appropriated by those who tried to relativize or normalize the Holocaust. The use of new dialectical approaches widened our gaze so that we looked at more than just a single unitary or positivistic framework, but it also meant that communities had to listen to "neo-Nazi revisionists" who argued that the "Holocaust never happened."[123]

Clearly the Eichmann trial was a catalytic event, but we need to remember that many different pedagogical lessons were being taught. Not everyone shared Judge Landau's views of the importance of separating politics from law, or theatrics from justice. Regardless of some of the participants' individual intentions, the narratives about the Holocaust that were circulated during the Eichmann trial took on lives of their own. Tom Segev once remarked that "with each passing year, popularization of the Holocaust increased. Form the *Heroism Quiz* on national television, live from Auschwitz, to the publication of a Hebrew edition of *Maus*, an American book that depicts the murder of the Jews in comic-book form, consciousness of the Holocaust became part of everyday life. . . . By the late 1980s there was hardly a day when the Holocaust was not mentioned in one of the newspapers."[124]

By that time, Israelis were also willing to contemplate the possibility that there would be more modern Holocaust trials that would bring some of the older war criminals to justice. In early 1986, an American worker by the name of Demjanjuk—described as "Ivan the Terrible"—would be extradited from the United States to stand trial in Jerusalem for crimes that were allegedly committed at Treblinka.[125]

Modern Israeli Memories of the Holocaust and the Demjanjuk Trials

When Jerusalem's District Court heard the case of John Demjanjuk in September 1986, the jurists were listening to arguments and hearing about evidence that had been collected on several different continents. For more than a dozen years, authorities had to sort through thousands of documents and photographs in order to help them make decisions about the legality of the defendant's denaturalization,[126] his extradition, the fairness of televising courtroom events, and the reliability of witness testimony. Unlike some of the other Holocaust trials, this one involved some questions of identification and the authenticity of materials that came from old enemies.

Skeptical observers complained that Israeli officials kept changing the charges that appeared in the Demjanjuk indictments.[127] Lawrence Douglas, who has defended many aspects of both the Nuremberg and Eichmann trials, averred that the "*Demjanjuk* trial was a tragic farce, a cautionary tale about the dangers of relying on the legal process to honor the pathos of memory."[128] Yet Avi Pazner, a spokesperson for Prime Minister Yitzhak Shamir, would tell one reporter that this proceeding would "become an obsession of a generation that seemed to have no feeling about the Holocaust—the third generation of Israelis, people [who] not only did not know [about] the Holocaust, but their parents did not know."[129] Demjanjuk would be tried for his alleged activities as a low-level functionary at the Treblinka camp in Poland, and Ehud Gol noted that he was waiting to take his eleven-year-old daughter to the Jerusalem courtroom on a day when one of the survivors was testifying.[130]

From a rhetorical standpoint, the Demjanjuk case is still a fascinating study in Holocaust memory work because it provides us with some excellent illustrations of the malleability of historical reconstruction in the face of multiple political pressures. These were highly evocative trials that asked audiences to deal with such issues as anti-Semitism, nationalistic pride, and the appearance of judicial propriety. One of the saddest parts of some trials came from the realization that out of the more than 800,000 people who went through Treblinka, fewer than a hundred survivors remained to tell their tales.

These would also be trials that would involve the reappropriation and reinterpretation of some controversial documentary materials that had been prepared in the 1940s and 1950s. Some of these governmental documents that made their way into Israeli courtrooms came from the U.S. Department of Justice, where officials had sifted through texts that came from the former Soviet Union. Some of these parcels had exchanged hands during the cold war, when trust was a rare commodity. Demjanjuk's various hearings and trials would last several decades, and many members of the Ukrainian communities in the United States and in Canada contributed millions of dollars to the defense fund that was used in the campaign to stop this "Soviet conspiracy."

It appears that government authorities first took an interest in Demjanjuk's potential culpability in 1975, when some Soviets sent the U.S. Department of Justice a list of seventy suspected war criminals who were believed to be living in the United States.[131] On this list were the names of several Ukrainians, including Demjanjuk, and at this time Soviet sources believed that he had been a guard at Sobibor. The U.S. Immigration and Naturalization Service interviewed twelve Sobibor survivors living in the United States, but none of them could positively identify Demjanjuk.[132] A year later, American officials sent to Israel a collection of seventeen photos with the hope that some Israeli survivors of Sobibor might recognize some of these faces. The Israelis thought that they were out of luck when none of these Sobibor survivors identified Demjanjuk, but things got complicated when several Treblinka survivors were certain that this was the man known in their camp as "Ivan the Terrible."[133]

By now, it was out in the open that both U.S. and Israeli governmental agents were trying to collect evidence against Demjanjuk, and in August 1976 a Ukrainian newspaper reported that during some of the early post-war crimes trials, a former guard at Sobibor (Ignat Danilchenko) had testified that he remembered a fellow guard by the name of Ivan Demjanjuk. Danilchenko would be executed after these trials, but he left some fragmentary records that indicated that Demjanjuk had also served at the Flossenburg concentration camp in Germany. This same newspaper article contained a photograph of a Demjanjuk who had been at the infamous Nazi training camp at Trawniki, Poland. Although this Soviet evidence did not link Demjanjuk to Treblinka, it clearly identified this person as someone who worked at Sobibor.[134]

Given these contradictory bits of information, we can readily see why some governmental officials worried about the reliability of these shards of memory, and why Allan Ryan, one of the key U.S. investigators, would later decide that he wasn't going to bring up some of these matters at Demjanjuk's denaturalization hearings.[135] During these early proceedings, legal and political decisions had to be made about the formal logic of these claims, the consistency of these vectors of memory, and the credibility of the sources who sometimes supplied this information. Various national organizations may have agreed that "Ivan the Terrible" needed to stand trial, but they often disagreed about his true identity, the framing of the specific charges, and the choice of forums. As one American informant told Gitta Sereny:

> [What the] Soviets could never understand was our pre-occupation with the murder of the Jews. For the Soviets, the Nazis were the murderers of twenty million Russians. For us in America, "Nazi" has really become synonymous with the genocide of the Jews, and our investigations of war crimes with a few exceptions were almost invariably connected with the Holocaust. This, apart from many other things, made for an enormous culture gap and distrust on both sides.[136]

It is perhaps no coincidence that Demjanjuk's name resurfaced at a time when many Americans were reevaluating the way that the entire nation thought about Holocaust consciousness-raising. In 1978, the Holtzman Amendment to the U.S. Immigration and Naturalization Act created the Office of Special Investigations (OSI), and this office would symbolically be housed within the Department of Justice.[137] The OSI's tasks included exposing, denaturalizing, extraditing, or deporting any Nazi collaborators.[138] As Neal Sher would note in the spring of 1987, the "passage of time does not mitigate what they have done, and doesn't excuse it. . . . We're dealing with people who would do it all over again."[139] These renewed efforts meant that America was joining the belated international search for surviving war criminals.

The Soviets did eventually decide that they would aid the Americans in their quest, and one of the key artifacts that was sent across the ocean was an identification card (the "Trawniki card") that purportedly showed that Demjanjuk had been at the Trawniki camp in Poland in 1942. Some observers argued that this card looked like a forgery, but other participants in this growing social drama were convinced of the document's authenticity.[140]

John Horrigan would later remark that "prosecuting Demjanjuk became an obsession for all of us."[141] In 1986, Demjanjuk was extradited to Israel so that he could face murder charges for his alleged activities as "Ivan the Terrible."[142] The Israelis put together a case that was based on affidavits, archival materials, historical research, photographs, and eyewitness testimony.

Between 1986 and 1988, the Jerusalem District Court would once again become a contested site of legal memories, and new generations heard stories about the horrors of the "Final Solution." Demjanjuk, like Eichmann, would be tried for violations of Israel's Nazi and Nazi Collaborators (Punishment) Law of 1950.[143] Prosecutors had to make sure that they had properly identified Demjanjuk, while his defense teams had their own difficulties—many of his own prior statements were filled with contradictory pieces of information. For more than a decade, the former autoworker and his family refused to admit that he had been involved in any war crimes at all, and they claimed that much of the evidence that had been collected by the Soviets was worthless.[144] During the pretrial phases of the investigations, Demjanjuk told Israeli authorities that during the war he served as a Soviet soldier, and that the Germans had captured him in 1942. This Israeli detainee then explained that he remained a German prisoner of war until 1944, when he was drafted into the Galician Waffen SS.

At first glance this appears to be a coherent tale, and it could have been an accurate chronology of Demjanjuk's life, but when officials began checking out some of the specific details of the story, they realized that he may have been leaving out some key pieces of this historical puzzle. First, the questionnaires that Demjanjuk had filled out in Germany in 1951 provided indications that he may have lived in Sobibor between 1937 and 1943. How could this textual evidence be reconciled with the statements that he had made about the two years that he supposedly spent in a German prison camp? Moreover, of all of the possible regions in Poland that could have been listed on these 1950s forms, why did he choose the word "Sobibor"? This was a place that was so small that it was not even "marked on any prewar maps."[145]

In December 1987, Demjanjuk's defense attorneys publicly expressed outrage when they learned that U.S. officials possessed some exculpatory evidence from the Soviets that could have helped free their client. In 1979, Soviet officials had handed over a statement from Ignat Danilchenko that clearly indicated that one of the Sobibor camp guards went by the name of "Demjanjuk." In part of Danilchenko's statement, we find these historical clues:

> Demjanjuk, like all guards in the [Sobibor] camp, participated in the mass killings of Jews. . . . While I was at the camp I repeatedly saw Demjanjuk, armed with a rifle, together with other guards and, in many cases, myself, guard prisoners in all areas of the camp, from the unloading platform to the entrance into the gas chamber. Demjanjuk escorted people until they

> reached the gas chamber. . . . Demjanjuk was considered to be an experienced and efficient guard. For example, he was repeatedly assigned by the Germans to get Jews in surrounding ghettos and deliver them in trucks to the camp to be killed.[146]

This type of documentary evidence provided what could be considered a double-edged sword—it showed that a person by the name of Demjanjuk committed some horrific acts, but not at the specific camp (Treblinka) that was the focal point of the Israeli prosecutorial narratives.

Once again we see how the establishment of a prima facie legal case against a single defendant can run into difficulties when authorities also want to provide historical records that document the magnitude of death camp horrors. Younger generations needed to know about the nature and scope of the Judeocide, and the culpability of "Ivan the Terrible," but how would they evaluate the conflicting narratives that were being told about Demjanjuk's whereabouts? Tom Segev would later complain that the Demjanjuk case, like "the *Eichmann* trial," showed that the "trial medium was very limited in its ability to tell history."[147]

The Jerusalem District Court became a forum for larger debates about the nature and scope of the entire Judeocide. "Ivan the Terrible" and camp survivor became key topoi as modern participants engaged in legal debates about this criminal's real identity and the morality of some of the choices that were made by survivors as well as perpetrators during these turbulent times. For example, when Eliahu Rosenberg testified about the difficulty of removing the bodies from gas chambers at Treblinka, he was asked by both defense attorney Mark O'Connor and Judge Dov Levin why he hadn't helped the victims escape.[148] These echoes from the Eichmann cross-examinations illustrate some of the ideological drifts that came from the polysemic nature of these proceedings—once more, searching for individuated guilt would prove to be just one of many motivations that activated these Holocaust trials.

In many ways, the Demjanjuk case also reopened the psychic wounds of a generation that had grown up with Holocaust remembrances, and the defense team members who tried to protect the American autoworkers' rights were vilified and personally attacked during the trial. At the same time, the defense argued that many of the prosecution's witnesses had been in touch with each other and had been talking about the case for years. When the lower court judges reviewed these allegations, they accepted the prosecutorial arguments that the witnesses who had identified Demjanjuk as "Ivan the Terrible" had "done so independently."[149]

When the defense attorneys put together their case, they relied on the testimony of historians, specialists on documents and signatures, a KGB expert, and even a psychiatrist, but the chief prosecutor, Yona Blattman, had two witnesses who personally identified Demjanjuk as the person they remembered as "Ivan the Terrible." As the trial progressed, audiences in the courtroom found out that some former death camp guards had tattoos for their blood types, and the defendant had to explain away a scar that looked like a tattoo had been removed.

In a desperate attempt to save his client's life, Yoram Sheftel, Demjanjuk's Israeli attorney, made a momentous decision—he would present his Israeli audiences with a third narrative. This new tale placed Demjanjuk at Sobibor and not Treblinka, and this legal defense relied on evidence from Danilchenko's earlier statement. This tactic was based on an extremely risky strategy, and when one of the Israeli judges asked Demjanjuk if he would admit to being at Sobibor, he steadfastly refused to budge from his prisoner-of-war story. The majority of the court seem to have negotiated their way through this thicket by concluding that "Ivan the Terrible" must have commuted between Sobibor and Treblinka—a distance of sixty-five miles.[150]

On April 18, 1988, the Jerusalem District Court determined that Demjanjuk was indeed "Ivan the Terrible." He would later be sentenced to death for his alleged transgressions.

These were incredibly volatile times for many Israelis, and the publicizing of the lower court decision served as a catalyst for legal and public commentary. Thomas Friedman reported that some liberal Israeli experts on the Judeocide questioned the educational value of the trial—the frameworks that were being used seemed to feed in to a "certain Israeli self-perception as victim," and they detracted attention away "from pressing domestic Israeli issues, such as Israeli power in the occupied territories."[151]

Several tragic events marred an already controversial trial. Just before the beginning of the appellate process, former judge Dov Eitan was said to have committed suicide by falling from the twentieth floor of the Jerusalem tower. Several days later, at Eitan's funeral, someone threw acid into Yoram Sheftel's eyes, and he had to undergo a number of operations in order to regain most of his eyesight.[152]

After several agonizing months of deliberation, the members of the Israeli Supreme Court announced to the press in 1993 that they believed that it was Ivan Marchenko, and not John Demjanjuk, who probably deserved the title of "Ivan the Terrible." The lack of positive proof of identification meant that Demjanjuk needed to be set free. Ironically, much of the evidence that was used to create this reasonable doubt came from Soviet documents and records.

In *Demjanjuk v. Israel,* the Israeli Supreme Court justices underscored the point that they were not trying to exonerate Demjanjuk. They weren't implying that he wasn't criminally culpable for the specific crimes outlined in the indictments—they were simply ruling that the prosecutorial evidence hadn't been strong enough to rule out the possibility that the defendant may not have been "Ivan the Terrible." Moreover, in July 1993, the Israeli Supreme Court determined:

> [Certain evidence] singles out [Demjanjuk] from hundreds of thousands of Russian prisoners of war held by the Germans and places him among the thousands who volunteered to serve in the S.S. within the framework of the *Wachmanner* unit that served the Germans in [Operation Reinhard], which was devised in order to establish and operate the extermination camps in Sobibor, Lodz and Treblinka. . . . [This] evidence shows that [Demjanjuk] served, contrary to his persistent denial, as a *Wachmann* of the S.S.[153]

The five Israeli Supreme Court justices determined that Demjanjuk should be acquitted, and for a while he was considered to be a "stateless" person who had lost his U.S. citizenship.

Three and a half months after Demjanjuk's acquittal, the U.S. Court of Appeals for the Sixth Circuit added a new wrinkle to the case when it decided in November 1993 that "the OSI attorneys [had] acted with reckless disregard for their duty to the court" and "committed fraud on the court."[154] For more than a year this appellate court had been looking into the possibility that several U.S. prosecutors in Demjanjuk's denaturalization hearings (1981) may have failed to disclose some exculpatory evidence.[155] Judge Gilbert Merritt remarked that just before the extradition hearings, the U.S. Department of Justice had been given some key documents that tended to show that another Ukrainian—Ivan Marchenko—was in fact "Ivan the Terrible." This was the same vector of evidence that became a key part of Yoram Sheftel's last-gasp defense.

After the end of the Israeli proceedings, Sheftel wrote a book that contained a devastating attack on the legal maneuvers of the Israeli, Soviet, and U.S. authorities. As Zayas noted in 1994 when he reviewed the British version of Sheftel's manuscript, the "book reads like a Perry Mason case study, replete with lucid procedural explanations, detailed evaluations of documents by expert witnesses, devastating cross-examinations, [and] revealing testimonies."[156] Outside observers averred that the Israeli prosecutors may have been misled by the "horror" of the "Ivan the Terrible" imagery, and not because of "any base motives."[157]

For those who believed that the Demjanjuk suit was providential in nature, the Supreme Court decision seemed to be profane and irreverent. If the Israeli authorities were going to take pride in the witnessing that was taking place in the courtroom, why not accept the victims' identification of the defendant? Peter Novick once observed that "much of the outrage which greeted the Israeli Supreme Court's overturning the verdict . . . was a result of the Court having based its decision on its plausible view that, while there was no subjective bad faith [on the part of victims-accusers], fifty-year old memories, however 'sacred,' were fallible. The decision was thus, literally, 'sacrilege.'"[158] Such cases remind us of some of the inherent difficulties that come from the intimate relationship that exists between public memories, legal principles, and retributional justice. Even if one grants that decisions like this serve some didactic purpose, the costs of carrying on prosecutions like this risk trivializing some of our Holocaust remembrances.

Moreover, given the convergence of varied interests, it should come as no surprise that the Israeli courts were not the only legal forums that were interested in Demjanjuk's wartime activities. Even if American authorities accepted the idea that John Demjanjuk may not have been "Ivan the Terrible," this did not mean that he couldn't have been an SS guard working in places like Sobibor or Flossenbürg. In May 1999, Justice Department attorneys filed a new lawsuit in a U.S. district court in Cleveland, claiming that Demjanjuk should once again have his citizenship revoked.[159] Two and a half years later, U.S. District Judge Paul Matia ruled that the U.S. government had shown "through clear, convincing and unequivocal evidence" that Demjanjuk had been a guard at several Nazi forced-labor camps and at the Sobibor extermination camp.[160] Ironically, some of the same evidence that saved Demjanjuk in the Israeli appellate process was now being used to take away his U.S. citizenship. Assistant Attorney General Michael Chertoff indicated that if this ruling was upheld, Demjanjuk could once again be extradited to a country that is interested in prosecuting him for war crimes. Demjanjuk was no longer "Ivan the Terrible," but he now was considered to be guard 1393, a criminal who worked at the Majdanek and Flossenburg concentration camps. In November 2004, the U.S. Supreme Court rejected Demjanjuk's attempt to keep his citizenship, and this decision will probably mean that he will be shipped to another country—

perhaps the Ukraine or Germany.[161] Some of the didactic lessons from Holocaust narratives were the same, but they had a different inflection.

Weighing the Costs and Benefits of Didactic Tales

When we follow the rhetorical progression of some of the legal and public arguments that provided the vectors of memory that circulated during the Kastner, Eichmann, and Demjanjuk trials, we begin to see several discernable patterns. Witness testimonials grow in importance, as so do the lists of potential Holocaust perpetrators. The Kastner affair would appear on a discursive horizon filled with stories about the Judenrate and the conflicting perceptions of "Yishuv-born Israelis and Holocaust survivors."[162] The Eichmann trial moved the spotlight away from the activities of Jewish leaders like Kastner and toward the Nazis themselves, while the Demjanjuk affair reminded us that all types of functionaries can end up in a legal courtroom.

If we are going to assess the positive benefits of these supposed didactic affairs, we need to attend to the costs as well. If we really believe in the importance of fair trials, how can we argue that these Holocaust trials protect the rights of defendants who have to face mounds of testimonial and documentary evidence on the Holocaust in general? Was the Israeli Supreme Court in 1993 telling us something we need to hear about the nature of survivor memories or legal historicizing? What did the younger generations learn from the Demjanjuk case that they couldn't get from reading or seeing other materials? How did any of these performances alter the ways that the younger generations thought about the Judeocide?

I firmly believe that such proceedings are inherently flawed, because they all attempt to hide the ideological pressures that are brought to bear in debates over Holocaust remembrance. Many of these tribunals end up using selective histories that become usable pasts, where the retrieval of "records" becomes a part of persuasive, ideological campaigns. The Kastner case was transformed into a critique of Jewish life in the diaspora and the alleged culpability of the Yishuv's Mapai Party. The Eichmann affair was used to explain the "uniqueness" of the Holocaust, and it also served as a countermemory that highlighted the shortcomings of the Nuremberg trials. By the time Demjanjuk took the stand, it was "Ivan the Terrible" who became the villain in new cautionary tales about the war criminals in the Holocaust. Were any of these proceedings really necessary?

5

Canada's Experiences with Holocaust Trials

I hope not everybody in Canada is as ready to abandon freedom of speech as this jury is.

—Douglas Christie, Zündel's Canadian Lawyer

The Canadian Jewish Congress once reported that about 10 percent of the more than 300,000 Jews living in Canada were Holocaust survivors, and many critics were convinced that some 3,000 Nazi war criminals[1] fled to Canada after the end of World War II.[2] Many of the diffuse vectors of memory that resonated with these audiences dealt with a number of issues—the mythic Canadian "haven" for fleeing war criminals, protecting the nation's multicultural heritage from the ravages of Holocaust revisionionism, and the preservation of Judeocide memories.

What made all of this very complicated for Canadian officials is the fact that there were many different communities living in that nation—including many German and Ukrainian immigrants—and these groups had very different didactic and dissident Holocaust memories. John-Paul Himka rebuked some writers in 1984 for forgetting that the "vast majority" of Ukrainians had not taken part in the extermination of Jews.[3] Himka was bothered by the fact that some members of the press were making blanket statements about Poles and Ukrainians, and he characterized such remarks as "demeaning ethnic generalizations."[4]

Yet Himka was writing at a time when many nations around the world had audiences that wanted more prosecution of war criminals. The ideological fragments that appeared in these modern commentaries contrasted sharply with the legal amnesias of the immediate postwar years. Stanley Barrett explains that during those earlier years, "Fascism had become a dirty word, and the world had had enough of racism and anti-Semitism."[5] Philip Wiess left us this survivor's record of Canadian life in the late 1940s:

> We had full freedom, but still from a point of spiritual satisfaction, there was a lot to be desired. . . . We were strangers in a strange land. You were not fully accepted, even in Jewish circles. There were barriers between Canadian citizens and those who survived. . . . For a certain period of time everything was dark, you could not be as happy as the Canadian who didn't go through the experiences of the Second World War. . . . Eventually the barriers broke down. For me it took a minimum of twenty years.[6]

Many interdisciplinary researchers have documented the traumatic problems experienced by the survivors who lived during these turbulent times,[7] and Wiess was not alone. Officially, Canada tried to encourage emigration to its sparsely populated areas, and some 5,000 war refugees crossed the Canadian border.[8]

Until the late 1960s and early 1970s, there were relatively few Canadians who openly talked about the perils of the Judeocide or called for trials of Nazi war criminals.[9] Cyril Levitt, a third-generation Canadian Jew, recalled that "the Holocaust was never broached directly in my house. It was a kind of disease that one didn't talk about. . . due partly to fear, partly pity, partly a sense of stigma."[10] Moreover, there were many residents who shared the notion that calling attention to Europe's "catastrophe" would only exacerbate the problems that were associated with anti-Semitism.

Yet with the passage of time, many Canadians would eventually join the ranks of those who did not want to forget, and organizations like B'nai B'rith of Canada and the Canadian Holocaust Remembrance Association were openly inviting their government to become more involved in the search for war criminals.

All of this was taking place at a time when Canadian officials were trying to find ways of protecting two cherished ideals—multiculturalism and freedom of expression.[11] For example, in 1966 the Special Committee on Hate Propaganda was formed (the Cohen Committee), and it released a report about how freedom of expression protection "stops this side of injury to the community itself and to individual members or identifiable groups innocently caught in verbal cross-fire that goes beyond legitimate debate."[12] On June 11, 1970, section 319 (2) of the Canadian Criminal Code was given royal assent, and anyone who willfully promoted hatred against an identifiable group could be fined or imprisoned.[13] By the mid–1980s, Canada's federal criminal code would be revised so that Canadian authorities could criminalize these three types of hate speech: the advocacy of genocide;[14] the public incitement of hatred likely to lead to a breach of the peace;[15] and the willful promotion of hatred.[16] When civil libertarians pointed out that the Canadian Charter of Rights and Freedoms protected "freedom of thought, belief, opinion, and expression," their critics responded that these rights were "subject only to such reasonable limits prescribed by law as can be demonstrably justified in a free and democratic society."[17] For the next five years, the courts were filled with cases challenging the regulation of hate propaganda.[18]

Given the unique nature of Canada's political and cultural milieu, we can readily understand why Canadians have crafted their own rhetorics about hate speech and Holocaust denial. Many of these postwar rules and regulations don't look anything like American court interpretations of the First Amendment of the U.S. Constitution, and Canadian jurists defend more restrictive, communitarian interpretations of freedom of expression that focus on the "duties" of rhetors and the "effects" of hate speech. When some of these lawyers and clerks quote American sources, they often select material from cases or theories that justify the placing of limitations on freedom of expression.[19]

Mayo Moran explains that in many of the Canadian narratives, legal commentators write and talk about the "profound harms of hate speech, the denial of the target's humanity."[20] Here critics argue that even traditional absolutists believe in some limits to free expression—such as libel, national security, sedition, and obscenity—and they contend that, by extension, Holocaust denial should be placed beyond the pale of free speech protection.[21]

These Canadian commentaries on war crimes and hate speech provide us with some unique sites of memory, and they help me extend some of the claims that I have been making about the role of didactic and dissident histories in courtrooms. In this chapter, I focus on some of the vectors of memory that surrounded three key Canadian Holocaust trials—the Keegstra, Zündel, and Finta cases. I begin by looking at some interesting legal and public commentaries on hate speech statutes, and then I turn my attention to salient Canadian discussions of war crimes.

James Keegstra and the Teaching of Revisionism in Canada

Between 1982 and 2000, a former Alberta high school teacher by the name of James Keegstra became one of the key figures in several Canadian Holocaust proceedings.[22] For more than a decade, Keegstra had been feeding students "in Eckville High School a steady diet of biased statements principally about Jews, but also about Catholics, Blacks, and others."[23] After some bitter school board meetings, Keegstra would eventually lose his teaching position, and it was alleged that he violated section 281 (12) of the Canadian Criminal Code, which criminalized the promotion of hate speech.[24] The indictment claimed that Keegstra had "wilfully" promoted hatred against "Jewish people" while teaching students at Eckville High School between September 1978 and December 1982.[25] Before his first trial, Keegstra tried to quash the indictment on the grounds that certain sections of the Canadian Criminal Code allowed for an infringement of his freedom of expression rights under the Charter.[26]

The facts that were presented in the Keegstra affair provided authorities with the types of moral and social complexities that law professors only dream of when they come up with hypotheticals for their classroom examinations.[27] For fourteen years, Keegstra had been telling students about the mystical power of the "international Jew" and the secretive power of banking conspiracies. In the early 1980s, Margaret Andrew told county authorities that her sons were being taught about the links between the Irish Republican Army and communism, and some of her children's class notes were filled with commentaries on how Jews "get what they can" and "will cut your throat."[28] Students learned about Talmudic inscriptions, but these were used in ways that questioned the nature and scope of the Holocaust. One class handout—which sadly echoed some of the claims that had been made by Eichmann (see chapter 4)—invited students to believe that the Zionists and the Nazis were active collaborators.[29]

In June 1984, Keegstra's preliminary hearing began in Red Deer's (Alberta) provincial courthouse, and many of his supporters sported "freedom of speech" buttons as they walked up the stairs. Bruce Fraser and Larry Phillippe were the Crown prosecutors, and Douglas Christie represented the defendant. The defense tried to argue that Keegstra was making selective comments about some, but not all, Jews, and that this didn't qualify as an attack on any identifiable group. Christie then quoted an article from Winston Churchill, entitled "Zionism versus Bolshevism," that appeared in the *Illustrated Sunday Herald.*[30] Fraser and Phillippe countered by reading sixty anti-Semitic fragments that came from Keegstra's various class assignments.

Interestingly enough, a few of Keegstra's former students didn't want to testify, and some even parroted back some of the claims that had been circulated in his lectures. For example, Danny Desrosiers told one Crown prosecutor that Keegstra "showed us pictures of the gas ovens," and they "were not very big. The Jewish people must have been very short."[31] When Fraser and Phillippe told Judge Douglas Crowe that they had some thirty other witnesses, the judge decided that he had heard enough. On the ninth day of the preliminary hearings, he announced that there "is, in my mind, no doubt these statements, or some of them . . . are capable of promoting hatred of the Jewish people."[32]

Some of the best narrative descriptions of both James Keegstra and his 1985 trial in the Court of Queen's Bench in Red Deer came from Alan Davies, who spent almost two weeks in the courtroom as a Crown witness. Davies never had to take the stand, but he would later write that he was able to observe the "defendant at close range" and formed these "indelible impressions":[33]

> Oblivious to the prosecutor's sarcasm, he [Keegstra] welcomed the opportunity to instruct everyone present, especially the media representatives, about the powers of darkness that are currently raging against Christian civilization, and which, at all costs, must be exposed and destroyed. . . . Keegstra was completely certain that he could identify these powers accurately, and no less certain that God fully agreed with his opinions. Indeed, any true Christian, he seemed to believe, must think as he thinks because the World of God itself plainly confirms every anti-Jewish assertion that has ever been uttered in history.[34]

Audiences in the courtroom heard about the power of the Illuminati, the many revolutions that were caused by Jewish manipulators, and the need for constant Christian vigilance.

Outside of the courtroom, things were much more explosive, as some communities began viewing this as a battle for the maintenance of their nation's multicultural heritage. Would Keegstra's Charter rights—which supposedly protected his "freedom of expression"—win out over the purported damage that was being inflicted by "hate propaganda"?[35] Bercuson and Wertheimer explain that some of the Jews living in Alberta were initially "shocked and dismayed by what happened in Eckville."[36] Like many marginalized communities, they had to decide just how much political pressure needed to be placed on Canadian legal officials:

> News was spotty at first, and press reports tended to concentrate on the Holocaust denial aspect of Keegstra's teachings. There was great uncertainty in the Jewish community about how much support Keegstra had, and fear that he represented a resurgence of the sort of virulent anti-Semitism that had been commonplace in Alberta in the 1930s. . . . [I]f the Jews responded too loudly, perhaps attacks on Jews would increase. . . . [O]ther Jews took a different, less cautionary approach. . . . These different approaches meant that the Jewish reaction to Keegstra was largely disunited and almost always *ad hoc.*[37]

The quick activities of the Crown prosecutors galvanized some of these factions when authorities sought out the help of public and private organizations that worried about the spread of anti-Semitism.

In many ways, this was a controversial case because it raised issues about the pervasiveness of anti-Semitism in Canadian society. Were the purveyors of these views living on the fringes of this multicultural nation, or was this a more endemic problem? Davies noted that "Keegstra did not invent this farrago of nonsense," and that the trial simply brought to the surface many of the latent tensions that have historically existed in Christian accounts of Judaism.[38]

In 1990, the Supreme Court finally held (in a four-to-three decision) that the criminal proscription of hate propaganda did not violate the Canadian Charter of Rights and Freedoms.[39] In her dissenting opinion, Justice Beverley McLachlin argued that courts should not be in the business of deciding whether certain types of "expression" advanced "in any way the values of truth, democracy, and self-realization which underlie the freedom."[40] Keegstra appealed, but after a second conviction in 1992, he was fined $3,000.[41]

Keegstra's appeals kept his name in the papers for half a dozen more years. In 1996, the Supreme Court of Canada—in a unanimous ruling—once again restored the former teacher's hate crime conviction, and this time observers were convinced that the case was finally being closed. Hal Joffe, of the Calgary Jewish Community Council, told reporters that "Keegstra has finally been adjudged by our highest court to be the hate monger that he is."[42] The defendant, now employed as a mechanic, talked about his "long fight," and he was convinced that all of his struggles were worth the effort.[43] In the end, noted Peeter Kopvillem, Keegstra remained "unrepentant."[44]

The Zündel Trials and the Limits of Canadian Freedom of Expression

At the same time that Canadians were hearing about teachers like Keegstra, they were reading about the legal trials and tribulations of Ernst Zündel, a worldwide disseminator of Holocaust revisionist material. Ernst Zündel is known internationally for his ideological battles with the Canadian government.[45] This former photo retoucher began associating with some of the world's leading anti-Semites,[46] and he allegedly claimed that "Nazi Germany never exterminated millions of Jews."[47] Before long, he was known as one of the leading popularizers of "revisionist" histories, and some of his material came from the famous think tank known as the Institute of Historical Review (IHR).[48] Although the vast majority of the material that Zündel was distributing was written by other neo-Nazis or Holocaust deniers, he did write two books, *The Hitler We Loved and Why* and *UFOS: Nazi Secret Weapons?*[49] By the early 1980s, he was sending Canadian parliamentarians some of these publications.[50] In 1994, he gained the attention of America's *60 Minutes* television program.[51]

Zündel's legal troubles began in the early 1980s when Sabina Citron went before a Canadian justice of the peace and pressed charges against him for willfully and falsely distributing damaging news.[52] Under a 1970 Canadian statute, a person could be prosecuted if he or she issued "a statement or tale known to be false and likely to cause mischief to the public interest in social and racial tolerance."[53] Zündel's materials were considered to be harmful because they allegedly hurt a variety of communities.[54] Zündel faced an indictment that involved two different but related charges:

1. He had published a four-page letter entitled "The West, War and Islam."[55] In it, he argued that there was an international Zionist conspiracy trying to control the world through bankers, Communists, and Freemasons.
2. He had also disseminated a thirty-page pamphlet entitled *Did Six Million Really Die?*[56]

Zündel would have to go through not just one, but several trials in the 1980s,[57] and in each of these the prosecution was in a difficult position because of formalistic requirements of the Canadian statutes. In these types of cases, prosecutors needed to show that the defendant was motivated by the willful intent to inflict harm on Jews.[58] The Crown thus had to proffer rhetorical narratives that showed how some of Canada's citizens were being stigmatized, and that this directly affected the Crown's goals of establishing social and racial tolerance. Some argued that Zündel was helping promote the idea that the Holocaust was a Zionist hoax.[59] Prosecutors therefore argued that these acts brought "injury or mischief" because Zündel was hurting Canadian Jewish survivors or the relatives of these survivors.

While some citizens might be mortified by having to appear in Court, it appears that Zündel relished the idea of doing battle with his critics. During his first trial in 1985, he appeared in court with a blackened face, carrying a cross that bore the inscription "Freedom of Speech."[60] When some of the Canadian jurists tried to halt these antics, this attracted a great deal of media attention, and Zündel helped catapult Canada into the international scholarly debates that focused on the free expression rights of revisionists and deniers.

On the surface, the Zündel trial may have looked like any other criminal prosecution based on a minor statute, but Canadian audiences were now going to hear discussions about the nature and scope of the Holocaust. This was because some of the jurists argued that the prosecution had to deal with the facticity of the Holocaust as they put together a prima facie case.[61] Other courts sidestepped some of these issues by taking "judicial notice" of some of these World War II facts, but in this first case the trial judge worried that taking judicial notice in this instance would mean that the prosecutor would no longer have to prove a key element of the case.[62] The original trial transcript contains these words from Judge Hugh Locke: "[T]o grant this motion . . . would have the effect, in the eyes of the public, as well as perhaps in the eyes of the jury and the accused, of not providing the defence and the accused with full answer and defence. It would have the effect of substantially eliminating the duty incumbent on the Crown insofar as the guilt of this accused is concerned."[63]

Locke decided that the prosecution was going to have to prove that the tract *Did Six Million Really Die?* contained false information. Zündel was also going to have to defend the truthfulness of some of the commentaries that he added to some "Richard Harwood" texts.[64] Harwood's pamphlet contained material that assumed that the Israelis were using the Holocaust "hoax" as leverage in their German compensation debates.[65]

In order to convict Zündel of having violated Canada's "false news" statute, the Crown had to create plausible narratives about the defendant's state of mind and his knowledge of the Holocaust. In one of the first trials, six concentration camp survivors talked about their horrible experiences,[66] and the prosecution showed a documentary film on the concentration camps that was once viewed by Nuremberg audiences.[67]

Therese O'Donnell has recently noted that one of the "fairly peculiar" features of "Holocaust denial" trials is that they often involve the use of "historians as witnesses,"[68] and in this particular instance the Crown prosecutors decided that they wanted to bring in some of the leading experts on the nature and scope of the Holocaust. Raul Hilberg, who was at that time a professor at the University of Vermont, told this Toronto jury in 1985 about some of the scholarly research on the "deeper architecture of the Final Solution,"[69] and he corroborated some of the evidence supplied by the survivor witnesses.

After having established the facticity of the Holocaust, the Crown shifted gears and tried to convince the Toronto jury that Zündel knew that he was distributing falsehoods. The prosecutors were claiming that no reasonable person who had researched the Holocaust could deny the extent of the Nazi devastation.[70] The Crown could then characterize Zündel as an anti-Semitic propagandist who threatened Canada's fostering of racial and social harmony.[71]

At these Canadian Holocaust trials, Zündel was represented by Douglas Christie,[72] who complained that some of the European restrictions on hate speech showed that narrow-minded people acted "as if we were living in an age when people were burned at the stake for their religious beliefs."[73] From Christie's point of view, Sabina Citron and the rest of Zündel's detractors were trying to defend some monolithic history.[74]

Zündel's first Toronto trial received a great deal of national and international coverage, and reporters recorded frequent clashes between Zündel's lawyer and Judge Locke. Rather than politely leaving the Holocaust survivor witnesses alone, Christie tried to test the memories of the prosecution witnesses by asking them to remember the names of relatives who were burned in Nazi ovens.[75]

The defense narratives were framed in ways that focused attention on the importance of dissent and open scientific inquiry. Christie called twenty witnesses to the stand,[76] and he even went to the trouble of bringing Robert Faurisson over from France so that this "expert" witness could support some of Zündel's assertions.[77] Faurisson appeared to have scored some points for the defendant, but during the cross-examination session he tried to answer one of the prosecutor's questions by claiming that while he did not know what happened to the 6,000,000 missing Jews, he was willing to take down the "names of family members" who had been lost so that he could try to find them.[78]

While the prosecutors focused on the effects of the circulation of denial materials, the defense responded by underscoring the importance of having liberal interpretations of Canada's free speech laws. Christie argued that the 1982 Canadian Charter of Rights contained a section that said that everyone had "freedom of thought, belief, opinion and expression, including freedom of the press and other media of communication."[79] The defense position rested on the assumption that during times of mass hysteria, empowered communities forget the importance of free speech rights.[80] Furthermore, Christie espoused the view that section 177 (which talked about injury caused by a "statement, tale or news") was "vague, imprecise and confusing."[81] For many of the supporters of the prosecution's case, one of the most maddening of Christie's assertions was his claim that the very existence of *any* historical disputes about the Holocaust provided proof that Zündel could not have knowingly violated Canada's "false news" statute.

If these defensive positions failed to convince the Toronto jury of Zündel's innocence, then Christie added to his legal arsenal by also claiming that Canadian courtrooms should not be involved in the business of refereeing historical disputes, and he questioned the constitutionality of restrictive legislation. In theory, even Zündel's allegedly "false" opinions should be protected from prosecutorial claims about possible harm.[82] At one point in his five-hour-long oration, Zündel's lawyer remarked that the "accused stands in place of anyone who desires to speak his mind. Even if you don't approve or agree with what he says, you must take it as a sacred responsibility not to allow the suppression of someone's honest beliefs."[83]

Because the facticity of the Holocaust had become an issue tied to the "false news" provisions of Canada's Criminal Code, both the prosecution and the defense spent a great deal of time discussing the extant historical and physical evidence that surrounded the existence of Nazi crematoriums, the official German memos on the "Final Solution," and the state of historiography in the 1980s. In many ways, this was the first time that Holocaust revisionists would go toe to toe with Holocaust historians, and it provides a perfect illustration of the difficulties that attend the balancing of the "interests of justice" and "didactic legality."[84] The Zündel trials offered new examples of how "the law" could be "enlisted in the project of safeguarding historical truth."[85]

During closing arguments, the Crown prosecutors tried to refocus attention on Zündel's love of Hitler, his identification with the Nazis, and his belief in an international Zionist conspiracy [86] Zündel's first trial would last eight weeks, and in February 1985 the jury would finally decide to acquit the defendant of the charge related to the pamphlet written by Zündel, "The West, War, and Islam." However, they also decided to convict him on the second charge, and in March he received a fifteen-month prison sentence.[87] Sabina Citron told the press that the "trial caused a lot of anguish and hard work—but it had to be done."[88] Near the end of the proceedings, Zündel claimed that the trial had helped him get "one million dollars worth of publicity."[89] Christie intoned that "tolerance cannot be legislated, understanding can't be legislated, kindness cannot be legislated."[90]

The first Zündel trial thus provides us with a textbook illustration of some of the costs and benefits that come from staging these public spectacles. Even decisions that end up protecting the procedural and substantive rights of defendants may have the unintended effect of distorting some of the histories of the Holocaust.[91] Given the temporal and monetary constraints of judicial proceedings, only some witnesses can appear on the stand, and only some of the documentary evidence can be presented. The juries, judges, and citizens who are told about the incomprehensibility of the Holocaust outside of the courtroom are now provided with legalistic frameworks that adjudicate between conflicting and partial representations and vectors of memory.

The passionate beliefs and combative attitudes of the court participants spilled over into the Canadian public sphere. Zündel's first trial was no longer just a criminal case that involved the possible violation of a few statutes—this was now a discursive war that involved a host of public Holocaust battles. For example, the treatment of the witnesses became an inevitable part of this complex dispute. Claude Adams thought that Christie's activities were "misdirected" and that his "witnesses were low-grade."[92] For several years, Canadian newspapers and journals were filled with stories that tried to gauge the impact of the first trial—had it increased or decreased the amount of Holocaust denial literature circulating within their national boundaries?[93]

The second Zündel trial (1988) attracted revisionists who realized that they now had a legal outlet that could help with the dissemination of their ideas. By now, even David Irving (see chapter 6) was showing an interest in these Canadian proceedings.[94] During the second Zündel trial, Judge Ronald Thomas took judicial notice of the Holocaust, and he justified his stance by noting that "the Nazi extermination of millions of Jews is so notorious as to not be the subject of dispute among reasonable persons."[95]

This, however, didn't mean that Zündel and his supporters couldn't interrogate some of the logistical or historical aspects of the Judeocide. This second trial is remembered as the legal affair that helped popularize the notorious "Leuchter Report"—a text filled with technical material on some of the Auschwitz facilities. Zündel paid Fred Leuchter thousands of dollars to go to Auschwitz and Birkenau and research the possible existence of the gas chambers. Leuchter claimed that he was an expert engineer, and his findings supported the controversial conclusion that the buildings at Birkenau could not have been used for massive killing.[96] As one might imagine, these were provocative claims, and Judge Thomas questioned Leuchter's credentials. When this four-week retrial ended in May 1988, Zündel was again convicted and sentenced.[97]

When the case of *Regina v. Zündel* reached the Canadian Supreme Court in 1992, a majority of the court decided that section 181 of the code infringed on the guarantee of freedom of expression that appeared in section 2(b) of the Canadian Charter of Rights and Freedoms, and they overturned Zündel's conviction.[98] Justice McLachlin, who spoke for the majority, opined that since Zündel's publications were a form of expression, this did not involve a "violent act." His words were covered by the section of the Charter that protected "the right of a minority to express its view, however unpopular it may be."[99] She went on to explain that section 181 of the code was based on some "anachronistic" positions that could be traced back to the Statute of Westminster in 1275, which introduced the notion that "false news or tales" threatened to bring "discord or slander" to the "King or his people, or the Great men of the Realm."[100] Section 181 had rarely been used in its long Canadian history, and this appellate court mentioned that this supported the view that it was "hardly essential to the maintenance of a free and democratic society."[101] In one key fragment, Justice McLachlin observed:

> To permit the imprisonment of people, or even the threat of imprisonment, on the ground that they have made a statement which 12 of their co-citizens deem to be false and mischievous to some undefined public interest, is to stifle a whole range of speech, some of which has long been regarded as legitimate and even beneficial to our society. . . . Such provisions [criminalizing racial slurs and hate propaganda] must be drafted with sufficient particularity to offer assurance that they cannot be abused so as to stifle a broad range of legitimate and valuable speech.[102]

The majority of the court was obviously bothered by legal regulations that included polarizing notions of "fact versus opinion" or "truth versus falsity."[103] This relatively liberal framing of events questioned the desirability of section 181 of the code because it allowed the virtually unlimited reach of the state based on the phrase "injury or mischief to a public interest."[104] Taken to the "ultimate extreme," these words could "render nugatory the free speech guarantee of the *Charter.*"[105]

The dissenting opinion, written by Justices Cory and Frank Iacobucci, followed portions of the Crown's narrative and focused on Zündel's apparent knowledge of the falsity of his Holocaust denial literature. According to these jurists, this "revisionist project" flew in the face of a united "international community" that had "cast a jaundiced eye on all forms of racism and has bonded together to reject and obliterate it."[106] Cory and Iacobucci argued that the lower courts had determined that Zündel had simply ignored the extensive documentation of the truth of the Holocaust. For example, Professor Hilberg had testified that while "some camps had labour facilities annexed to them, Belzec, Treblinka, Sobibor and Chelmno were exclusively 'killing factories.'"[107] One Holocaust survivor, Rudolf Vrba, replied during cross-examination that he "saw 1,765,000 people walk into the space before my eyes, knowing that space is absolutely closed and no road out. . . . [W]ould you perhaps suggest that they are still there?"[108] From the point of view of the dissent, the "Crown showed that the appellant misrepresented the work of historians, misquoted witnesses, fabricated evidence, and cited non-existent sources."[109]

Supporters of both the Crown position and the dissent contended that before 1992, Canada seemed to be joining the ranks of the international communities who wanted stricter regulations for some types of expression. As Fogo-Schensul once observed, "an absolutist position on freedom of expression" might be appropriate for the United States, but "many other nations have come to a different conclusion."[110] When civil libertarians tried to talk about the inviolable nature of freedom of expression, people like Kenneth Stern responded that "Holocaust education alone" was not enough, because this was an issue that involved "anti-Jewish hatred as part of a political agenda."[111]

A review of the public and legal reactions to the Zündel trials also shows that a surprising number of scholars and ordinary citizens around the world supported the efforts of the Canadian government. Prutschi, for example, claimed that prosecuting Zündel had brought "greater sympathy for the Jewish community."[112] Responding to claims that such actions violated national and international norms of freedom of expression, Hill noted:

> Many observers have argued that the purveyors of "hate propaganda" would languish in obscurity if they were not given prominence by the publicity of the trial. This is partly wishful thinking; they had already obtained much publicity. It is also the same as telling those who believe they suffer an injustice for which there is a remedy in law that they should remain silent or struggle with their attackers in other ways outside the courts.[113]

Hellmut Schade, writing in the *Ottawa Citizen*, claimed that "Mr. Zündel's ideas are remnants" of a time when "*Weltanschauung* Canadians and their allies" had "fought in the Second World War."[114] Given the persuasive power of racist speech, "it is not enough for societies that claim to be committed to the ideals of social and political equality and respect for individual dignity to remain neutral and passive when threats to these values exit."[115] Kenneth Lasson, a believer in the importance of group libel, has argued that "Holocaust denial is not an attempt at free inquiry, but at distortion."[116] Vera Ranke echoed these sentiments by observing that Zündel's anti-Semitic publications are considered to be extremely detrimental to the well-being of many communities.[117]

Obviously, the strongest defenses of a revisionist/denier's rights would come from absolutist positions that argue for maintaining the presumptive protection of the marketplace of ideas. Morris Manning, for example, observed that if a person did not have the right to criticize a historical event, then "freedom of speech is meaningless."[118] Defenders of an open marketplace of ideas claim that exposure to such material might actually reduce "racial hostilities," because the presence of such shocking material could act as a catalyst and be the "first step in awakening us from this slumber."[119] Alan Borovoy takes a very consequentialist angle when he opines that it is "unwise from square one to prosecute this kind of thing."[120]

Others might argue that some of these restrictions have created administrative nightmares for government officials who try to close down Web sites located within their own borders.[121] In spite of these problems, throughout 2003–2004 Zündel's work was considered to be so controversial that he would face Canadian deportation hearings, so that Germany could prosecute him for the circulation of his neo-Nazi and "Holocaust-denying activities."[122]

Those who defend the civil liberties of Holocaust deniers/revisionists might also argue that the Zündel trials helped legitimate and popularize the work of institutions like the IHR.[123] Fogo-Schensul reluctantly admitted that by 1997, the IHR's Web site was linked to twelve other sites.[124] It could be argued that those Web sites would have been created in spite of these Canadian trials, but the visibility of these proceedings may have had an adverse impact in that the publicity encouraged the creation of controversial Web sites.

Critics also note that some of these trials may also have raised the stature of some of these revisionists and their "experts," who can now claim that they have done intellectual battle with titans like Hilberg. As Heinrichs observed in 1988, "[W]hile many Canadians think it is good that Zündel was convicted, a substantial segment of the community suspects" that "the price paid for conviction was too high."[125] An editorial writer for the *Toronto Star* made these incisive comments during the middle of the proceedings:

> The appeal [*sic*] court found that the trial judge had erroneously rejected evidence that Zündel wished to introduce—such as photographs and books that Zündel claimed he relied on in forming his belief what he published was true. Accordingly, Zündel will be in a better position the next time around to establish his defence, and obtain an acquittal. . . . What more do we need to convince us that there are better ways of dealing with the Zündels of the world than using the criminal law?[126]

These are the types of arguments that I have found to be persuasive in my analyses of didactic and dissident trials, and even Douglas has had to admit that some courts end up treating "the Holocaust as just another historical event about which unpopular claims can be made."[127]

Liberal defenders who object to the Zündel trials might also point out that we can always support the efforts of those who provide counterspeech networks or who monitor and critique hate speech sites. These could be part of what some call extrajudicial remedies. For example, two of the most effective organizations involved in such rebuttals include Ken McVay's Nizkor Project[128] and the Simon Wiesenthal Center.[129]

Unfortunately, it looks as though the Zündel trials were only the beginning of Canada's involvement with Holocaust denial proceedings. A relatively new site, the 1996 "Zündelsite," became the first Internet target of an inquiry by the Canadian Human Rights Commission.[130] Citizens and scholars living in the United States may soon hear similar clarion calls for stricter regulations of the Internet.[131]

Regina v. Finta *and* *Canadian War Crimes Legislation*

Canadian authorities decided in 1986 that they were going to create a commission that looked into allegations that Canada was still a haven for former Nazis, and the Deschenes Commission (directed by Quebec Superior Court judge Jules Deschenes) put together a report that indicated that at least twenty suspected war criminals might be living in Canada.[132] The commission's report indicated that the government needed to look at the war records of several hundred potential suspects.[133] Special teams of police, prosecutors, and historians were set up to begin investigating Canadian war crime allegations.[134] The Deschenes Commission suggested that investigators should have access to confidential pension records, and it asked that officials streamline denaturalization and deportation processes.

The Deschenes Commission's findings became the basis of a 1987 amendment of the criminal code in Ottawa,[135] and some onlookers hoped that Canada was now going to be viewed as one of the international leaders in the prosecution of all types of war criminals. In December 1987, Canadian authorities showed that they were serious about stepping up efforts to prosecute war criminals when they arrested seventy-six-year-old Imre Finta at a Hamilton, Ontario, bus terminal. The former restaurant owner was considered to be the first person to be prosecuted under Canada's new laws, and several of his relatives had to post $100,000 bail before he could temporarily leave Toronto's Don Jail.[136] Upon hearing of Finta's arrest, Sabina Citron—the same activist who had helped initiate proceedings against Zündel—exclaimed that this was "indeed a historical [*sic*] day for Canada. It restores a sense of justice for all who suffered under the Nazis."[137] Citron had earlier remarked that Finta had been involved in World War II atrocities, and Finta had responded that these were "awful, dirty lies."[138] As Irwin Cotler noted in 1996, the Finta case turned out to be a "multilayered legal inquiry," where the "factual backdrop" included "an exercise in Holocaust historiography and the implementation of the Nazi 'final solution' in Hungary."[139] I would of course argue that the affective dimensions of these "mournful and accusatory" memories highlight the problematics of some of these didactic historicizations.[140]

Take, for example, the vectors of memory that were used in the creation of the Crown's didactic renditions of Finta's role in the Judeocide. The prosecutors' narratives take us back to 1944, when Finta served as a captain in the Hungarian Mounted Police. He was supposed to have kidnapped, robbed, and confined 8,617 Jews while they waited to be sent to Nazi death camps in Auschwitz and Strasshof.[141] It took almost two years for this case to make its way through Canada's pretrial system, and observers learned that the omnipresent Douglas Christie would be Finta's lawyer. Part of the holdup in bringing Finta to trial stemmed from the fact that Christie was already preparing for Zündel's second trial.[142]

The initial trial proceedings against Finta began in November 1989, and Justice Archibald Campbell of the Ontario Supreme Court supervised these proceedings. The defendant pleaded not guilty to four counts of war crimes and four counts of crimes against humanity.[143] When he was asked by the court to enter a plea, Finta responded in Hungarian: "I have saved Jews, never molested them."[144]

The thin line that purportedly separates judicial and extrajudicial interests was crossed when officials learned that a popular film, *Music Box*, arrived in movie theaters in Canada in January 1990. Was it mere coincidence that the plot line of the movie involved the legal defense of a Hungarian American who was accused of having committed atrocities in Hungary during World War II? Jessica Lange played the part of a Chicago lawyer who tries to defend her father against these charges, but eventually she begins to suspect that her client might be guilty. Interested onlookers could have interpreted the daughter's awakening as a representative anecdote that symbolized Canada's belated anamnesic practices. Justice Campbell, who worried about the possible effect that the movie might have on jurors' perceptions, instructed them to avoid seeing *Music Box*.[145]

At least in this particular case, it looked like Canadian prosecutors would have little trouble identifying Finta as the abusive Hungarian policeman. At least three witnesses said that the defendant had helped facilitate the loading of Jews into boxcars at a brickyard,[146] and some witnesses claimed that Finta knew that these boxcars were destined for the Nazi death camps. One witness, Margit Hahn, even admitted having dated Finta for several months, and she testified that Finta had "called me a stinking whore, a Jewish whore, all kinds of dirt."[147]

In many ways, the Finta case was one of the first didactic trials where Canadians heard about some of the specific horrors of Nazi deportations and exterminations. Tibor Drucker, who was fifty-nine years old at the time of the trial, was initially considered to be one of the best witnesses because of his articulateness. He told his Ontario audiences that his train was headed for Auschwitz before it was diverted to a different location in Austria.[148] On direct examination, Drucker said that he remembered that the brickyard was so crowded that you couldn't help stepping on other people, and that the enclosure had little food or water.[149] Yet when Christie asked Drucker about his own social agency, this prosecution witness admitted that he had not searched for any water at that time.[150]

Christie also took advantage of the forty-five-year gap in time by asking the prosecution witnesses about their activities since the time of the Judeocide. Had they seen or read anything about these wartime events during these interim years? Drucker, for example, was asked about his reading of history books and his understanding of the Eichmann trial. Could this witness be sure that his testimony was based on his own remembrances, or was he recollecting material that might have been produced by others?[151] After some intense cross-examination, it "emerged that his recollection of dates was based on documents that he studied."[152]

In the same way that French defense attorneys in their own Holocaust cases tried to reduce the social agency of Vichy officials,[153] Christie tried to argue that Finta was simply obeying "superiors' orders." The judges and prosecutors at the Nuremberg trials had heard similar claims, but this defense attorney persuasively argued that his client's job primarily involved the collection of jewelry and other valuables from Jewish prisoners.[154]

The Crown prosecutors may have thought that they had positively identified Finta, but Christie tried to create some doubt in the courtroom when he introduced into evidence some conflicting material that had been presented in a prior 1948 Hungarian court case.[155] Some of this earlier evidence came from a mysterious man named Imre Dallos, who recalled that the Szeged brickyard camp was controlled by a Hungarian lieutenant by the name of Bodolai. Dallos—who died in 1963—told the Hungarian court that another lieutenant by the name of Narai was also a powerful figure in the brickyard. The only prosecutorial witness who was asked about these names, Livia Fonyo, remembered the name of Narai, but denied that Bodolai had been the commander of the brickyard.[156]

During his closing peroration, Christie reminded jurors that the Hungarians were a people who lived under Nazi rule, and that some of the witnesses had testified that there was a German officer present in the brickyard when these atrocities had taken place. The defense pointed out that some of the prosecutorial documents had also mentioned that a German commandant had been on the scene.[157] Christie was clearly implying that the Hungarian police were not acting on their own initiative when they loaded people into the boxcars.

In many ways, Christie was trying to deploy some familiar functionalist arguments—here was a Hungarian subaltern caught up in the fog of war. Within the defense scenarios, Finta's choices resembled those that had confronted the Royal Canadian Mounted Police (RCMP) officers who were ordered to round up Japanese Canadians during World War II.[158]

Christie was on a roll, and he now averred that Canada's war crimes legislation was "convoluted and diabolical."[159] Jurors were told that the authorities in Canada, Australia, and Britain were watching these proceedings, and that if they "resurrect the grievances of the Second World War" by convicting Finta, there would be "an outpouring of unjust charges in those three countries against other men."[160] As far as this defense attorney was concerned, alleged war criminals could not be found guilty unless prosecutors showed that it could be proven "beyond a reasonable doubt" that the defendants knew that they were in violation of international law.[161]

After hearing the evidence that was presented by both sides in the controversy, Justice Campbell told the jury that they needed to remember that forty-six years had indeed passed, and that sometimes innocent people had been convicted because of false identifications.[162] The jury was also cautioned to remember that it would be "dangerous to convict" Finta for the deaths in the boxcars, because they had not heard any medical evidence on the causes of these deaths. At the same time, jurors were not supposed to be sending their compatriots any larger metamessage about international war crimes.[163]

In May 1990, an Ontario jury determined that Imre Finta should be acquitted of manslaughter and other atrocities charges.[164] The jury had been composed of eight women and four men, and they had discussed the facts and issues in the case for more than twelve hours.[165] Eventually, Finta was found not guilty on each of the eight counts that had been based on the transporting of the more than 8,000 Hungarian Jews in 1944.[166]

The reactions from the victims who had testified against Finta were surprisingly mixed. Patricia Chisholm of *Maclean's* reported that they "ranged from relief to stunned disbelief."[167] Zsuzsa Szendrei, an Auschwitz survivor, noted that while she was "furious," she could "imagine that Finta has already suffered a lot."[168]

This forgiving attitude was not something that was shared by those who wanted to see Canada more involved in these war crimes trials. Tibor Drucker claimed that "when he gave evidence" in the trial, he had "the feeling it was a big thing that in Canada, 45 years after the war, [that] such a process could even be started."[169] Drucker was only sixteen years old when he was taken from his home in Hungary to an Austrian concentration camp. He was fortunate enough to have survived, but he lost one of his siblings and his mother.

This clash of Canadian didactic and dissident memories brought to the surface some conflicting traumatic memories. After the jury announced its decision in the Ontario courtroom, Finta was said to have broken into tears, exclaiming that "nobody believes Finta a Nazi."[170] The chairperson of the Canadian Holocaust Remembrance Association, Helen Smolack, proclaimed that such a decision "makes us lose faith in the justice system of Canada."[171] When news of the verdict reached Austria, Simon Wiesenthal told reporters that he could not believe the verdict.[172] Retired Quebec judge Jules Deschenes remarked, "They charged him. He was acquitted. Justice was served."[173]

Other observers thought that this jury verdict spelled the end of Canada's pursuit of Nazi criminals, and perhaps that was not such a bad thing. Barbara Amiel, writing a week after the end of the trial, provided this interesting commentary:

> Now that he is acquitted, I wondered about all those Canadian schoolchildren who watched the trial as a part of their history courses. How will their teachers explain the reaction of the Canadian Jewish community to the decision of 12 jurors good and true? Will they be told the Jews made a mistake in calling Finta a horrid Nazi? Somehow, I don't think so. . . . Imre Finta was charged as a criminal for performing his legal duties as a policeman in Hungary during the war. . . . As for the manslaughter charges, they referred to people who were said to have died during the train journey to the concentration camp because of several conditions in the cattle cars into which Finta's gendarmerie had loaded them. Those charges should never have been brought.[174]

Perhaps the Crown prosecutors would drop the matter.

That did not happen. Just a few days after the reading of the initial verdict, Christopher Amerasinghe, the lead prosecutor, began sifting through the evidence. Apparently, Finta made some key admissions to RCMP officials, but during the pretrial hearings Justice Campbell was forced to throw these out because of tainted police evidence.[175] After evaluating the Crown's case, the prosecutorial team decided that it had found thirty-six grounds for appeal, and it asked the five-member Ontario Court of Appeals to look into the possibility that Finta be retried.[176] Several of the key grounds for appeal included:

1. Judge Campbell's allowance of the 1948 evidence from Imre Dallos on Bodolai and Narai;[177]
2. Douglas Christie's quotation from a Bible passage in which Jesus doesn't answer his accusers—which allegedly created the unfair inference that Finta was being falsely accused by Canada's Jews;[178]
3. Christie's intimidation of the jury when he told them that "if you convict, you are going to suffer, too";[179] and
4. The judge's final instructions had not gone far enough in trying to neutralize Christie's inflammatory remarks regarding the alleged "convoluted, diabolical" Canadian war crimes legislation.[180]

In April 1992, a divided Ontario Court of Appeals (three to two) decided that Finta's prior acquittal would stand. The court determined that although the trial judge may have made a legal error when he called in some evidence that was not introduced by the Crown, this did not result in any substantial "miscarriage of justice."[181]

By this time, many government officials and interested parties were convinced that changes needed to be made in the ways that Canada handled any future investigations of war criminals. Obviously, the complexities of these cases were hindering trial prosecutions, so writers like David Matas and Paul Marcus suggested that the government needed to consider expanding its remedies to include denaturalization and deportation options.[182] The Crown prosecutors didn't give up, and they decided that they were going to appeal the Finta case. This time it would be the seven judges on the Canadian Supreme Court who would hear about the problematics of Christie's position, and the appellants argued that the jury should have been able to make some key decisions about whether certain offences constituted war crimes or crimes against humanity.[183] "This is an important case for the crown," noted Amerasinghe, "because the subject has given rise to much controversy in the nation."[184]

During oral argument before the seven judges, Christie once again claimed that Finta had only been following orders when he participated in the round up of Hungarian Jews. The defendant was characterized as someone who couldn't have thrown "people into burning pits." The Canadian authorities were dealing with someone who simply "confiscated property."[185] From a technically legal standpoint, Finta had little choice because his actions in 1944 were a part of "a legitimate exercise in state security for the preservation of the battle zone."[186] Christie went on to claim that because Hungary was an ally of the Nazis, this meant that the Jews were considered their "joint" enemies.[187] This obstinate attorney also recirculated the comparisons that he had been making about Finta's situation and the Canadian officers who participated in the internment of 22,000 Japanese Canadians during the war.[188]

Amerasinghe responded to Christie's arguments by trying to magnify Finta's role in the round up of the more than 8,000 Jews from the Hungarian village of Szeged. Amerasinghe told the court that the legality of Finta's activities in 1944 was beside the point, especially when judges were evaluating issues involving moral wrongs.[189]

In March 1994, the Supreme Court in Canada rendered its first decision regarding the interpretation of Canada's war crimes laws.[190] The country's highest appellate court upheld the constitutionality of Canada's war crimes statutes, but by a vote of four to three they also upheld Finta's acquittal.[191] As long as the orders of a superior were not "manifestly illegal," then the accused was going to be presumed to have little volition during wartime. Moreover, the prosecution had to show that the accused somehow knew that he or she was committing a *Canadian* crime when engaging in potentially culpable acts.[192]

In one of the most intriguing parts of the Canadian Supreme Court opinion, Justice Cory argued that Finta had been living during a very stressful period in Hungary's history.[193] A survey of newspaper accounts during 1944 showed that the dominant public opinion at the time supported the deportation of Hungarian Jews. Because the confiscation of Jewish property was done openly, this tended to show the historical legality of Finta's activities.[194] This was a rare and fascinating way for a jurist to have put together select vectors of memory.

B'nai B'rith Canada's legal counsel, David Matas, averred that the decision "sounds the death knell for the made-in-Canada solution of prosecuting war criminals. . . . The law has been so wound up with complexities . . . that it's virtually impossible to get a conviction."[195] From the point of view of Crown officials, it had taken seven years to test Canada's new war crimes statutes, and the only successful conviction had involved Jacob Luitjens's deportation proceeding. Irving Abella told reporters that he was "dismayed" because the Supreme Court seemed to be "lessening" the "uniqueness of the Holocaust" and the "moral suasion of the Nuremberg Courts and the *Nuremberg* decisions."[196] Matas told reporters that in spite of the legal impediments, "we have to deal with these murders like any others. Otherwise, we're saying killing is wrong, unless you're killing Jewish victims."[197]

Conclusion: Didactic Spectacles can't Provide Definitive Holocaust Accounts

As I looked over the legal and public arguments that surrounded the Keegstra, Zündel, and Finta trials, I had to ask myself this question—had these didactic spectacles really served the interests of either the victims of the Judeocide or future generations? A synoptic look at some of these Canadian cases provides ample evidence of the specific problems that attended these proceedings—problems with identification, the passage of time that erodes some memories, the prejudicial reading of outside materials in the interim, the unintentional bracketing out of some facts, the selective use of witness testimonials, and so forth. These problems in and of themselves would justify my skepticism, but we also need to take into account some of the more general issues that come from legal historicizing. Vivian Curran notes how

> [j]udicial reification . . . banalizes by eliminating the unspoken, and by equating the judicial record with reality itself. This problem generally affects the relation between the judicial event and adjudicated life occurrences, but it is a particularly acute problem with respect to the holocaust [*sic*]. . . . To reduce the unspeakable to words is to transmute it into material which must fit within a previously constructed system for the assimilation of data, but one that has been constructed of categories that cannot encompass events or ideas of the order of magnitude of the holocaust.[198]

Perhaps silence is not always the answer, but we do not need to think of courtrooms as the key public forums that will provide us with the exclusive or definitive didactic lessons about the Judeocide.

6

Understanding England's Holocaust Memories

"[T]he reality of the Holocaust, which is overwhelmingly documented, doesn't hinge on the outcome of this trial."

—Walter Reich, "The Stakes in the Holocaust Trial"

"During the 1930s and World War II," argues Tony Kushner, "the British government and its apparatus" often "downplayed the fate of the Jews under Nazi control."[1] British nationalists like to remember that they provided a haven for political refugees during this conflict, but these same mythic tales glossed over some of the political ambiguities that surrounded the Allied responses to the Judeocide. After the war, Britain was considered to be one of the victorious "liberators" of the concentration camps, but in recent years this image has been tarnished by those who contend that the British could have done more either to prevent the "Final Solution" or to aid the victims of the catastrophe.[2]

In this chapter, I analyze some of the rhetorics surrounding several key British Holocaust trials and review how some communities within the United Kingdom have reacted to the Sawoniuk (1999)[3] and Irving (2000) trials.[4] I begin by writing about the liberation of Bergen-Belsen and contemporary commentaries on British attitudes toward war crimes trials.

Bergen-Belsen and British Postwar Forgetfulness

As World War II progressed, governments in exile continued to push for war crimes proceedings, but it would be the massive press coverage that followed the liberation of Bergen-Belsen, Buchenwald, and Dachau that would galvanize public opinion against the Nazis. For example, after Winston Churchill received a letter from Dwight D. Eisenhower describing some of the camps, he announced that a parliamentary delegation was going across the Channel so that they "might have ocular and first-hand proof of the atrocities."[5]

On April 15, 1945, the British liberated the concentration camp of Bergen-Belsen, and Raymond Phillips would write that Belsen "became the archetype of the rest; and a proof that it was not an imaginary evil which the Allies had been fighting for almost six years."[6] After a lengthy trial, Belsen's former commandant and several other Germans would be hanged, while others received lengthy prison sentences. Unfortunately, these types of cases had the unintended effect of blurring the perceptual lines that separated death camps from concentration camps.

For the next half-century, there would be relatively few British trials that touched on questions involving Holocaust memories.[7] While the Americans conducted dozens of trials that tried to extend some of the Nuremberg "principles," the British tried "lesser" war criminals, and they quickly phased out some of these programs.[8]

Postwar England should have been an inhospitable place for former enemies, but this may not have been the case. Jon Silverman noted that when "it comes to dealing with the greatest act of mass-murder [in] this century, the Holocaust, English justice has not exactly distinguished itself."[9] In the aftermath of the postwar Nuremberg trials, many politicians and civil servants in Great Britain "insisted that no war criminals had entered the United Kingdom."[10]

By the 1980s, things were beginning to change as a number of organizations began sending the British government lists of alleged war criminals. England's Sir Thomas Hetherington and Scotland's Thomas Chambers were asked to review the existing British laws on war crimes,[11] and their committee determined that investigators needed to "mount a number of criminal prosecutions for clear violations of long-standing international law."[12] The British *Report of the War Crimes Inquiry* stated that it was "a generally recognized principle of international law that belligerent and neutral states have a right to exercise jurisdiction in respect of war crimes since they are crimes *ex jure genium*."[13] This meant that any citizen or resident of the United Kingdom should face criminal charges on the basis of having violated international laws or customs of war.[14]

The commission's findings helped usher in debates over the legitimacy of the British War Crimes Act. Geoffrey Howe asked how courts were going to sift through evidence that came from witnesses and defendants "who were already in the twilight of their lives."[15] One journalist complained that the act was not being considered to "redress an injustice in any ordinary sense of the word" but was being used "to assuage a political appetite."[16]

The debates over the War Crimes Act were very divisive,[17] and ultimately Margaret Thatcher and several of her cabinet members overruled some of the Lords and reintroduced the bill. Thatcher had recently visited Babi Yar in Kiev, and she had learned about how 30,000 Jews had been killed by the Nazis at that location.[18] This tour strengthened her resolve, and she was convinced that the British needed the War Crimes Act of 1991.

Detractors of the War Crimes Act understood the motivation behind the legislation, but they wondered whether this type of legislation created new heritage industries. James Heartfield would write that

> the other modern development which was reflected in the War Crimes legislation is our growing cultural fascination with the Holocaust. As the memory of the event itself recedes, Holocaust films, plays, documentaries and museums increase in number. . . . From the Washington Museum to the Berlin memorial, the public appetite for recollection of the Holocaust is growing. . . . With the war crimes law, the hope was that unalloyed evil would be put in the dock.[19]

Before the passage of the War Crimes Act, British jurisdiction had extended to some types of war crimes trials on the European continent,[20] but now the act allowed for trials of many more citizens.[21] Once these British laws were on the books, it was only going to be a matter of time before some former enemy would stand trial for alleged war crimes. In this instance, that person would be Anthony Sawoniuk. The Sawoniuk trial would become the first completed prosecution of a war crimes defendant in Britain's history.

The Sawoniuk Trial

Anthony Sawoniuk, a retired rail worker, was initially accused of having murdered hundreds of Jews in Belarus during World War II. British officials found that Sawoniuk had made his way to Britain in 1946, and by that time he was already on Belarus's list of its most wanted criminals.[22] British authorities believed that they had evidence that tended to show that Sawoniuk had been a member of a "Nazi-organized police outfit," and he would be accused of four counts of murder that contravened the British common law as outlined in the War Crimes Act.[23] His trial signaled that "many thousands just like him" helped perpetrate genocide.[24] Christopher Browning, an American historian who would later take the witness stand in this trial, remarked in November 1998 that "the admirable efforts of the prosecution" would help erase the memories of the absurd sentences that had been imposed by a West German court in the 1960s.[25]

Many of these investigators began to realize that they needed to focus their attention on Sawoniuk's activities in the small town of Domachevo. Today Domachevo is considered to be a resort town, but during World War II it was contested space between German and Russian forces. When the Nazis came through this region, they were looking for volunteers who might be interested in fighting the Communists, and Sawoniuk was said to have been so dangerous that his fellow police officers feared him.[26]

Didactic Histories and the Prosecution's Case in the Sawoniuk Trial

Vivian Curran has commented on some of the "ideological drifts" that float "under the frozen surface of legal texts,"[27] and the *Sawoniuk* case would be filled with unanticipated twists and turns. Many British audiences expressed their ambivalence as they watched this new World War II war crimes trial. John Morris, an early opponent of the War Crimes Act, had to switch gears and make sure that the government could put together some prima facie cases. This was not always an easy task, given the legal biases of those believed in the differences between testimonial memoirs and judicial evidence,[28] the passage of time, and the occasional lack of some documentary authentication.

Sawoniuk was trying to characterize himself as a Polish freedom fighter, a young innocent living in a border town. When Sawoniuk was first notified that he was under investigation, he tried to claim that he was a victim of mistaken identity. While he admitted that he had given some "information" to the Nazis, he was "very, very upset" and steadfastly denied ever wearing a German uniform or having killed anyone.[29]

By the time that Sawoniuk's trial actually got under way in February 1999, the charges against the defendant had been whittled down so that he would be tried for four counts of murder.[30] The defendant was now charged with having murdered several Jewish men and women "in circumstances constituting a violation of the laws and customs of war."[31] One of Sawoniuk's barristers, William Clegg, pointed out that this former Belorussian was entitled to raise his own defenses, and he argued that potential defense witnesses were intimidated by politically motivated officials who were "keen" on the idea of conviction.[32] Many of the prosecutorial witnesses came from the town of Borisy—considered to be a "partisan village"—and some claimed that Sawoniuk had "freely admitted to having killed partisans."[33] To borrow a phrase from Marita Sturken, what we got was a "tangle" of histories and memories, where there was a great deal of "traffic" depending on "political intent."[34]

During the first day of these proceedings, Sawoniuk "limped" into Court One. The lead prosecutor explained that he would soon be calling Christopher Browning to the stand, and audiences were informed that Browning was "an expert in matters relating to the Holocaust and the Final Solution of the Jewish people."[35] A key issue, of course, was whether Browning knew anything about Sawoniuk's individuated activities or his guilt.

The prosecutors wanted to provide the jury with both documentary and testimonial evidence, and during his opening statement, the Queen's Counsel noted that he was convinced that Sawoniuk had been an important part of the Nazi war machine.[36] The prosecutorial narrative punctuated time by focusing attention on the events of September 1942 and "search-and-kill operations."[37] Sir John Nutting claimed that the "evidence indicates, in our submission, that the defendant not only was prepared to do the Nazi bidding, but carried out their genocidal policy with enthusiasm."[38] The Queen's Counsel painted a picture of a prewar idyllic haven, where the Jewish majority lived side by side with Poles, Ukrainians, and Belarussians.[39] Sawoniuk could therefore be caricatured as one of those collaborators who broke this peace.[40]

Nick Hopkins noted that the "horror of the Holocaust" had been "described in harrowing detail at the Old Bailey."[41] The retired British rail ticket collector was portrayed as an inhuman beast who shot dozens of women in the back with a machine gun. Nutting implied that Sawoniuk was responsible for many murders that might escape documentation, and that the defendant had worked with the German army's *Einsatzgruppen*.[42]

Several days into the trial, the jury was shown photographs of Domachevo, so that they could see both the layout of the village and the surrounding area.[43] One photograph, identified as photograph number 33, showed the crowded conditions of the town's Jewish ghetto. Another photo illustrated the vantage point of those who would later testify about the death march to Sandy Hills.[44] From a critical rhetorical perspective, these types of theatrics helped magnify the scope and magnitude of the defendant's alleged crimes.

At the same time, the entire court began to make preparations for an unusual 1,000-mile trek to the Republic of Belarus.[45] For several days, millions of readers were provided with daily summaries of the activities of the migrating Sawoniuk court.[46] One newspaper reported that the small Russian obelisk that memorialized the massacre of thousands at Domachevo only talked about the "victims of the German Fascist terror" because "Soviet memorials never mention Jews."[47]

The Sawoniuk entourage braved bitterly cold temperatures of minus 14 degrees so that they could see and feel what life must have been like when the Wehrmacht's 487 Infantry and 22nd Cavalry came to the town in 1941.[48] Judge Humphrey Potts and the other participants got to see the buildings that once housed the Nazis, and they also visited the site of the old Jewish ghetto. Maureen Messent wrote:

> A British jury trudged through the snow in a far-flung corner of what used to be a Soviet satellite country this week. . . . Those who say they witnessed his killings are in their 70s and 80s. . . . Add to the forgetfulness of old-age the dreadful spirit of vengeance they show, and there is surely danger of a great miscarriage of justice. Isn't it better . . . , in cases like this . . . , [to] leave retribution to the God whom old Sawoniuk and they are now well on their way to meeting?[49]

This was, of course, not the dominant view of the participants who entered Old Bailey. Ben-Zion Blustein, one of the first individuals to take the stand, described how "Andrusha" (Sawoniuk) had once been "a man of power, a master, a lord."[50] David Hirsh, who attended many of these trial sessions, would later recall that Blustein "seemed to me to be a very typical Jewish Holocaust survivor. He appeared tough, but now old. . . . [H]e had a definite confidence in his story, combined with a nervous vulnerability."[51] Hirsh contends that Blustein tried to tell the type of story that might be described as a "memoir," a genre that might entail the uninterrupted telling of a story that would resonate with Yad Vashem chroniclers, ghost writers, or schoolchildren.[52]

After having positively identified the defendant and some of his deeds, the prosecution then turned its attention to the issue of volition. For example, one prosecutorial witness, Galina Puchkina, testified that she thought that Sawoniuk "joined" the Nazis "voluntarily" because of the way that "he behaved afterwards."[53] Moreover, Puchkina could talk knowledgeably about the 1942 massacre of many Jews, and she told the jury that by April 1944, Sawoniuk was in charge of the local police.[54] Another witness, Aleksandr (Ivan) Baglay, told Nutting that he remembered seeing Sawoniuk order the killing of two Jewish men and one Jewish woman.[55]

The prosecution decided to end the presentation of its case by calling Fedor Zan to take the stand. Zan proved to be a very animated witness, and he told his listeners that he had watched as more than a dozen women were machine-gunned to death by "Andrusha."[56] Zan had seen his own aunt's family being taken out of the ghetto by the local police.

After hearing the prosecution's case, Judge Potts directed the jury to find Sawoniuk not guilty on two of the four charges of murdering Jews. The two charges that remained involved the alleged murder of the fifteen Jewish women and the separate killing of the two men and one woman. The burden of rejoinder now shifted to the defense, and they tried to advance their own dissident narratives that could perhaps recontextualize the case.

The Defense's Claims in the Sawoniuk Trial

William Clegg, who led Sawoniuk's defense team, tried to minimize the role that Sawoniuk played in Operation Barbarossa. Operation Barbarossa was the name given to the German Eastern First Campaign that began in 1941. For instance, during his cross-examination of Browning, Clegg tried to get some admissions that Sawoniuk and the other local police members could not automatically resign from their posts, because a refusal to join the Nazis could mean death or slavery.[57]

This type of argument was supplemented with material that came from difficult cross-examination of prosecutorial witnesses. For example, after listening to Baglay's testimony, Clegg asked this witness if he could be mistaken about what took place during the day Sawoniuk was supposed to have supervised the shooting of the three Jews. When Baglay responded that he remembered the day "beautifully," Clegg showed him a death certificate of a friend who had died several years *before* the dates that had been mentioned by Baglay.[58]

When he gave his opening presentation, Clegg noted that "there can be no trial in our history that has been more emotive than this," and that nobody could be left unmoved after hearing about the accounts of the murders in Eastern Europe.[59] This was not supposed to be a trial about Holocaust denial or Hitler's victims—the sole issue here was Sawoniuk's personal guilt or innocence. As he pointed to the defendant, Clegg proclaimed that "it was not his fault that it [the Holocaust] happened."[60] In theory, Domachevo's police force was a "ramshackle local defence unit,"[61] and Hitler didn't have any "hotline to a hut in Domachevo."[62]

At this point in the trial, the defense decided to take a calculated risk, and Sawoniuk took the stand. Audrey Gillan and Libby Brooks have written that the "dramatic evidence of Anthony Sawoniuk marked a pivotal point in the nation's approach to the Holocaust."[63] Perhaps this testimony, combined with Clegg's withering attack, would help counter the suasory power of the prosecution's case.

Unfortunately for the defense, Sawoniuk ended up hurting his own case. He perhaps felt that he had suffered in silence for five long years, listening to the testimony of former neighbors.[64] He hobbled to the witness stand, and once again lashed out at his accusers. "I have been accused by people who have come to this country," observed Sawoniuk, and "they should be locked up for lying."[65]

In Sawoniuk's narration of events, he did not want to go to Germany, and he did not have any interest in any forced labor group. Sawoniuk's own wife had died in one of the partisan attacks on the local police station, and he told the jury: "They tried to kill me, so I killed them first."[66]

So far so good, but as soon as the cross-examination period began, the defense's case quickly unraveled. When Nutting asked Sawoniuk to speculate about the motivations of the former classmates and neighbors who testified against him, Sawoniuk claimed that they were all "told by the Russian KGB to say that there was a ghetto."[67] Furthermore, he thought that his accusers were liars, criminals, or alcoholics—people who would not admit that he "was the best friend of the Jews."[68]

The longer Sawoniuk stayed on the stand, the worse things got for the defense. Hirsh recalls that he was "simply absurd," and he "routinely denied everything," even in cases where some of these denials clashed with "established historical fact."[69] When the defendant was asked about his competency as a police officer, he responded that he had done his duty, even though he had been treated like one of the "cleaners, floor scrubbers."[70] At one interesting point in his exchange with the prosecutor, Sawoniuk wondered why he was the only policeman who was being accused of murdering Jews, and he hoped that Nutting would remember the name "Andrusha" for the rest of his life.[71]

By the third day of this cross-examination, there were few observers who thought that Sawoniuk had any chance of winning. Nutting had once again saved some of his devastating evidence for the very end, and he asked the defendant about a document that purportedly showed that Sawoniuk had become a member of the Waffen SS.[72] The defendant threatened to walk out if the prosecutor kept questioning him about being in the German army, and Sawoniuk told the jury that he hated both the Germans and the Russians, because they had both occupied his beloved Poland.[73] Tim Jones remarked that although the defendant was now "a sick man, there was a moment at the Old Bailey when it was easy to see why, almost 60 years ago, the Jews that Anthony Sawoniuk persecuted so ruthlessly had good cause to fear him."[74]

On April 1, 1999, Sawoniuk was given two life sentences for the murders that he had allegedly committed. As he read out the sentence, Judge Potts talked about low-level functionaries, the Jews in Eastern Europe, and the fears of the Jews living in Domachevo.[75] Martin Lee, one of Sawoniuk's lawyers, told reporters that he was thinking about appealing the case because "millions had been wasted by the government on prosecuting a nobody from south London."[76]

Reactions to the Sawoniuk Trial and the War Crimes Act

More than 11,000,000 pounds had been spent on British war crimes investigations,[77] and half of that amount was spent on the Sawoniuk trial. Initially there had been 393 possible suspects on some of the lists that had been put together by researchers in the late 1980s, but by April 1999 there was only one name left on that list. Tim Jones predicted that the nation's "efforts to track down the Nazi killers of the Second World War is now certain to be closed."[78] By the beginning of 2004, British authorities noted that some war crimes units had been disbanded "after a series of controversial investigations and trials," and in the wake of 9/11 some war crimes investigations would fall under the jurisdiction of antiterrorism squads.[79]

An analysis of the press reports during and after the trial reveals that the War Crimes Act and the Sawoniuk proceedings were still divisive issues in many public and elite spheres. One representative for the Simon Wiesenthal Center in Jerusalem told reporters that there was "satisfaction" in knowing that Britain was serious about prosecuting war criminals.[80] Lord Janner noted that "this trial and the jury's just verdict vindicated our war crimes procedures."[81] Niall Mulvihill argued that the investigations had "given a lot of reassurances to families."[82] The *Birmingham Post* reported that the name of "Anthony Sawoniuk" could now be added to the "Nazis on the war crimes roll of dishonour"—"Adolph Eichmann, the 'Butcher of Lyons' Klaus Barbie, [and] Maurice Papon."[83] Fergal Keane was sure that the Sawoniuk case showed "the beauty of the law" where voices from the past "reminded us that the law is about witnessing."[84]

Defenders of these proceedings also opined that the Sawoniuk trial would influence the trajectory of other war crimes trials. For example, Alasdair Palmer informed his readers that this was "exactly how the Serbs killed thousands of Muslims" in Bosnia and Kosovo.[85] Jay Rayner speculated that this case would show the dictators in Yugoslavia and Chile that "there was no statute of limitations on evil."[86] David Cesarani chastised the opponents of the War Crimes Act for buying "time for the Nazis," but he ultimately thought that the ruling would mean that "neither the heads of state nor the foot soldiers responsible for crimes against humanity will ever again find refuge on these shores."[87]

Yet detractors had no shortage of missives, and they could arm themselves with the types of critical arguments that had been circulating for decades. Was Britain dispensing victor's justice, providing another example of prosecutions that were being "brought purely for revenge?"[88] Matt Wells claimed:

> The conviction of Anthony Sawoniuk has renewed the debate over what his trial achieved. For those opposed to the 1991 War Crimes Act, the scenes played out in court number 12 at the Old Bailey over the past eight weeks—elderly witnesses contradicting their stories, prosecution lawyers struggling to shore up their case and a jury forced to pass judgment on events which occurred before many of them were born—have simply reinforced their views.[89]

Even before the participants' Eastern European trek, there were journalists and other critics who wondered about the costs of these trials. Anne Applebaum observed as early as February 14, 1999:

> We are not, after all, Mr. Sawoniuk's peers; just as it ought to be up to the Chileans, and not the Spaniards, to decide what they want to do about General Pinochet, and up to the Poles to decide what they want to do about Helena Brus, the former Stalinist prosecutor whose extradition from Britain has recently been requested by the Polish government. It is up to his contemporaries and his alleged victims to try Mr. Sawoniuk.[90]

Several days later, James Heartfield admitted that the "dead need memorials," but he thought that "the Statute Book is not the place to erect them."[91] Sawoniuk's trial was simply the "product of the demand for moral absolutes."[92] An anonymous editorial writer for the *London Daily Telegraph* thought that the "law under which he [Sawoniuk] was tried and convicted remains unsatisfactory. . . . We do not have the authority to judge all crimes wherever they may have been committed."[93]

In sum, many British publics had ambivalent feelings about both the legality and social desirability of the Sawoniuk case. Within a year, British audiences would once again be reading about the Holocaust in judicial courtrooms. This time the case would involve a civil suit.

Irving v. Penguin Books and Lipstadt *and Holocaust Revisionism in England Courtrooms*

Many different nations around the world have been preoccupied with problems related to various international Holocaust denial movements.[94] Lawrence McNamara has recently opined that debates about defamation and truth inevitably get caught up in disputes about national "identity."[95] In the English courtrooms of the late twentieth century, the vectors of memory that carried key ideological fragments were configured in ways that reminded audiences of the aggression of the Nazis and the dangers of Holocaust revisionism.

We already have several excellent studies that have documented some of the historical and legal dimensions of the *Irving v. Penguin Books and Lipstadt* case[96]—we now need to supplement these analyses with scholarly investigations that look at the rhetorical dimensions of this decision.[97] This case would provide another example of courts and prosecutors enlisting "the coercive power of the law to protect the truth and sacral memory from hateful distortion."[98]

Why, for example, did this case attract so much attention in various national and international press outlets, and why would so many countries later decide that they would bar David Irving's entry?[99] Were his ideas and actions that dangerous? In the same way that some observers worried about the belatedness of modern war crimes trials, other commentators argued that Holocaust denial or revisionism might erode our generational memories of places such as Auschwitz, Belsen, and Buchenwald.[100] While Irving viewed himself as a dissident historian who was fighting an uphill battle against England's academic and legal elite, the British press often portrayed him as a wayward historian who fell from grace.

In many ways, the participants in the Irving case were also engaged in a battle between competing national narratives, where the plaintiff was trying to create a self-image of a liberal defender of English free speech principles, while the defense attorneys countered with tales that emphasized the communitarian "judicialisation of the past."[101] From a formalistic legal vantage point, Irving could be characterized as a "claimant" who argued that Lipstadt and her publishers were conspiring to take away his reputation and his livelihood.[102] We read about how David Irving, "an English author and self-professed expert on the Third Reich,"[103] was suing Penguin Books and Deborah Lipstadt for libel in England.[104] Yet here was a case where the various parties were reliving England's past, as Irving commented on the bombing of Dresden, or the social agency of Churchill, Goebbels, and Hitler.

Guttenplan notes that if Irving had been simply a "sophist" or "clown," then "it would hardly have been necessary to commission a team of scholars to oppose him,"[105] but in this particular case British officials were dealing with a person who at one time was considered to be a competent and thorough military historian.[106] Irving's stance sometimes created nightmares for many of his British and international defenders, because they wanted to believe in the virtues of Anglo-Saxon principles of fair play and freedom of expression, and yet they had to be cognizant of the fact that Irving was no longer welcome in places like Austria, Canada, Germany, or Italy.[107]

In some of the defendant's didactic tales, Deborah Lipstadt was portrayed as a specialist who wrote about America's press coverage of Hitler's "Final Solution."[108] In *Denying the Holocaust,* she claimed that Irving had been an associate of neo-Nazis, that he had a political agenda, and that he twisted or omitted evidence so that he could shield Hitler from blame for the Holocaust.[109]

In the Irving case, the defense team included Richard Rampton, Heather Rogers, Davenport Lyons, and Anthony Julius. Rampton, a veteran of many other famous British libel trials, would do the vast majority of the speaking and would be involved in most of the key cross-examinations. Justice Charles Gray served as the sole judge presiding in the case, and during the first day of the proceedings he observed that the outcome of the case would not depend to a very great extent on "oral evidence."[110] By this, he meant that the court would not hear any testimony from Holocaust survivors.

In spite of assurances by the judge in this case that his courtroom would not be turned into a historical battleground, both the procedural requirements of putting together British libel cases[111] and the perceived symbolic importance of the case created situations where there were conflicts involving pedagogical memories. Guttenplan, who sat through much of this thirty-two-day-long affair, wrote that if "David Irving [had] won, a British court would have lent its imprimatur to his version of events, in which the survivors of Auschwitz are branded as liars, and the suffering of the victims of the gas chambers is simply erased from the pages of history."[112] Although the judge in this case would later write in his summary that he did not see it as a part of his function "to make findings of fact as to what did or did not occur during the Nazi regime in Germany,"[113] England's highest judicial court was going to have to intervene.

For observers who were interested in issues of freedom of expression, this was also a case that involved a clash between at least two cherished "rights"—Irving's right to talk and write about the Auschwitz gas chambers, and Lipstadt's right to label such views as "denial" or dangerous revisionism. One writer observed that this affair was going to investigate the ideas of a "maverick British historian" who on numerous occasions had argued that hundreds of thousands rather than millions of Jews were killed in places like Auschwitz.[114]

The lines between formalistic reasoning and judicial decision making are blurred in cases where the Holocaust takes center stage. As Lawrence Douglas insightfully noted in 1998, efforts "to proscribe Holocaust denial remind us that the very legal grammar of harm, jurisdiction, culpability, and proof that permits the law to order our social world effectively, may frustrate the law's efforts to speak reliably on behalf of that world's most difficult histories and most traumatic memories."[115] Yet Irving perhaps thought that Britain's libel laws could help him restore his reputation.

An Overview of Modern British Libel Law and the Reasons for Irving's Choice of Forums

For hundreds of years, British legal tradition has prioritized the importance of protecting an individual's "reputation," and yet Anglo-American systems of justice have had to balance a number of competing societal interests. As Douglas Vick and Linda MacPherson argued in 1996:

> A society's defamation laws reflect the relative weight that society assigns to certain fundamental and conflicting values. On the one hand, these laws represent a commitment to protect the dignity of the individual against insult and scurrilous attacks. . . . On the other hand, overprotective defamation laws can deter legitimate investigative journalism, inhibit free discussion, and discourage criticism of governmental policy and policy makers.[116]

In recent years, claimants have used these laws to win large damage awards.[117]

Plaintiffs who use the British courts for libel suits usually have to show that a defendant has published a defamatory statement, that this was publicized, and that this publication irreparably damaged the reputation of the aggrieved party. These forums generally begin with the presumption that these are false and defamatory claims.[118] The defendants therefore have the burden of showing that such statements were true, privileged, or justified.

In the Irving trial, the defendants decided to argue before Justice Gray that even if Irving had established a prima facie case of libel, they were going to assert the "defense of justification by proving that the statements about Irving were true."[119] Defendants who use this legal tactic "cannot simply rely on the knowledge that what was said was true, but rather must provide the truth of its statements with evidence that will satisfy a court of law."[120] Dennise Mulvihill contends that the English law recognizes this defense because it helps to preserve "the interests of free speech and free press."[121] Changes in the Defamation Act of 1952 modified the British common law so that a defendant could avoid liability by showing a court that a statement is justified or "substantially true."[122]

As noted above, the defense attorneys in *Irving* were dealing with a case that was quickly taking on nationalistic dimensions—would British legal protection be extended to those "Jews and other maligned ethnic groups" who wanted to "respond robustly" when their communal histories were under attack?[123] The case appeared on the horizon at the same time that many European nations were grappling with issues such as immigration restriction, the rise of neo-Nazi societies, anti-Semitism, and renascent nationalism. The Austrian victories of Joerg Haider and the Stockholm International Forum on the Holocaust were just two events that were taking place at the same time that Irving's case was coming to trial.[124] "In effect," Guttenplan predicted, Irving was "seeking to put not just Lipstadt but the Holocaust itself on trial—an effort in which he will receive considerable support from British libel law."[125]

On several different occasions during the trial, Irving offered to settle the case out of court, yet Lipstadt remarked that if this had happened, Irving "would have won by default, and his definition of the Holocaust would have become the standard definition recognized by the High Court of London."[126] After some four years of waiting, Irving finally got the chance to try and take apart the passages in Lipstadt's *Denying the Holocaust,* but he made the mistake of lavishing too much attention on his own words and deeds. This meant that in the early stages of the proceedings, the focus of the trial would shift away from the words of the second defendant (Lipstadt), and toward Irving's own narrative version of Hitler's "Final Solution." McNamara explains that both sides were "operating on the same methodological assumption that the past is objectively knowable,"[127] which meant the interrogation of select historiographical methods.

"Pictures of an Execution": British Libel Law and Irving's Dissident Memories

During the first few days of the Irving trial, the bulk of the claimant's opening remarks should have been tailored to answering the defendants' claims about the justification defense, but his courtroom performances were filled with subnarratives about his own scholarly activities. Audiences heard about various research trips to key archives, conversations with former Nazis, and visitations to hundreds of libraries that once stocked his biographical histories. At one point in his opening peroration, Irving told Justice Gray that Lipstadt and her supporters had contributed to the termination of one of his contracts with St. Martin's Press.[128]

Irving tried to create the impression that he was just a hardworking British "historian" who willingly battled batteries of aggressive defense lawyers.[129] An analysis of the trial transcript reveals that he seemed to enjoy talking about the contingent nature of scholarly interpretations of Nazi histories and Nazi historiographies, although he noted that he believed in the modernist tenets of objectivity and the need for accurate interpretations of historical events. His basic position was that while there were several different ways of conducting research on important historical pasts, his was the preferred method because it was based on primary sources. He implied that while ivory-tower types were busy citing each other's work on the events of World War II, he was out interviewing the Germans who had actually fought the war or helped with the planning of some of the key wartime operations. From a legal standpoint, he seemed to be trying to argue that if he sincerely believed in what he wrote about the Holocaust, then he should not be labeled a "denier." Moreover, Judge Gray and the rest of Irving's audiences needed to judge his work by looking at contemporary records and available manuscripts, and not by the evolutionary growth of all types of interdisciplinary Holocaust studies.

Irving claimed that other historians were constantly involved in disagreements over the nature and scope of the Holocaust, and that his critics were just having trouble dealing with the dissemination of some unpleasant and unvarnished "truths." Moreover, the defense barristers failed to recognize the fact that he had "never held myself out to be a Holocaust expert," and that he had not written any books on "what is now called the Holocaust."[130] He wanted the court to think of him as merely an expert on the "role that Adolph Hitler played in the propagation of World War II," and Hitler's decision making.[131]

In Irving's mythic world, he was simply one of many self-trained and hardworking British historians, and at one point in the trial, he claimed that to his "utter distaste," it had become "evident that it is no longer possible to write pure history, untrammeled and uninfluenced by politics."[132] During the presentation of these introductory remarks, he alleged that "far from being a 'Holocaust denier,'" he had "repeatedly" drawn "attention to major aspects of the Holocaust," and that he did not mind sharing this work with others.[133]

One of the most interesting and often overlooked aspects of the trial is the way that Irving appeared to be trying to create symbolic linkages between the words and deeds of Hitler and some of the diplomatic positions of British leaders who sometimes had ambivalent feelings about nazism and Allied intervention. Like many other revisionists, Irving tried to normalize some of the actions of the Nazis by commenting on the alleged war crimes that were perpetrated by the Allied forces during World War II. If Lipstadt had helped popularize the word "denier," then he should be given credit for having "imported Dresden into the vocabulary of horror."[134] His arguments were perhaps crafted in such a way that they tried to give the impression that this proceeding was adding to Britain's heritage of freedom of expression—Irving, after all, was trying to demythologize some of the most sacrosanct of memories.

Yet if Irving had the right to write about Hitler and Dresden, then why was he suing Lipstadt for her publications that labeled him a "denier"? What guidance was he going to give Justice Gray in outlining the specific legal standards that were going to be used in this particular libel case? Irving tried to argue that Lipstadt and the other defendants had to show that Irving "misrepresented what happened" during the Holocaust; "knew what happened"; and had "perversely and deliberately" portrayed the Holocaust differently from how he "knew it to have happened."[135]

As long as Irving was talking about his former reputation and his research methods, he was at least working on some of the prima facie elements of his case, but when he tried to connect Lipstadt's writings to a larger international conspiracy, he apparently started to lose some persuasive ground. The claimant opined that he was being persecuted by a cabal of critics who were encouraging the defendants to "vandalise" his "legitimacy as an historian."[136] At one point in the trial, he even told Justice Gray that an apt title for this particular "libel action" was "Pictures at an Execution," because the defendants were destroying his livelihood.[137]

Irving argued that Lipstadt and her supporters had "coined," "crafted," and "embedded in the vernacular" the term "Holocaust denial," and this damaged his reputation in ways that were worse than "the more usual rhetoric."[138] In his harangue, he claimed that the actual word "Holocaust" was "an artificial label commonly attached to one of the greatest and still most unexplained tragedies of this century."[139] In a twist of reasoning that must have infuriated many of his listeners, he remarked that this labeling may be "less lethal than a hypodermic with nerve gas jabbed in the neck," but it was still a "verbal Yellow Star."[140] This rhetorical maneuvering meant that Irving was trying to identify himself with the very people that he is accused of forgetting, while at the same time casting the defendants in the role of the authoritarian Nazis.

Irving also must have realized that the defense had found some damaging information during the discovery stages of the pretrial proceedings, because he tried to blunt the damage by arguing:

> Your Lordship will hear no doubt that in the course of my speech, of which apparently no full transcript survives, I uttered the following remark: "We now know that the gas chambers shown to the tourists in Auschwitz is [*sic*] a fake built by the Poles after the war, just like the one established by the

> Americans at Dachau." Those are two concentration camps my Lord. This may well raise eyebrows. . . . The fact remains that these remarks are true. The Poles admitted it in January 1995, and under English law truth has always been regarded as an absolute defence.[141]

So how would the defendants respond when they heard these contentions?

The Defendants' Legal Arguments

The leading defense barrister, Richard Rampton, claimed that Irving should have been paying attention to the research that was being disseminated by orthodox historians. This stance framed the legal standards in such a way that if the claimant willfully left out or ignored some key materials about the Holocaust, then by this definition he was a "liar" who manipulated history for ideological ends. When Justice Gray asked the defense about their views on the burden of proof in cases like this, Rampton seized the moment to tell the court that Irving was "not an historian at all, but a falsifier of history."[142]

In the nationalistic narratives that were being constructed by the defense teams, the Irving who might have provided some acceptable research in the 1970s had been transmogrified into the 1990s falsifier who had betrayed his country's principles. The fact that Irving was giving speeches in front of right-wing organizations around the world helped give the impression that he had lost his moral compass. Even worse, Irving was so far down the road that he was denying "that the Nazis planned and carried out the systematic murder of millions of Jews."[143]

Obviously, the Holocaust is a huge topic that conceptually stitched together a number of spaces and times, and in this case Irving and the defendants seemed to be focusing their attention on questions involving the accurate representation of one key former death camp in Poland—Auschwitz. As Robert Jan van Pelt has recently observed, the historical facts surrounding Auschwitz appeared to be a key part of the "bedrock of Irving's claim that the Nazis had no systematic program to murder all of the Jews of Europe."[144] A close reading of many of Irving's fragmentary remarks might lead one to conclude that he viewed Auschwitz as a concentration camp rather than a death camp. This is one of the reasons why the defense argued that the vast majority of real historians never disputed the facticity of the gas chambers.

The defense teams averred that Lipstadt was "substantially" accurate in her characterization of Irving. During his opening remarks, Rampton claimed that Irving's political proclivities had clouded his judgment, and that he had gone to "considerable lengths to achieve his exoneration of Hitler."[145] For example, an entry in Heinrich Himmler's daily logbook contained this intriguing command: *"Judentransport aus Berlin. Kiene Liquidierung."* In Irving's interpretation of this entry, Hitler was telling his subalterns that "Jews are to stay where they are" and that there would be "no liquidation" of the Jews. Rampton argued that the more accurate interpretation was that this was merely a single order from Himmler to Reinhard Heydrich discussing a particular trainload of Berlin Jews, and that this was therefore not a "general prohibition against the liquidation of Jews."[146] The defense was therefore arguing that Irving's method of analysis was allowing him to make hasty generalizations about Hitler's state of mind.

Rampton also claimed that between 1977 and 1991, Irving began eliding any discussions of the Holocaust or the systematic murder of Jews from the later editions of his work. For example, the claimant attended the Canadian trials of Ernst Zündel and defended the Leuchter Report.[147] The defense took the position that the "Leuchter Report" had been discredited by reputable scholars in many different countries, and that Irving's obstinate refusal to treat this document as "rubbish" showed that he was purposely ignoring inconsistencies. Rampton remarked that Irving was willing to resort to "lies, distortions and misrepresentations and deceptions in pursuit of his exoneration of Adolf Hitler and his denial of the Holocaust."[148]

In the end, Justice Gray decided that the defense had shown that the statements made by Lipstadt were "substantially true" and that the defendants were justified in making the defamatory statements about Irving. In his summary, Gray noted that Irving had "deliberately misrepresented and manipulated historical evidence" for his "own ideological reasons," and that he had "portrayed Hitler in an unwarrantedly favourable light." Moreover, the claimant was "an active Holocaust denier," an "anti-semitic [*sic*] and racist" who associated with "right-wing extremists who promote neo-Nazism."[149] Irving would later lose on appeal.[150]

Speculating about the Future of Legal Proscriptions of Holocaust Denial Materials

Just months before the advent of the Irving trial, Elli Wohlgelernter wrote that the "outcome will echo long after the survivors and perpetrators are no longer around."[151] James Dalrymple similarly remarked that

> what is happening in Court 73 is more than just another libel action. . . . For the first time, in a major British arena, we have been forced to enter the strange and flourishing landscape that has come to be known as historical revisionism. It is an area of study with only one subject. The Holocaust. And it is a place where tiny flaws can be found—and magnified—in large structures, where great truths can be tainted and wounded by small discrepancies, where millions of dead people can be turned into a chimera.[152]

Yet, as long as we continue to defend the existence of some libel laws, or allow them to be turned into forums that debate the facticity of the Holocaust, there are only winners of pyrrhic victories, where the most orthodox, didactic, or popular histories became the Archimedean yardstick for measuring the truths of fragile memories. Irving's presence reminds us that revisionists come on to the scene for a variety of reasons, and that this will not be the last legal trial that will involve Holocaust remembrances.

Many critics of such trials find Irving's views to be abhorrent but are willing to defend his right to circulate these ideas. This is another legal case that illustrates how counterspeech, and countermemories, are needed in any future debates with revisionists or deniers. If decision makers are going to salvage anything from the Irving case, it is not going to be this nationalistic victory for some single, state-established "truth," but the more modest goal of having detailed records of some of the most popular arguments that are used by members of the Holocaust denial movement. Otherwise, Irving "sets up a standard of proof for his enemies which no human event could ever fully satisfy."[153] Legal proscriptions that try to establish equally unrealistic standards for historical inquiry are not the answer.

If Lipstadt is right when she argues about the importance of "canaries in the mines,"[154] then public officials and private citizens will need to present audiences with nonlegal information on the systematic nature of the Holocaust. Whether we like it or not, we live in the age of the Internet, and trying to judicially quarantine the ideas that circulate in these future generational battles merely reproduces the very conditions that produced the Zündels and Irvings in the first place.

Conclusion: British Remembrances of the Irving and Sawoniuk Cases

Obviously, I believe that the British *Sawoniuk* and *Irving* trials are some of the most fascinating of the Holocaust proceedings, and I agree with those who worry that idealism has sometimes triumphed over realism. R. E.

Boustred remarked that sending "a jury and lawyers to Belarus" had involved a "ridiculous waste of public money."[155] This British citizen went on to explain:

> {W]hat right have we, who, but [for] the grace of God, were not invaded, to moralise? Can we honestly declare that, had Britain been occupied, the Nazis would have found it difficult to recruit ignorant, unemployed oafs into their extermination squads, with the prospect of a uniform and more power than they could otherwise ever hope to acquire? . . . Is it not a little ridiculous to judge wartime actions by peacetime standards? While no one will condone Nazi atrocities, the war crimes legislation . . . is one of the silliest acts.[156]

Michael Naumann told one reporter that perhaps Britain's fascination with World War II involved some national personality disorder, "an example of obsessive-compulsive behaviour from a country that cannot wash its hands of the past."[157] This goes too far, but clearly there are skeptics.

These types of critiques—which offered some functionalistic assessments of some of the choices that were made during the war—were often overshadowed by the more eulogistic defenses of these trials. Yet these critiques have provided us with some of the fragments that may surface in future dissident or didactic commentaries.

Such criticisms were augmented by arguments that focused on the lack of fairness in any process that involved prejudicial trips overseas. One writer admonished readers to remember that "a photograph of Mr. Sawoniuk's house, or [a] visit to his town, or even a silent moment spent standing by the mass grave of the Jews of Domachevo can't tell us whether the witnesses sound credible, or whether his testimony sounds true."[158] Pious declarations in British courtrooms were being used to "re-run historical events," satisfy emotional needs, and avoid critical engagement.[159]

In June 1999, some legal jurists began talking about how England's courts needed to think about providing "an earlier release" for Sawoniuk. Lord Bingham, the chief justice, disagreed with Judge Potts's earlier ruling that the retired British rail ticket collector should die in jail.[160] Was "retribution" going to help matters?

Sawoniuk's conviction has been sustained.[161] A three-judge court of appeal ruled that there were no abuses of process at the lower trial level. William Clegg had based much of the appeal on the claim that Aleksandr Baglay had not mentioned the shooting to anyone until 1996. Lord Bingham responded that it was "not easy to imagine any event which, if witnessed, would impress itself more indelibly on the mind of a 13-year old boy."[162] This meant that the lower court jury was entitled to believe that the witness was "honest and reliable."[163]

In spite of staff cuts at the Metropolitan Police War Crimes unit and vociferous complaints, the War Crimes Act is still on the books, and there have even been international discussions of how extradition proceedings can be used to bring suspected Nazi war criminal Konrad Kalejs back to Britain to stand trial.[164] Meanwhile, symbolic gestures and public displays that involve Holocaust remembrances continue to be a part of Great Britain's contemporary image making. Queen Elizabeth II visited the opening of a new exhibit within the Imperial War Museum in London that is devoted to the history of the Holocaust.[165] Rumor has it that the exhibit seems to be presenting a balanced view of such topics as Jewish refugee bank accounts, British immigration policy, and the wartime discussions of the Holocaust. One can only wonder if the Sawoniuk trial will receive similar memorialization.

7

The Future of Legal Involvement in Holocaust Memories

Each trial will be a masterpiece, and masterpieces frequently take a long time to complete. In the meantime, the biological clock is ticking.

—Sol Littman, Canadian representative for the Simon Wiesenthal Center of Los Angeles

As David Cesarani has recently observed, during the last quarter of the last century, war "crimes investigations into Nazi collaborators" were "commenced on a large scale in the United States, Canada, Australia and Britain," and the "opening of archive collections" shed new "light on Nazi occupation policy, [and] ousted Eichmann from preeminence and replaced him with the *Einsatzgruppen* killer, the East European auxiliary and the reserve policeman."[1] As he opened the Nuremberg trials of the major war criminals, Robert Jackson had hoped that the "record on which we judge these defendants today is the record on which history will judge us tomorrow,"[2] but some observers readily acknowledge that we are quickly losing our potential defendants as well as witnesses.[3]

Yet there are still those who keep track of global trends and the international pursuit of war criminals, and readers of the *Jerusalem Post* were told in April 2004 that the number of investigations that were opened in the preceding year increased by 20 percent. Incentive programs like Operation Last Chance provide awards of $10,000 or 10,000 Euros for information that helps bring about the arrest and conviction of Nazi war criminals, and by the spring of 2003 Austria had opened up 60 new investigations.[4] In some nine countries there were more than 160 ongoing investigations. The recent U.S. revocation of John Demjanjuk's citizenship shows us that there is plenty of work for potential Nazi hunters.[5]

Moreover, there are still many scholars, politicians, and laypersons who willingly ask for more "monumental spectacles."[6] While some of the participants in the *Nuremberg* proceedings tried to avoid defining crimes "in terms of religion or nationality of the victim,"[7] the inherent politicalization of these forums meant that we would be left with countless rhetorical figurations that would recirculate in many future vectors of memory. Given a host of presentist needs, the deaths of the last witnesses who lived through these horrors will not mean the end of clarion calls for vengeance,[8] vicarious memory work, or legal remembrance. Marianne Hirsch's notion of the "postmemory" captures the idea that second and third generations care about the transmission of key post-Holocaust histories and memories,[9] and there are obviously many communities around the world who still want Holocaust trials.

As we have seen in previous chapters, there are a host of reasons that are proffered by those who advocate the continued use of these Holocaust trials—observers write of the duty to remember, the importance of trauma or catharsis, the dispensation of retributive justice, and the deterrence of future war crimes.[10] The rising influence of trauma studies, recovered memory investigations, and the victims' rights movement are just some manifestations of much larger scholarly and societal shifts in the ways that we think about the balancing of formal and informal rights of defendants and victims.

I tried to counter these types of arguments by underscoring the inherent problematic nature of these Holocaust trials, and my comparative approach has provided me with a synthetic view of some of the competing legal histories and memories that dot our rhetorical landscapes. I illustrated the repetitious nature of many of these arguments, as a way of critiquing the supposed pedagogical value of these trials. I purposely highlighted the partial and contingent nature of our nationalist memories. As Michael Schudson once averred in one of his studies of collective memories, "a way of seeing is not seeing, a way of remembering is a way of forgetting."[11]

Oftentimes the use of key nationalistic forums has meant that a number of politically volatile choices had to be made in selecting venues, witnesses, relevant defenses, admissible evidence, and so forth. Formalistic-looking rules and principles are tied to hidden legal histories and collective memories, as various nations use these trials as a way of expiating guilt or apportioning blame. The popularity of many of these proceedings has meant that certain vectors of memory have been instantiated as shards in our collective legal remembrances. Note, for example, how the Kastner affair set the stage for the Eichmann trial, and how a shifting of attention away from the Judenrate could help magnify the social agency of a Nazi "desk" murderer. Several years later, the West German authorities in the Auschwitz trial faced their own cultural pressures as they tried to craft a national narrative that would resonate with Allied occupiers and local populations.

If we compare the various rhetorics surrounding the Nuremberg trials and the Auschwitz trials, we find that the search for judicial closure meant that prosecutors had to use their discretion in the creation of select recordings of the past. Scholars may be interested in discovering and interrogating these various competing and contradicting stories of culprits and victims, but jurists and prosecutors are primarily interested in defending a single coherent picture of the "truth" (based on formalistic and/or positivistic assumptions), where polysemic readings are viewed as obfuscatory, erroneous, or irrelevant. Empowered judicial actors are supposed to be making final decisions about the guilt or innocence of defendants,[12] and the "establishment of facts by legal process" is supposed to carry "special authority."[13] Closure in war crimes trials is tied to the idea that we can "wrest law from political ideology and . . . invest it with neutrality."[14]

A half-century has passed, and nationalistic communities are still trying to "widen the range of the trial" so that we can deal with "the noblest of ulterior purposes,"[15] but these forums have become so didactic that the defendants end up being minor characters in much larger morality plays. Vivian Curran elegantly explains how "the perpetrators' acts themselves, which one might have supposed and hoped to be the dominant legal issue, have become a small and generally insufficient attribute of legal cognizance."[16] This is happening at a time when critics like Marie Bénédicte Dembour and Emily Haslam are arguing that many proponents of these trials are "too easily" assuming "that the legal arena provides a superior platform for victims to recount their stories."[17]

The proliferation of these nationalistic trials has also created a fascinating conundrum—we now have so many legal framings of the Holocaust that future generations are still going to have to choose between competing, and sometimes exclusionary, legal histories and judicial memories. My guess would be that when state authorities catch a "big fish," they will selectively appropriate some of the discourse from the Nuremberg trials or the Eichmann proceeding, and when they catch lower functionaries they will consult the records from the Auschwitz or Sawoniuk affair.

As various national judiciaries have created rhetorics that apportion blame between victims, bystanders, and perpetrators, they have simultaneously deflected blame away from themselves or others. Contests over the "terrain of victimhood"[18] can be used as strategies for deferral—why forgive and forget, or master the past, when culpability can be symbolically condensed in teleological narratives that simplify matters for nationalistic audiences? Isn't there some vicarious pleasure, some sense of pride, that comes from tales of Warsaw ghetto uprisings that were heard during the Eichmann trial, or small acts of resistance that were commented on in the Sawoniuk case?

Didactic tales that are filled with heroes and villains can be framed as explanatory stories about Manichaean struggles between the forces of good and evil, but the use of these reductionist interpretative tools creates massive problems for those who want to understand the complexities of administrative massacre. This is why it is imperative that we understand the rhetorical dimensions of these trials, and recognize that all of us have blinders that filter the ways that we think about crimes against humanity or war crimes. As Arno Mayer has recently observed:

> Clearly the issue is not just the "relativity of evil," but also the evil one selects as a point of entry into a comparison: for Russians, Stalingrad; for Jews, Babi Yar; for non-Jewish Polish, Katyn; for Czechs, Lidice; for the French, Oradour-sur-Glâne; for the English, Coventry; for the Japanese, Hiroshima; for the Germans, Dresden. . . . This is why I make a special point of quoting the speech acts of the rhetoricians, commandants, and perpetrators of violence and terror in the context in which they formulated and articulated them.[19]

When David Irving decided to sue Penguin Books and Deborah Lipstadt, he may have thought that this would provide him with a forum that would allow him to engage in debates with the defendants and other historians, but he quickly found out that legal authorities have the power to decide what evils need to be addressed and what topics are relevant.

One can easily imagine the difficulties that all of this creates for the defendants in criminal trials or the "revisionist" who ends up in civil court. Whether we believe in the importance of scientific methodologies (with principles of open inquiry, skepticism, and the value of negative findings), or humanistic approaches to knowledge production (valuing constructivism, self-reflexivity, personal/communal interventions), we should all worry about the ossification of contingent Holocaust remembrances. In best-case scenarios, these proceedings can only help "define the parameters of subsequent historiography and collective memory."[20] Mark Osiel once admitted that "contemporary historians, whether focused on impersonal structures of complicity or intimate survivors' sensibilities, have found that the legal record of Nuremberg and other such trials, gathered with a view to criminal prosecution, is not particularly useful for current purposes of description or explanation."[21]

Yet shifting the contingency of Holocaust information away from courts and toward "historians" ignores a key part of our comparative puzzle—the assumed scholarly consensus that might exist about the role of collective or individual perpetrators might itself depend on the power (material and symbolic) behind those narratives. For example, the establishment of the vaunted Nuremberg "record" didn't just depend on the epistemic information contained in Nazi files—its believability depended on the imprimatur of the victors who won on the battlefield. I agree with John Zimmerman's claim that we need to evaluate and critique the legitimacy of the deniers' arguments[22]—I just believe that we don't need courtrooms when we engage in these critical exercises.

From the outset, I tried to make it abundantly clear that I believe that *all* trials are inherently political or ideological. Perceptual notions of fairness and justice involve the coproduction of knowledge, and there simply are no universal "rules of law" that exist outside the vagaries of our mundane world.[23] Is it any coincidence that many of the defenses that were considered to be foundational principles of international law in the first half of the twentieth century—including the following of "superior orders" and *tu quoque* (accusers also committed similar crimes)—mysteriously vanished when victor's justice was demanded?[24]

As I review the various claims that I made throughout this book, I would have to defend the following subclaims.

1. *Holocaust trials are not needed for the preservation of World War II memories.*

In the post–World War II decades, there were proponents of war crimes trials who openly admitted some of the public and ideological dimensions of these controversial proceedings. For example, Ben-Gurion candidly admitted:

> We are not out to punish Eichmann; there is no fit punishment. . . . [O]ne of our motives in bringing Eichmann to trial is to make the details of his case known to the generation of Israelis who have grown up since the holocaust [*sic*]. It is necessary that our youth remember what happened to the Jewish people. . . . They should be taught the lesson that Jews are not sheep to be slaughtered but a people who can hit back—as Jews did in the War of Independence.[25]

This seems to be a perfect example of how a rhetor can explicitly defend the privileging of the didactic dimensions of a trial over the issue of individual justice. Ben-Gurion is not just interested in the retrieval of accurate Holocaust histories—he wants these memories to serve as illustrations of what happens when younger generations don't want to fight for independence or when they have forgotten about the resistance spirit of the Warsaw ghetto warriors.

Clearly the Nuremberg and Eichmann trials were catalytic events that gained the attention of millions of viewers, but were these the best places to establish a "record" that would serve pedagogical purposes? Haven't many different generations learned about the Holocaust through oral reports, diaries, textbooks, novels, books, plays, films, and other extrajudicial mediums?[26] John Zimmerman, in a letter to the *Los Angeles Times,* told readers in January 2000 that only 5 percent of the Americans who participated in a Roper poll "expressed some degree of doubt but even they believed the Holocaust occurred."[27] The reasons for this heightened public Holocaust consciousness are manifold. Samantha Power noted in 1999:

> Perched among the nation's most treasured sites, the Holocaust Museum has a budget of $51 million and receives an average of two million visitors a year—nearly double the number of visitors tallied annually by the White House. The companion educational efforts have been immense. Since 1990, chairs in Holocaust Studies have been established at Emory University, the Richard Stockton College of New Jersey, the Florida Atlantic University in Boca Raton, the University of California at Santa Cruz, and Clark University. . . . Seven states either mandate or recommend Holocaust programs in their schools.[28]

Given the growing cultural, political, and social importance of Holocaust remembrance, there is little likelihood that Americans, Israelis, or any other nationalistic communities are going to forget the facticity of these events.

2. *Even if Holocaust trials were procedurally fair and helpful in the past, the passage of time has created too many moral and legal conundrums.*

I have written about how a host of critics have complained about the inherent or operational unfairness of many of the Holocaust trials, and I have touched on a number of issues—the choice of nationalistic venues, the selection of witnesses, the credibility of some witnesses, the authenticity of archival information, the bracketing out of defenses, the choice of applicable procedures, and so forth. For the sake of argument, let us assume that empowered prosecutors and judges in these cases can be fair and that policy makers have determined that such show trials are worth the expense. Was the late twentieth century the best time to be conducting these proceedings? Listen, for example, to the way that Tom Segev talks about the problematics of the first Demjanjuk trial:

> Was there ever any chance that Demjanjuk would be acquitted, even on the basis of reasonable doubt? The atmosphere surrounding the trial and the witnesses called to identify him made acquittal almost impossible. Their testimony raised the question of whether it is at all feasible to identify a man after so many years, especially since during the last ten years that preceded the trial he had been mentioned in the press and even seen on television. The procedures used to identify him were in many ways irregular, and there were some questions as to whether to believe the witnesses' assurance that they had not coordinated their testimony or coached one another.[29]

With the passage of time, we have fewer witnesses who can testify about the horrors of Auschwitz or the other death camps, and even those survivors will have heard many previous tales that may have prefigured the ways that they remember the culpability of particular defendants.

Even if I grant the argument that at one time having trials like this might have made sense, I could still argue that belated justice benefited very few individuals. Heartfield was persuasive when he noted that

> frail old men with thick, foreign accents are put on trial for crimes allegedly committed half a century earlier. These recent trials do not teach any useful moral lesson. If anything, they make a mockery of the real importance of the Holocaust. The original Nuremberg hearings have *gravitas,* with the Nazi elite such as Goering and Hess in the dock. Today we have a sorry spectacle of pensioners on trial. . . . These elderly East Europeans, even if guilty, are hardly representative of the might of Nazi Germany.[30]

Obviously, I disagree with Heartfield on the purported gravitas of the Nuremberg proceedings, but he does point out the importance of some of the relational dimensions of Holocaust memories. The complexities of Europe's ethnic and national histories often influence the ways that we apportion war guilt and criminality. At the same time, one group's denial or evasion may be another's remembrance—and one nation's didactic memory may be another's dissenting recollection.

Even if we bracketed out some of the procedural difficulties that were associated with the selection of witnesses or defendants, we would have to look at the inherent fairness that is involved when judicial actors are supposed to look into the scope and causes of the Judeocide. Note, for example, how few witnesses in the Eichmann trial could testify about any of the defendant's specific acts, or how a courtroom can be turned into a forum for reductionist debates about holes in crematoria (Zündel).

The very magnitude of the Holocaust means that defendants often become ciphers for larger debates about the culpability of Jews living in the diaspora (Kastner), or the complicity of Eastern European auxiliary forces (Demjanjuk, Sawoniuk). Audiences who are trying to make determinations about the guilt or innocence of particular individuals are also bombarded with a welter of material from films, models, expert witnesses, archival documents, witness testimony, and so forth, and in some cases they even travel to distant lands so that they can view the scene of the crime. Vicarious memories mix with experiential memories as courtroom participants try to piece together partial—and sometimes contradictory—rhetorical fragments.

These moral and legal problematics have plagued what are viewed as legitimate trials of war criminals or Holocaust revisionists/negationists, but what happens when some of these same procedural or substantive issues are used in novel types of didactic trials? Once we start using the courts as forums for "settling" the facticity of the Holocaust or combating "denial," we create new double-edged swords. Take, for example, the case of Bernard Lewis, a historian who found himself in an unexpected place—a law court in Paris. This famous scholar got into trouble in France when he publicly expressed "doubts that the massacre of 1.5 million Armenians early in this century by the Ottoman Empire could correctly [be] termed a 'genocide.'"[31] Lewis is perhaps trying to defend the uniqueness of the Judeocide, but in the process of establishing his case, he became involved in those victimhood debates that symbolically tie him to another volatile topic—remembrance of the Armenian atrocities. If we do not protect the rights of those defendants who do not share our ideological viewpoints, we risk losing our own rights.

Given the protean nature of shifting political allegiances, the fluidity of historical accounts, and the malleability of collective memories, we are going to have a difficult time coming up with the formalistic and equitable rules and procedures that will theoretically govern future Holocaust trials. For example, what happens when jurists around the world start hearing cases about denials of Palestinian claims, Armenian atrocities, horrors in Rwanda, or genocide in the Americas?[32] The instantiation of select holocaust narratives as the "historical record" of the Holocaust will mean that those dominant didactic tales can be used to critique alternative dissenting tales. Amos Funkenstein provided one illustration of some of these difficulties when he talked about the historicism involved with Zionism and Israeli remembrances:

> In the beginning, Zionist ideology labored hard to construct a new, positive Jewish self-image, to restore a Jewish "self-respect" (Pinsker) so as to achieve "autoemancipation." It was a noble and timely endeavor, which at its worst could be blamed for disregarding the fact that the land of Israel was not empty and barren, and that it was already populated by indigenous Arabs. By now, however, the collective self-identification of many Israelis—not of all—is inextricably tied to a downright negation of the national identity of the Palestinians.[33]

In part, this is obviously an ideologically driven argument, but it provides us with an insightful example of what happens when even well-intentioned jurists or juries become participants in historical disputation. Samantha Power has recently studied what she calls the "Holocaustizing" of various genocides, where journalists, advocates, and policy makers consistently link together "contemporary cases of genocide and the Holocaust."[34]

3. *Holocaust trials are ineffectual deterrents.*

Throughout this book, I have provided numerous examples of claims that have been made about the supposed deterrent effect of Holocaust trials, but I wonder about the empirical backing for these assertions. Priscilla Hayner, who looked at the discourse surrounding truth commissions in twenty countries, has recently argued that the passage of time and reparations may be more influential in helping nations grapple with their pasts than any "cathartic" experiences.[35] Perhaps we need to reevaluate the claims that have been made about the psychic benefits of the Holocaust trials and the linkages that have been made between these trials and pedagogical lessons that have supposedly been learned.[36]

There are even those who worry about the exaggerated claims that are made about the symbolic impact of Holocaust proceedings. For example, Barbara Amiel has reluctantly admitted: "Those people who still do not believe the awful bloodstained reality of the Holocaust will never accept it. If Finta had been convicted, they would simply have seen him as a martyr to the Jewish conspiracy."[37] Nine years later, Michael Siegel would write that "hate groups lurk in the background, trying to find new ways to avoid censorship imposed by governments."[38]

4. *Holocaust denial trials may interfere with rights associated with freedom of expression.*

In a world filled with commentaries on the need for more multicultural sensitivity, we will see an erosion of public and elite support for absolutist positions on freedom of expression. Changes in academic fashions and public perceptions of the need for "balance" will mean that in the first quarter of the twenty-first century, restrictionist denial legislation will grow in popularity. American officials are now going to be bombarded with legal briefs filled with discussions of the importance of the Keegstra, Zündel, and Irving "precedents." Supporters of the decision in Reno v. ACLU[39] will be able to temporarily stem this tide, but the existence of the Internet will mean that many parents may be persuaded that hate speech and Holocaust denial should be restricted.

For the purposes of protecting our national and international rights of freedom of expression, we need to resist these temptations. If we have to, we may want to decouple the ways that we think about Holocaust war crimes and Holocaust denial trials. We should recognize the importance of protecting the rights of those who express opinions that seem to us to be lies. Restricting criticism—even in cases of overt racism or disingenuous skepticism—can quickly lead to some pernicious practices. "Silencing Mr. Irving," noted Gordon Craig in 1996, "would be a high price to pay for freedom from the annoyance that he causes us. . . . [S]tudents of the years 1933–1945 owe more than they are always willing to admit to his energy as a researcher and to the scope and vigor of his publications."[40]

I may disagree with Craig about the influence that Irving has had on our understanding of Hitler or Goebbels, but I share his concern about the potential dangers of censoring such criticism. Edward Countryman reminds us that while libel cases are not the best means of resolving such contests, those who claim to be "serious" scholars "cannot be considered so if they have to use the power of the state to silence their critics."[41] Ironically, the silencing of Irving is based on some of the same logic that he himself used in bringing his case against Lipstadt and Penguin Press in the first place.

When it comes to legal issues involving the Holocaust, how do we decide when an individual or group is "willfully" disseminating "false" information? Aren't we implicitly being asked to choose between nationalistic didactic and dissenting narratives? Alan Dershowitz gives us some needed insight when he avers:

> The Holocaust was full of complexity. It was full of cynicism. It was full of heroes. It was full of devils. It was full of heroes on the German side. And devils on the Jewish side. It was full of extraordinary complexities. The Holocaust itself was a metaphor. What does it mean? It's a word for inflamed and engulfed. It's not even a word that one can give precise meaning to. . . . So what are we to do? What are we to take judicial notice of? . . . The very issue of whether or not we should litigate the Holocaust creates for me an uncomfortable situation. . . . [N]o government should sit in final historical judgment over its parameters, its boundaries, and its truth.[42]

Perhaps we need to reevaluate the ways that we think about international tribunals or Holocaust truth and reconciliation commissions.

The traditional linkages that are made between select nationalist memories and show trials may be part of the reason that the advocates of didactic trials have encountered the arguments of critics who want some type of international adjudication of these issues. Vivian Curran, for example, has eloquently opined that we have much to lose when "we erroneously assume them [the didactic trials] to be immutable, perpetual pillars of our national life."[43] After all, if courts have participants who are talking about administrative massacres, war crimes, crimes against humanity, and so forth, then why do we need more local, nationalistic trials? If advocates of these Holocaust trials truly believe that some didactic proceedings can balance the interests of defendants and victims, then why not participate in international dialogues?

Given the continued interests of both elites and laypersons in the preservation of Holocaust memories, those of us who critique these trials may need to accept the fact that these trials will not go away. So as a fallback position, we may need to think about reformation in the place of abolition. We need to find judicial forums that do more than focus attention on the historical views of one party or the presumed need for collective "retributive" justice. In his evaluation of the Eichmann trial, Telford Taylor suggested that the Israeli government be allowed to conduct an "inquest" following the Continental model of criminal practice, so that the Israelis would not sit as prosecutors and jurors in the Eichmann proceeding. The Israelis could therefore present their prosecutorial case in front of a "special international tribunal" based on the "Nuremberg principles which the General Assembly affirmed in 1946."[44]

If memory work involves the active participation of bystanders, victims, and perpetrators, then we need venues that provide for the coproduction of legal and social knowledge, where various audiences are involved in the performance of restorative justice as well as retributive justice. Many communities around the world will accept the idea that didactic trials are desirable, and yet they worry about the legitimacy of holding local, nationalistic trials. More than a hundred nations met in 1998 and talked about the importance of creating an International Criminal Court (ICC), and that type of venue has already been used for debates about the genocidal acts committed in Rwanda, the former Yugoslavia, and South Africa.[45]

Given the volatile nature of Holocaust memory work, policy makers and scholars may also want to think about the possibility of having what might be called "Holocaust Truth and Reconciliation Commissions," modeled after some previous types of commissions. If scholars are going to be serious about the importance of traumatic memories or didactic histories, then why not use forums that don't always have to make choices between binary histories or exclusionary collective memories? In recent years, more than a dozen countries have been actively promoting truth commissions to deal with the processes of healing and reconciliation. These truth commissions are considered to be a "third way" of dealing with both civilian and military violations of human rights—they avoid the extremes of blanket amnesties and the harshness of Nuremberg-style proceedings. As Audrey Chapman and Patrick Ball explain:

> Truth Commissions are temporary bodies, usually with an official status, set up to investigate a past history of human rights violations that took place within a country during a specific period of time. In contrast with tribunals or courts, truth commissions do not have prosecutorial powers to bring cases to trial. Nor do they act as judicial bodies to investigate individuals accused of crimes.[46]

Ideally, such forums would have commissioners who would serve as facilitators, advancing conversations on how various communities identify with particular World War II narratives. Despite all of the problems that have been countered by the participants in these commissions, they are better than Holocaust trials.

My comparative study of criminal war crimes trials and Holocaust denial proceedings in places like Germany, Israel, Canada, and England has shown some of the difficulties that attend nationalistic solutions to these complex situations. If we truly want a balance of idealism and realism, and we want to find some of the best ways of dealing with war crimes or crimes against humanity, we need to recognize both the strengths and weaknesses of these Holocaust trials. Hopefully, the twenty-first century will teach us that healing involves more than retributive justice. Perhaps there is a time for forgiving and selective forgetting.

Notes

Chapter One. The Role of Legal Trials in the Preservation of Select Holocaust Histories and Memories

1. Herbert Adam, "Divided Memories: Confronting the Crimes of Previous Regimes," *Telos* 118 (Winter 2000): 93.
2. Throughout this book, I follow Arno J. Mayer's suggestion that we use the term "Judeocide" to refer to Nazi Germany's genocide of the Jews. Arno J. Mayer, *Why Did the Heavens Not Darken?: The "Final Solution" in History* (New York: Verso, 1988), vii.
3. Shoshana Felman, *The Juridical Unconscious: Trials and Traumas in the Twentieth Century* (Cambridge, Mass.: Harvard University Press, 2002), 7.
4. For an interesting analysis of the exaggerated claims about the deterrent impact on many prosecutions of perpetrators of atrocities, see Jack Snyder and Leslie Vinjamuri, "Trials and Errors: Principle and Pragmatism in Strategies of International Justice," *International Security* 28 (2004): 5–44.
5. See, for example, how some courts have been involved in the compensation of the victims of the Nazis. Regula Ludi, "Waging War on Wartime Memory: Recent Swiss Debates on the Legacies of the Holocaust and the Nazi Era," *Jewish Social Studies* 10 (2004): 116–152.
6. For excellent overviews of some of these functions, see Donald Bloxham, *Genocide on Trial: War Crimes Trials and the Formation of Holocaust History and Memory* (New York: Oxford University Press, 2001), 1–16; Lawrence Douglas, "Book Review: *Genocide on Trial,*" *Holocaust and Genocide Studies* 18 (2004): 135–138; Nancy Wood, "Crimes or Misdemeanours? Memory on Trial in Contemporary France," *French Cultural Studies* 5 (1994): 21.
7. Bloxham, *Genocide*, 2.
8. Gerry Simpson, "The Balance between Forgetting and Remembering," *Political Quarterly* 72 (2001): 505.

9. For an overview of how popular Holocaust trials engage in this balancing, see Hanna Yablonka, "The Development of Holocaust Consciousness in Israel: The Nuremberg, Kapos, Kastner, and Eichmann Trials," *Israel Studies* 8 (2003): 1–24. Lawrence Douglas avers that these trials help us as we cope with the "mass atrocities in Bosnia, Kosovo, and Rwanda." Lawrence Douglas, "History, Memory and Crimes against Humanity: A Response to Todorov," *Salmagundi* 129 (2001): 326.
10. Tzvetan Todorov, "A Rejoinder: French Trials," *Salmagundi* 129 (2001): 327–330.
11. Stephen Howard Browne, "Arendt, Eichmann, and the Politics of Remembrance," in *Framing Public Memory*, ed. Kendall R. Phillips (Tuscaloosa: University of Alabama Press, 2004), 45.
12. Stiina Löytömäki, "Book Review: *Barbie, Touvier, Papon: Des Procès Pour la Mémoire*," *European Journal of International Law* 15 (2004): 613.
13. Austin Sarat and Thomas R. Kearns, "Writing History and Registering Memory in Legal Decisions and Legal Practices: An Introduction," in *History, Memory, and the Law* (Ann Arbor: University of Michigan Press, 2001), 11.
14. Daphne Eviatar, "The Show Trial: A Larger Justice?" *New York Times*, July 20, 2002, web.lexis-nexis.com/universe (January 3, 2005). Leora Bilsky explains that within legal professions, "Holocaust trials were dealt with cautiously, as trials in which purely legal considerations are often sacrificed for pedagogical and political goals." Leora Bilsky, "Book Review: *The Memory of Judgment*," *Journal of Modern History* 75 (2003): 398.
15. Sarat and Kearns, "Writing History," 11.
16. For some brief commentaries on both postmodern and positivistic perspectives on these trials, see Lawrence McNamara, "History, Memory, and Judgment: Holocaust Denial, the History Wars and Law's Problems with the Past," *Sydney Law Review* 26 (2004): 353–394.
17. Eviatar, "Show Trial."
18. See Felman, *Juridical Unconscious*, 226–227.
19. Douglas, "History," 325.
20. Löytömäki, "Book Review," 613.
21. Michael A. Bernstein, "Not Beyond the Law," *Times Literary Supplement*, April 12, 2002, 5.
22. Mark Osiel, *Mass Atrocity, Collective Memory, and the Law* (New Brunswick, N.J.: Transaction, 1997), 65.
23. Bernstein, "Not Beyond the Law," 5.

24. For an interesting critique that acknowledges the "political" role of these genocidal trials and still argues that we need to try Saddam Hussein and many other mass murderers, see Daniel Goldhagen, "Put Saddam's Willing Executioners on Trial," *London Times*, December 28, 2003, http://web.lexis-nexis.com (December 10, 2004).
25. Jamie Mayerfeld, "Book Review: *The Memory of Judgment*," *Punishment and Society* 5 (2003): 228.
26. Patricia Chisholm, "Verdict on the Past," *Macleans*, June 4, 1990.
27. See Eric Stein, "History against Free Speech: The New German Law against the 'Auschwitz' and Other 'Lies,'" *Michigan Law Review* 85 (November 1986): 277–324.
28. For an insightful discussion of some of the legal conundrums that attend realistic and idealistic interpretations of "victor's justice," see Gary Jonathan Bass, *Stay the Hand of Vengeance: The Politics of War Crimes Tribunals* (Princeton, N.J.: Princeton University Press, 2000), 8–16.
29. Idith Zertal, "From the People's Hall to the Wailing Wall: A Study in Memory, Fear, and War," *Representations* 69 (2000): 98–99.
30. The phrase "theatre of justice" has also been used in critiques of America's military tribunal system. See Edward J. Klaris, "Justice Can't Be Done in Secret," *Nation*, June 10, 2002, http:www.thenation.com. (December 10, 2004).
31. Lawrence Douglas, *The Memory of Judgment: Making Law and History in the Trials of the Holocaust* (New Haven, Conn.: Yale University Press, 2001), 1–7.
32. Douglas, *Memory of Judgment*, 2.
33. By "extrajudicial," I mean those public, official, and intellectual commentaries that become fragments in some of the public debates that take place outside the confines of judicial proceedings. Douglas notes how some scholars have argued that the law "cannot productively engage with the most disturbing and fundamental issues raised by traumatic events, issues more satisfactorily explored through the discourses of history, philosophy, literature, theology, or psychoanalysis—or in alternative forums, such as truth commissions." Douglas, "Book Review," 136. I feel comfortable placing myself within this camp, with the proviso that we take into account public and official commentaries as well.
34. These types of issues remind us of one of the key dangers that attend these type of show trials—reductionism. If we go back to the Eichmann example, we need to note that Arendt was complaining about

the reductionism that came from the theological demonization of Eichmann—a legal/political framework that focused too narrowly on a single perpetrator's intentions, abilities, and social agency. This deflected attention away from the other parties who might be involved in administrative massacres—the "desk" murderers, the Kapo functionaries in the death camps, etc. Hannah Arendt, *Eichmann in Jerusalem: A Report on the Banality of Evil* (New York: Penguin Books, 1983).

35. Sarat and Kearns, "Writing History," 5.
36. For an overview of some of the tragic and romantic possibilities that are associated with legal forums, see William Lewis, "Of Innocence, Exclusion, and the Burning of Flags: The Romantic Realism of the Law," *Southern Communication Journal* 60 (Fall 1994): 4–5.
37. Arendt, *Eichmann*, 3, 5.
38. As David Cesarani recently averred, the "trial of the Nazi war criminal Adolf Eichmann in Jerusalem in 1961–2 is widely regarded as a crucial step along the path that leads to Milosevic and Saddam facing justice today." David Cesarani, "Comment: Why Tyrants Must Stand Trial," *London Observer*, July 11, 2004, http://web.lexis-nexis.com (December 10, 2004).
39. Douglas, "History," 320.
40. Osiel, *Mass Atrocity*, 242.
41. Bloxham goes as far as to argue that the Allied trials may have inadvertently helped accommodate or fortify the German process of "mastering the past." Bloxham, *Genocide*, 225–226.

    For key overviews of some of the "didactic" functions of various Holocaust trials, see Vivian G. Curran, "The Legalization of Racism in a Constitutional State: Democracy's Suicide in Vichy France," *Hastings Law Journal* 50, no. 1 (November 1998): 1–96; Gerry J. Simpson, "Didactic and Dissident Histories in War Crimes Trials," *Albany Law Review* 60 (1997): 803.
42. See, for example, Paul Vallely, "Tens of Thousands of Corpses," *London Independent*, February 20, 2004, http://web.lexis-nexis.com (December 10, 2004).
43. For an insightful commentary on the potential legal and political implications of Saddam Hussein's "judicial theater," see Gary J. Bass, "At Saddam's Trial, the Law Is Just One Part of the Picture," *Washington Post*, January 18, 2004.
44. Yablonka, "Development of Holocaust Consciousness," 1–24.
45. Douglas, *Memory of Judgment*, 144.

46. Vivian Grosswald Curran, "Atoms of the Law," *University of Toronto Law Journal* 53 (2003): 319.
47. Peter Novick, *The Holocaust in American Life* (Boston: Houghton Mifflin, 1999), 1.
48. Tim Cole, *Selling the Holocaust* (New York: Routledge, 1999), 1.
49. Tom Brokaw, *The Greatest Generation* (New York: Random House, 1998).
50. Yablonka, "Development of Holocaust Consciousness," 7.
51. Saul Friedlander, "Trauma, Transference, and 'Working Through' in Writing the History of the Shoah," *History and Memory* 4 (1992): 48.
52. For an excellent overview of the iconic and discursive images that circulated in Europe during the end of the war, see Barbie Zelizer, *Remembering to Forget: Holocaust Memory through the Camera's Eye* (Chicago: University of Chicago Press, 1998).
53. Ian Buruma, *The Wages of Guilt* (New York: Penguin Books, 1995), 5.
54. Curran, "Atoms," 318.
55. T. G. Ashplant, Graham Dawson, and Michael Roper, *The Politics of War Memory and Commemoration* (New York: Routledge, 2000), 3.
56. See, for example, Raymond Phillips, ed., *Trial of Joseph Kramer and Forty-four Others: (The Belsen Trial)* (London: William Hodge, 1949), xxiv.
57. Benjamin Robinson, "*The Specialist* on the Eichmann Precedent: Morality, Law, and Military Sovereignty," *Critical Inquiry* 30 (2003): 65.
58. Douglas believes that responsible collective memory can balance legal justice with didactic legality. Douglas, *Memory of Judgment*, 1–7. I clearly do not share his optimism about the existence of jurisprudential norms and rules that guide and constrain human behavior in ways that maintain that balance. I would be one of those individuals whom he characterizes as a "votary of the critical legal studies" movement, who might see his "model of obligation" as a "mere fetishization of law" (304). Throughout this book, I defend the position that Douglas and other defenders of the didactic elements of these trials often inadvertently bracket out the power dimensions and the selective nature of judicial Holocaust memories. Moreover, they take it as empirical fact that audiences see the trials through the same eyes and lens that are supplied by elite lawyers and jurists in cases like the Eichmann and the Nuremberg trials. Holocaust trials will never provide us with "responsible" collective memories as long as the victors in wars are the only ones empowered to provide the theaters,

artifacts, documents, testimony, witnesses, and standards for judgments in these contested cases.

59. Norman Finkelstein avers that there is a difference between the "Nazi holocaust" (the "actual historical event") and "the Holocaust"—its ideological "representation." Norman G. Finkelstein, *The Holocaust Industry: Reflections on the Exploitation of Jewish Suffering* (London: Verso, 2000), 3.
60. Some observers complain about the politics of the second and third generations that vicariously remember the Judeocide. See Alain Finkielkraut, *The Imaginary Jew,* trans. K. O'Neill and D. Suchoff (Lincoln: University of Nebraska Press, 1994), 22–23.
61. Osiel, *Mass Atrocity,* 3.
62. Snyder and Vinjamuri argue that a balancing of principled and pragmatic concerns would invite us to acknowledge that sometimes the prosecution of perpetrators "risks causing more atrocities than it would prevent." Snyder and Vinjamuri, "Trials and Errors," 5.
63. Douglas, *Memory of Judgment,* 261.
64. See Michael L. Siegel, "Comment: Hate Speech, Civil Rights, and the Internet: The Jurisdictional and Human Rights Nightmare," *Albany Law Journal of Science and Technology* 9 (1999): 375.
65. Curran, "Atoms," 306. For an excellent overview of the dangers that attend some forms of consciousness-raising, see Judith E. Doneson, "Holocaust Revisited: A Catalyst for Memory or Trivialization," *Annals of the American Academy of Political and Social Sciences* 548 (November 1996): 70–77.
66. See Kenneth Lasson, "Holocaust Denial and the First Amendment: The Quest for Truth in a Free Society," *George Mason Law Review* 6 (1997): 35–86. I see this as an incredibly weak argument. There are many different research paradigms that could be historically and epistemically connected to Holocaust denial. For an excellent analysis of the positive contributions that can be made by "deconstruction" and "structuralism" in the battle against anti-Semitism, see Vivian Grosswald Curran, "Deconstruction, Structuralism, Antisemitism and the Law," *Boston College Law Review* 36 (1994): 1–52.
67. Ludi, "Waging War," 116–117.
68. For a fascinating examination of how discussions about genocide can degenerate into personal attacks and tarring with the label of "denier," see David E. Stannard, "Uniqueness as Denial: The Politics of Genocide Scholarship," in *Is the Holocaust Unique*? ed. Alan S. Rosenbaum (Boulder, Colo.: Westview Press, 1996), 163–208.

69. Yablonka, "Development of Holocaust Consciousness," 8.
70. In the concluding chapter of this book, I note that this 20 percent figure has been disputed by those who claim that the polls that collected this data used several double negatives.
71. Deborah Lipstadt, *Denying the Holocaust: The Growing Assault on Truth and Memory* (1993; New York: Plume Press, 1994).
72. Kenneth S. Stern, *Holocaust Denial* (New York: American Jewish Committee, 1993), 10.
73. Lasson, "Holocaust Denial," 72.
74. Gerald Tishler, et al., "When Academic Freedom and Freedom of Speech Confront Holocaust Denial and Group Libel: Comparative Perspectives," *Boston College Third World Law Journal* 8 (1988): 70. For an excellent analysis of this quotation, see Vera Ranki, "Holocaust History and the Law: Recent Trials[,] Emerging Theories," *Cardozo Studies in Law and Literature* 9 (1997): 31.
75. Some observers, like Douglas, understand the fluidity of history and the importance of the "process of legal renegotiation," while at the same time defend the fact that "individual trials must necessarily aspire to empathetic closure in the form of a verdict." Douglas, "History," 326.
76. Curran, "Legalization," 86–87
77. Curran, "Atoms," 306.
78. Simpson, "Didactic," 803.
79. Ibid., 804.
80. Ibid., 833.
81. Curran, "Legalization," 88.
82. Ibid., 95.
83. Zelizer, *Remembering*, 188.
84. Douglas, *Memory of Judgment*, 259.
85. For example, in Israel many survivors have had emotional difficulties in dealing with societal denial and recognition of the Holocaust. See Zahava Solomon, "From Denial to Recognition: Attitudes toward Holocaust Survivors from World War II to the Present," *Journal of Traumatic Stress* 8 (1995): 215–228.
86. Gerald Tishler, et al., "When Academic Freedom and Freedom of Speech Confront Holocaust Denial and Group Libel: Comparative Perspectives," *Boston College Third World Law Journal* 8 (1988): 71.
87. Nadine Fresco, "The Denial of the Dead: On the Faurisson Affair," *Dissent* 28 (1981): 481.
88. Bloxham, *Genocide*, 2.

89. Èric Conan and Henry Rousso, *Vichy: An Ever-Present Past,* trans. Nathan Bracher (Hanover, N.H.: University Press of New England, 1998), 210–211.
90. Felman, *Juridical Unconscious,* 4–5.
91. For a detailed discussion of the methods involved in ideographic approaches, see Celeste M. Condit and John L. Lucaites, *Crafting Equality: America's Anglo-African Word* (Chicago: University of Chicago Press, 1993).
92. Before the 1970s there were very few legal discussions of the constitutive role of rhetoric in jurisprudence, but today there are hundreds of essays on this topic that appear annually in legal texts and journals. Many believe that the work of James Boyd White helped facilitate this renaissance of interest in rhetoric and law. See, for example, James Boyd White, *The Legal Imagination: Studies in the Nature of Legal Thought and Expression* (Boston: Little, Brown, 1973). Obviously, there are a number of different disciplines and movements that have influenced these trends, including the law and literature movement (see Guyora Binder and Robert Weisberg, *Literary Criticisms of Law* [Princeton, N.J.: Princeton University Press, 2000]) and the 1980s critical legal studies movement.
93. E. Culpepper Clark and Raymie E. McKerrow, "The Rhetorical Construction of History," in *Doing Rhetorical History: Cases and Concepts,* ed. Kathleen J. Turner (Tuscaloosa: University of Alabama Press, 1998), 35.
94. Dominick LaCapra, *History and Criticism* (Ithaca, N.Y.: Cornell University Press, 1985), 17.
95. Within the field of communication, note the work on "memory" that appears in Carole Blair, Marsha S. Jeppeson, and Enrico Pucci, "Public Memorialization in Postmodernity: The Vietnam Memorial as Prototype," *Quarterly Journal of Speech* 77 (1991): 263–288; Stephen H. Browne, "Reading, Rhetoric, and the Texture of Public Memory," *Quarterly Journal of Speech* 81 (1993): 237–250; J. Robert Cox, "Memory, Critical Theory, and the Argument from History," *Argumentation and Advocacy* 27 (1990): 1–13; Greg Dickinson, "Memories for Sale: Nostalgia and the Construction of Identity in Old Pasadena," *Quarterly Journal of Speech* 83 (1997): 1–27; Marouf Hasian Jr. and Robert E. Frank, "Rhetoric, History, and Collective Memory: Decoding the Goldhagen Debates," *Western Journal of Communication* 63 (1999): 95–114; Victoria J. Gallagher, "Remembering Together: Rhetorical Integration and the Case of Martin Luther King, Jr. Memorial," *Southern*

Communication Journal 60 (1995): 109–119; Tamar Katriel, "Sites of Memory: Discourse of the Past in Israeli Pioneering Settlement Museums," *Quarterly Journal of Speech* 80 (1994): 1–20; Barbie Zelizer, "Reading the Past against the Grain: The Shape of Memory Studies," *Critical Studies in Mass Communication* 12 (1995): 214–235.

96. Some of the leading historical discussions of memory include Sacvan Bercovitch, *The Rites of Assent: Transformation in the Symbolic Construction of America* (New York: Routledge, 1993); Paul Fussell, *The Great War and Modern Memory* (New York: Oxford University Press, 1975); Eric Hobsbawn and Terrance Ranger, eds., *The Invention of Tradition* (Cambridge: Cambridge University Press, 1983); Michael Kammen, *Mystic Chords of Memory* (New York: Vintage Books, 1993); Pierre Nora, "Between Memory and History: Les Lieux de Memoirè," *Representations* 26 (1989): 7–25.
97. Eugenio Donato, "The Ruins of Memory: Archeological Fragments and Textual Artifacts," *MLN* 93 (1978): 575–596; Shoshana Felman, and Doris Laub, eds., *Testimony: Crises of Witnessing in Literature, Psychoanalysis, and History* (New York: Routledge, 1992).
98. Michael L. Mezey, "Book Review: *Watergate in American Memory*," *Journal of Politics* 56 (1994): 513–583.
99. For some psychological discussions of memory, see F. C. Barlett, *Remembering: A Study in Experimental and Social Psychology* (Cambridge: Cambridge University Press, 1932); Cathy Caruth, ed., *Trauma: Explorations in Memory* (Baltimore: Johns Hopkins University Press, 1995); Nancy Potter, "Loopholes, Gaps and What Is Held Fast: Democratic Epistemology and Claims to Recovered Memories," *Philosophy, Psychiatry, and Psychology* 3 (1996): 237–254.
100. Sociologists have been some of the leading scholars who have paved the way for "memory" studies. See John Bodnar, *Remaking America: Public Memory, Commemoration, and Patriotism in the Twentieth Century* (Princeton, N.J.: University of Princeton Press, 1992); Maurice Halbwachs, *The Collective Memory*, trans. Francis J. Ditter Jr. and Vida Yazdi Ditter (New York: Harper and Row, 1980); Maurice Halbwachs, *On Collective Memory*, trans. Lewis Coser (Chicago: University of Chicago Press, 1992); I. Irwin-Zarecka, *Frames of Remembrance: The Dynamics of Collective Memory* (New Brunswick, N.J.: Transaction, 1994); Kurt Lang and Gladys Engel Lang, "Collective Memory and the News," *Communication* 11 (1989): 123–139; George Lipsitz, *Time Passages: Collective Memory and the American Popular Culture* (Minneapolis: University of Minnesota Press, 1990); Michael Schudson, *Watergate in American*

Memory: How We Remember, Forget and Reconstruct the Past (New York: Basic Books, 1992); Barry Schwartz, "The Social Context of Commemoration: A Study in Collective Memory," *Social Forces* 61 (1982): 374–402; Barry Schwartz, "Deconstructing and Reconstructing the Past," *Qualitative Sociology* 18 (1995): 263–270; Yael Zerubavel, *Recovered Roots: Collective Memory and the Making of Israeli National Tradition* (Chicago: University of Chicago Press, 1995).

101. See, for example, Peter Burke, "History as Social Memory," in *Memory: History, Culture, and the Mind*, ed. Thomas Butler (Oxford: Blackwell, 1989), 97–98.
102. Nora, "Between Memory," 17. Unfortunately, such an approach intentionally or unintentionally has the potential for essentializing "memories" or "histories" and treating them as antirhetorical concepts. As Alonso once averred, "history is rhetorical in that it aims to convince." A. M. Alonso, "The Effects of Truth: Re-presentations of the Past and the Imagining of Community," *Journal of Historical Sociology* 1 (1988): 37.
103. James E. Young, *The Texture of Memory: Holocaust Memorials and Meaning* (New Haven, Conn.: Yale University Press, 1993), 2.
104. Milner S. Ball, "Judge Posner, Professor Fish, and Law as Rhetoric," *Poetics Today* 12 (1991): 336. See also Stanley Fish, *Doing What Comes Naturally* (Durham, N.C.: Duke University Press, 1989); Robert Hariman, ed., *Popular Trials: Rhetoric, Mass Media, and the Law* (Tuscaloosa: University of Alabama Press, 1990).
105. Robert Weisberg, "Proclaiming Trials as Narratives: Premises and Pretenses," in *Law's Stories: Narrative and Rhetoric in the Law*, ed. Peter Brooks and Paul Gewirtz (New Haven, Conn.: Yale University Press, 1996), 61.
106. For one of the best discussions of how entire legal theories have their social contexts, see Robert W. Gordon, "The Politics of Legal History and the Search for a Usable Past," *Benchmark* 4 (1990): 269–281.
107. For an illuminating discussion of the national reactions to the *Brown* decision, see Gary Peller, "Cultural Imperialism, White Anxiety, and the Ideological Realignment of *Brown*," in *Race, Law, and Culture*: Reflections on Brown v. Board of Education, Austin Sarat, ed. (New York: Oxford University Press, 1997), 190–194.
108. See Hayden White, *Tropics of Discourse: Essays in Cultural Criticism* (Baltimore: Johns Hopkins University Press, 1985). It is perhaps no coincidence that White has recently backtracked on some of his relativist claims when confronted with the example of the Holocaust. Hayden

V. White, "Historical Emplotment and the Problem of Truth," in *Probing the Limits of Representation: Nazism and the "Final Solution,"* ed. Saul Friedlander (Cambridge, Mass.: Harvard University Press, 1992), 37–53.

109. Marita Sturken, *Tangled Memories: The Vietnam War, the AIDS Epidemic, and the Politics of Remembering* (Berkeley: University of California Press, 1997), 1.
110. Some of the best overviews of the importance of "commemoration" can be found in Bodnar, *Remaking America*; J. R. Gillis, ed., *Commemorations: The Politics of National Identity* (Princeton, N.J.: Princeton University Press, 1994); and Schwartz, "Social Context," 374–402.
111. Barry Schwartz, "Postmodernity and Historical Reputation: Abraham Lincoln in Late Twentieth-Century American Memory," *Social Forces* 77 (1998): 94.
112. Ibid., 94–95. For a recent discussion of the "Good War" and *Saving Private Ryan,* see Charles Krauthammer, "Debating 'Pvt. Ryan,'" *Washington Post,* August 14, 1998.
113. Peter Ehrenhaus, "The Wall," *Critical Studies in Mass Communication* 6 (1989): 96. For other work on symbolic meaning of the Vietnam Memorial, see Richard Morris and Peter Ehrenhaus, eds., *The Cultural Legacy of Vietnam* (Norwood, N.J.: Ablex, 1990).
114. Alonso, "Effects," 42.
115. Stephen H. Browne, "Remembering Crispus Attucks: Race, Rhetoric, and the Politics of Commemoration," *Quarterly Journal of Speech* 85 (1999): 175.
116. Ibid., 175–176.
117. For example, even those who have not lived through the Holocaust may participate in what Young has called "vicarious memory." J. E. Young, "Introduction," in *The Art of Memory: Holocaust Memorials in History,* ed. J. E. Young (New York: Prestel-Verlag, 1994), 19.
118. Schwartz, "Deconstructing," 270.
119. Dickinson, "Memories for Sale," 1.
120. Remo Bodei, "Farewell to the Past: Historical Memory, Oblivion, and Collective Identity," *Philosophy and Social Criticism* 18 (1992): 251.
121. Gillis, *Commemorations,* 4.
122. For example, see the importance of memory work in the creation of Zionism and Israeli national identity. Zerubavel, *Recovered Roots.*
123. On the figurative importance of Echo, see J. Greenberg, "The Echo of Trauma and the Trauma of Echo," *American Imago* 55 (1998): 319–347; J. Hollander, *The Figure of Echo* (Berkeley: University of

California Press, 1981); J. Lowenstein, *Responsive Readings: Versions of Echo in the Pastoral, Epic, and the Johnsonian Mask* (New Haven, Conn.: Yale University Press, 1984); Ovid, *The Metamorphoses*, trans. A. Mandelbaum (New York: Harcourt, Brace, 1993), 92–93.

124. Ovid, *Metamorphoses*, 92–93.
125. Judith Lewis Herman, *Trauma and Recovery* (New York: Harper Collins, 1992); Doris Laub, "An Event without a Witness: Truth, Testimony and Survival," in Felman and Laub, *Testimony*, 75–92; Robert J. Lifton, "An Interview with Robert Jay Lifton," in Caruth, *Trauma*, 128–147.
126. Greenberg, "Echo," 319.
127. See Cathy Caruth, *Unclaimed Experience: Trauma, Narrative, and History* (Baltimore: Johns Hopkins University Press, 1995); E. L. Santner, "History beyond the Pleasure Principle: Some Thoughts on the Representation of Trauma," in Friedlander *Probing the Limits*, 143–154.
128. For an excellent discussion of some of the conundrums that are involved when courts try to grapple with postmodern or poststructural interpretations of legal history, see Lawrence Douglas, "The Memory of Judgment: The Law, the Holocaust, and Denial," *History and Memory* 7 (1996): 100–120; Alain Finkielkraut, *Remembering in Vain: The Klaus Barbie Trial and Crimes Against Humanity*, trans. Roxanne Lapidus with Sima Godfrey (New York: Columbia University Press, 1992).
129. For a discussion on the importance of "working through" rather than mastering the past, see Friedlander, "Trauma," 39–59.
130. Laub, "Event," 75.
131. Austin Sarat, "Rhetoric and Remembrance: Trials, Transcription, and the Politics of Critical Reading," *Legal Studies Forum* 23 (1999): 355–356.
132. See, for example, the press coverage of the International Military Tribunal (IMT) at Nuremberg. Brian K. Feltman, "Legitimizing Justice: The American Press and the International Military Tribunal, 1945–1946," *Historian* 66 (2004): 300–319.
133. For an excellent overview of the Nuremberg trials, see Ann Tusa and John Tusa, *The Nuremberg Trial* (New York: Atheneum, 1986).
134. Douglas, "History," 321.
135. Novick, *Holocaust*, 129.
136. Lipstadt, *Denying the Holocaust*, 157.
137. Arendt, *Eichmann*, 288.
138. Conan and Rousso, *Vichy*, 210.

Chapter Two. The Nuremberg Trial of the Major War Criminals and Early Legal Remembrances of the Holocaust

1. For an intriguing look at how Holocaust memories are even tied to the terrorist attacks of 9/11, see Eva Hoffman, *After Such Knowledge: Memory, History, and the Aftermath of the Holocaust* (New York: Public Affairs, 2004).
2. See, for example, Stephen Goodell, Kevin A. Mahoney, and Sybil Milton, *1945: The Year of Liberation* (Washington, D.C.: U.S. Holocaust Memorial Museum, 1995).
3. William D. Rubinstein, *The Myth of Rescue: Why the Democracies Could Not Have Saved More Jews from the Nazis* (London: Routledge, 1997), 2.
4. Lipstadt, *Denying the Holocaust*, 2–3.
5. Jacob Robinson argued that by January 1942, the Allies realized that they needed to send the Axis powers strongly worded messages condemning the exterminations that were taking place in Europe. Jacob Robinson, "The International Military Tribunal and the Holocaust," *Israel Law Review* 7 (1972): 1–2. For a contemporary example of what was being discussed in the Allied presses, see "Mass Butchery in Poland," *London Times*, June 10, 1942.
6. Nancy Wood, *Vectors of Memory: Legacies of Trauma in Postwar Europe* (New York: Berg, 1999), 2.
7. Some of the key legal vectors for many of our histories and memories of Nuremberg can be found in International Military Tribunal, *Trial of the Major War Criminals before the International Military Tribunal, Nuremberg, 14 November 1945–1 October 1946*, 42 vols. (Nuremberg: International Military Tribunal, 1947).
8. Michael R. Marrus, "The Holocaust at Nuremberg," *Yad Vashem Studies* 26 (1998): 5. For the specific cataloging of Holocaust references from Nuremberg, see Jacob Robinson, "The International Military Tribunal and the Holocaust: Some Legal Reflections," *Israel Law Review* 7 (1972): 1–13; Jacob Robinson and Henry Sachs, *The Holocaust: The Nuremberg Evidence* (New York: YIVO Institute for Jewish Research, 1976).
9. Robinson, "International," 6.
10. Bass, *Stay the Hand*, 203.
11. For an early contemporary commentary that questions the deterrent value of Nuremberg, arguing that aggressors always feel certain of

"victory," see L. B. Namier, "The Nuremberg Trial—History or Law," *Manchester Guardian*, November 23, 1945.

12. Bloxham, *Genocide*, viii. Arno J. Mayer claims that Auschwitz began as a concentration camp, but when the Germans began to lose the war they turned "Auschwitz into the unprecedented human inferno of industrial production, hyperexploitation, death, and extermination whose memory haunts the civilized world." Mayer, *Why Did the Heavens Not Darken?*, 462.
13. Howard Ball, for example, notes that during these "post–World War II trials," the defenses associated with "sovereign immunity," "military necessity," and "following a superior's orders" were of "little help to the defendants." Howard Ball, *Prosecuting War Crimes and Genocide: The Twentieth-Century Experience* (Lawrence: University of Kansas Press, 1999), 217–218.
14. See, for example, Eugene Davidson, *The Trial of the Germans: An Account of the Twenty-two Defendants before the International Military Tribunal at Nuremberg* (New York: Macmillan, 1966); Michael R. Marrus, *The Nuremberg War Crimes Trial 1945–1946: A Documentary History* (Boston: Bedford, 1997); Bradley F. Smith, *Reaching Judgment at Nuremberg* (1977; New York: Meridian, 1979); Telford Taylor, *The Anatomy of the Nuremberg Trials* (Boston: Little, Brown, 1992).
15. See "Rise and Fall of the Nazis: Nuremberg Court Sees Film," *Manchester Guardian*, December 14, 1945.
16. Bass, *Stay the Hand*, 203.
17. Marrus, *Nuremberg*, 57-58.
18. Raul Hilberg, *The Destruction of the European Jews* (1961; Chicago: Quadrangle Books, 1967), 688.
19. Werner Maser, *Nuremberg: A Nation on Trial*, trans. Richard Barry (1977; New York: Charles Scribner's Sons, 1979).
20. Ibid., 28. Steven Fogelson elaborates by noting that the Allies were trying to create a system where individual members of criminal organizations would be tried, but all of these individual defendants had to show why they should not be found guilty because of their membership in those criminalized groups. Steven Fogelson, "The Nuremberg Legacy: An Unfilled Promise," *Southern California Law Review* 63 (1990): 848
21. Maser, *Nuremberg*, 74.
22. Ibid., 97-98.
23. Ibid., 125.
24. Ibid., 286.

25. The ruling out of the "superior orders" defense is something that had been discussed in the Anglo-American presses for years. See, for example, "Rules Out 'Superior Orders,'" *New York Times,* February 19, 1943.
26. For example, this meant bracketing out a well-known international law principle, where defendants wanted to talk about *tu quoque* (others engaged in this activity).
27. Contemporaries noticed this as well. See "The Law of Nuremberg," *New York Times,* December 6, 1945.
28. Wood, *Vectors,* 21.
29. Maser, *Nuremberg,* 283.
30. Simpson, "Didactic," 803.
31. Tadeusz Cyprian and Jerzy Sawicki reported in 1967 that out of the tons of documents, the Allies "picked a few thousand for translation in English, French, and Russian." Tadeusz Cyprian and Jerzy Sawicki, *Nuremberg in Retrospect* (Warsaw: Western Press Agency, 1967), 43.
32. The term "genocide" comes from the melding of the Greek term "genos," meaning race or tribe, with the Latin "cide," the word for killing. Raphael Lemkin is credited with having helped popularize the term. Raphael Lemkin, *Axis Rule in Occupied Europe: Laws of Occupation, Analysis of Government, and Proposals for Redress* (Washington, D.C.: Carnegie Foundation for International Peace, 1944), 79. See Ball, *Prosecuting,* 25–26.
33. For an excellent overview of these early wartime debates about Nazi war crimes, see Arieh J. Kochavi, *Prelude to Nuremberg: Allied War Crimes Policy and the Question of Punishment* (Chapel Hill: University of North Carolina Press, 1998).
34. "What Now?" *Jewish Chronicle,* December 25, 1942, 8. These types of arguments would resurface in more modern commentaries that defended or critiqued the Allied efforts. See, for example, Henry L. Feingold, *The Politics of Rescue: The Roosevelt Administration and the Holocaust, 1938–1945* (New Brunswick, N.J.: Rutgers University Press, 1970); Haskell Lookstein, *Were We Our Brothers' Keepers?: The Public Response of American Jews to the Holocaust, 1938–1944* (New York: Vintage, 1988); Verne W. Newton, ed., *FDR and the Holocaust* (New York: St. Martin's Press, 1996); David S. Wyman, *The Abandonment of the Jews: America and the Holocaust, 1941–1945* (New York: Pantheon Books, 1984), xiii.
35. Breckinridge Long, quoted on the cover of a popular video entitled *America and the Holocaust: Deceit and Indifference* (Boston: WGBH Educational Foundation, 1994).

36. For an interesting counterargument that critiques the position of those who believe that more rescues should have been attempted by the Allies, see William Rubinstein's claim that the "Jews of Nazi-occupied Europe were prisoners, not refugees." Rubinstein, *Myth.*
37. Lookstein, *Were We,* 115.
38. Robert H. Jackson, "The Challenge of International Lawlessness," *International Conciliation* 374 (1941): 683.
39. Ibid., 684-685.
40. Ibid., 686.
41. Ibid., 687.
42. Raphael Lemkin, "The Legal Case against Germany," *Nation,* February 24, 1945, 205–206.
43. Harris, quoted in "'You Have No Chance': Warning to German People," *London Times,* July 29, 1942.
44. Roosevelt, quoted in Quincy Wright, "War Criminals," *American Journal of International Law* 39 (1945): 260.
45. One of the best analyses of the Leipzig trials can be found in Bass, *Stay the Hand,* 58–105.
46. "The Nürnberg Confusion," *Fortune,* December 1946, 120.
47. Franz von Papen, *Memoirs,* trans. Brian Connell (New York: E. P. Dutton, 1953), 570.
48. Simpson, "Didactic," 804.
49. Marshall Harris, R. Bruce Hitchner, Michael P. Scharf, and Paul R. Williams, quoted in Ball, *Prosecuting,* 225.
50. Telford Taylor, "The Nuremberg Trials," *Columbia Law Review* 55 (1955): 493-494.
51. Ibid., 522.
52. Douglas, *Memory,* 257.
53. Simon, quoted in "Rules Out."
54. Jackson, quoted in John H. E. Fried, "The Great Nuremberg Trial," *American Political Science Review* 70 (1976): 192.
55. Lawrence Douglas, "Film as Witness: Screening Nazi Concentration Camps before the Nuremberg Tribunal," *Yale Law Journal* 105 (1995): 480.
56. Robert H. Jackson, "Opening Statement for the United States of America by Robert H. Jackson, Chief of Counsel for the United States at the Palace of Justice, Nürnberg, Germany, November 21, 1945," in Robert H. Jackson, *The Nürnberg Case* (1947; New York: Cooper Square, 1971), 33–34.
57. Ibid., 31.

58. On Lord Justice Lawrence's role, see "The Lesson of Nuremberg," *New Statesman and Nation,* October 5, 1946, 237.
59. Jackson, "Opening Statement," 40.
60. Ibid., 35.
61. Ibid., 31–32.
62. Ibid., 32.
63. Ibid., 83.
64. Ehard, quoted in William E. Benton and Georg Grimm, eds., *Nuremberg: German Views of the War Trials* (Dallas: Southern Methodist University Press, 1955), 100.
65. Jackson, "Opening Statement," 83.
66. Ibid., 34.
67. Ibid., 38-42.
68. Ibid., 54.
69. Ibid.
70. Ibid., 71.
71. Note how American newspapers characterized this portion of Jackson's argument. "Germans Plotted in '40 to Fight U.S., Jackson Charges," *New York Times,* November 22, 1945.
72. Jackson, "Opening Statement," 72.
73. The fact that the Allies were willing to critique militarism and aggression but not colonialism or imperialism did not go unnoticed. See Radhabinod Pal, *Dissentient Judgment of Justice Pal: International Military Tribunal for the Far East* (Tokyo: Kokusho-Kankokai, 1999).
74. Henry Rousso, *The Vichy Syndrome: History and Memory in France since 1944,* trans. Arthur Goldhammer (Cambridge, Mass.: Harvard University Press, 1994), 11.
75. Taylor, quoted in James Podgers, "Remembering Nuremberg," *American Bar Association Journal* 79 (October 1993): 90.
76. Marrus, *Nuremberg,* 234.
77. Edward M. Morgan, "Retributory Theater," *American University Journal of International Law and Policy* 3 (Spring 1988): 41, 43.
78. Feltman, "Legitimizing Justice," 300.
79. Arthur L. Goodhart, "Letters to the Editor: Justice at Nuremberg," *Spectator,* May 17, 1946, 505.
80. "Judgment," *Manchester Guardian,* October 4, 1946.
81. Arthur L. Goodhart, "The Legality of the Nuremberg Trials," *Juridical Review* 56 (1945): 1, 5.
82. Russell Hill, "Berliners Feel Trial of Leaders Shifts War Guilt," *New York Herald Tribune,* December 13, 1945.

83. "Lesson of Nuremberg," 237.
84. Taylor, quoted in "Convincing Germans of Guilt Held Futile," *New York Times*, March 7, 1947.
85. See, for example, how various public opinion polls and other measures gauged Allied or German attitudes toward Nuremberg. William J. Bosch, *Judgment on Nuremberg: American Attitudes toward the Major German War-Crimes Trials* (Chapel Hill: University of North Carolina Press, 1970).
86. Davidson, *Trial*, 36.
87. Feltman, "Legitimizing Justice," 300.
88. Gerald Reitlinger, *The Final Solution: The Attempt to Exterminate the Jews of Europe, 1939–1945* (1953; New York: A. S. Barnes, 1961), 183, 489.
89. Whitney R. Harris, *Tyranny on Trial* (1954; Dallas: Southern Methodist University Press, 1999), 281–315.
90. Judith N. Shklar, *Legalism* (Cambridge, Mass.: Harvard University Press, 1964), 170–171.
91. Davidson, *Trial*, 583-584.
92. Martha Minow, *Between Vengeance and Forgiveness: Facing History after Genocide and Mass Violence* (Boston: Beacon Press, 1998), 34.
93. Robert H. Jackson, "Justice Jackson Weighs Nuremberg's Lessons," *New York Times Magazine*, June 16, 1946, 12.
94. Max Radin provided a much more detailed account of the types of critics who complained about Nuremberg—open or covert sympathizers, humanitarians and pacifists who wanted to outlaw all wars, academics who worried about violations of American constitutional principles and international norms, or conservatives who just wanted to see hangings instead of formal trials. Max Radin, "Justice at Nuremberg," *Foreign Affairs* 24 (1946): 373–374.
95. Jonathan Bush, "Nuremberg: The Modern Law of War and Its Limitations," *Columbia Law Review* 93 (1993): 2059. For a rhetorical analysis that looks at Taft's arguments about Nuremberg, see Donald K. Enholm, "Robert Taft and Nuremberg: The Verdict of Time," *Communication Studies* 51 (2000): 35-54.
96. Stone, quoted in Minow, *Between Vengeance and Forgiveness*, 30.
97. Quincy Wright, "The Law of the Nuremberg Trial," *American Journal of International Law* 41 (1947): 45.
98. Vivian Grosswald Curran, "Competing Frameworks for Assessing Contemporary Holocaust Era Claims," *Fordham International Law Journal* 25 (2001): 110.
99. Ehard, quoted in Benton and Grimm, *Nuremberg*, 101.

100. Francis Biddle, *In Brief Authority* (Garden City, N.Y.: Doubleday, 1962), 455.
101. Maurice Hankey, *Politics, Trials, and Errors* (Oxford: Pen-in-Hand, 1950), 99; Cyprian and Sawicki, *Nuremberg*, 160.
102. F. A. Voigt, "Nuremberg," *Nineteenth Century and After* 140 (1946): 252–253.
103. Some of these neutral states during the war included Portugal, Sweden, and Switzerland.
104. Montgomery Belgion, *Victors' Justice* (Hinsdale, Ill.: Henry Regnery, 1949), 17.
105. For a defense of German trials, see Rustem Vambery, "Law and Legalism," *Nation*, December 1, 1945, 574.
106. Jesse Joseph Silverglate, "The Role of the Conspiracy Doctrine in the Nuremberg War Crimes Trials" (Ph.D. diss., University of Wisconsin–Madison, 1969), 263–265.
107. Smith, *Reaching*, 138.
108. Ibid., 137–138.
109. "The Nuremberg Judgment," *Economist*, October 5, 1946, 531.
110. Cyprian and Sawicki, *Nuremberg*, 151. See also "Aggressor Nations," *Chicago Tribune*, October 2, 1946.
111. Belgion, *Victors'*, 61.
112. Otto Kranzbühler, quoted in Benton and Grimm, *Nuremberg*, 115–116.
113. Maser, *Nuremberg*, 284.
114. Caption on picture in Tusa and Tusa, *Nuremberg Trial*, 288.
115. Kranzbühler, quoted in Benton and Grimm, *Nuremberg*, 335–339.
116. Ibid., 344.
117. Ibid., 347.
118. Taylor, "Nuremberg Trials," 488.
119. David Luban worried the American "conspiracy idea"—the "brainchild of Murray Bernays"—was based on some "shallow, Hollywood conception of history and politics—one, moreover that missed the moral challenge of organizational responsibility." David Luban, "The Legacies of Nuremberg," *Social Research* 54 (1987): 818.
120. Podgers, "Remembering Nuremberg," 88.
121. For the symbolic and legal links that tied the Nuremberg trials with the Eichmann proceeding, see Robert K. Woetzel, *The Nuremberg Trials in International Law with a Postlude on the Eichmann Case* (London: Stevens and Sons, 1962).

122. Robert L. Birmingham, "The War Crimes Trial: A Second Look," *University of Pittsburgh Law Review* 24 (1962): 133.
123. Bradley, *Reaching,* 301.
124. Bloxham, *Genocide,* 185.
125. Simpson, "Didactic," 821.
126. *Bloxham,* Genocide, 185.
127. Jacob Robinson and Henry Sachs, *The Holocaust: The Nuremberg Evidence* (New York: YIVO Institute for Jewish Research, 1976), 8.
128. Mark J. Osiel, "Ever Again: Legal Remembrance of Administrative Massacre," *University of Pennsylvania Law Review* 144 (1995): 464.
129. The Katyn massacre took place when thousands of Polish POWs were murdered in a forest near Smolensk in Russia. During the Nuremberg proceedings, Colonel Y. V. Pokrovsky introduced document U.S.S.R. 34, which was a report that claimed that the Nazis had murdered the Polish POWs. Joseph E. Persico, *Nuremberg: Infamy on Trial* (New York: Penguin, 2000), 250.
130. For some of the key works that have reminded us of the complexities of prewar and wartime immigration, see Yehuda Bauer, *American Jewry and the Holocaust: The American Jewish Joint Distribution Committee, 1939–1945* (Detroit: Wayne State University Press, 1981); Henry L. Feingold, *Bearing Witness: How America and Its Jews Responded to the Holocaust* (Syracuse, N.Y.: Syracuse University Press, 1995); Rafael Medoff, "New Perspectives on How America, and American Jewry, Responded to the Holocaust," *American Jewish History* 84 (1996): 253–266; Sarah E. Peck, "The Campaign for an American Response to the Nazi Holocaust, 1943–1945," *Journal of Contemporary History* 15 (1980): 367-400; Efraim Zuroff, *The Response of Orthodox Jewry in the United States to the Holocaust: The Activities of the Vaad-Ha-Hatzala Rescue Committee, 1939–1945* (Hoboken, N.J.: KTAV, 2000).
131. Bloxham, *Genocide,* ix.
132. István Deák, "Misjudgment at Nuremberg," *New York Review of Books,* October 7, 1993, 46-52.
133. Ibid., 49.
134. Ibid., 52.
135. Franz von Papen would later recall that every time the defense "protested about the unfair advantages which the charter seemed to accord the prosecution, we were reminded that we were lucky to get any trial at all." Von Papen, *Memoirs,* 557.
136. Deák, "Misjudgment," 52.

Chapter Three. The Difficulties of "Mastering the Past": Contemporary and Modern Vectors of Memories and the Auschwitz Trial

1. Wood, *Vectors*, 41.
2. Edward T. Linenthal, *Preserving Memory: The Struggle to Create America's Holocaust Museum* (New York: Viking, 1995).
3. For a very insightful overview of some of the key controversies that surround tourism and the scholarly debates about the physicality of Auschwitz, see Ian Traynor, "Death and Its Detail," *London Guardian*, January 21, 1995, http:web.lexis-nexis.com/universe (January 26, 2004).
4. Aleksander Lasik, quoted in "Frankfurter Trial of the Former Adjutant to the Auschwitz Concentration Camp Commandant," http://www.auschwitz.orgpl/html/eng/aktaulnosci/news.php?rok=2002 (December 25, 2004).
5. Alexander Victor Prusin, "'Fascist Criminals to the Gallows!': The Holocaust and Soviet War Crimes Trials, December 1945–February 1946," *Holocaust and Genocide Studies* 17 (2003): 19.
6. Ibid., 5.
7. Bernd Naumann, *Auschwitz: A Report on the Proceedings against Robert Karl Ludwig Mulka and Others before the Court at Frankfurt*, trans. Jean Steinberg, intro. Hannah Arendt (New York: Frederick A. Praeger, 1966), vii.
8. Gerd Wilcke, "Auschwitz Trial of 22 Is Started," *New York Times*, December 21, 1963.
9. Osiel, *Mass Atrocity*, 2–3.
10. Henry Friedlander, "The Judiciary and Nazi Crimes in Postwar Germany," *Simon Wiesenthal Center Annual* 1 (1984): 30–31. On the Allied Control Council System, see Rebecca Elizabeth Wittmann, "The Wheels of Justice Turn Slowly: The Pretrial Investigations of the Frankfurt Auschwitz Trial 1963–65," *Central European History* 35 (2002): 348.
11. These comparative types of arguments would resurface in a number of scholarly and political engagements. See Caroline Wiedmer, *The Claims of Memory: Representations of the Holocaust in Contemporary Germany and France* (Ithaca, N.Y.: Cornell University Press, 1999), 82.
12. Robert G. Moeller, *War Stories: The Search for a Usable Past in the Federal Republic of Germany* (Berkeley: University of California Press, 2001).

13. For an excellent overview of how postwar Europeans were reacting to news about the Holocaust in the late 1940s and early 1950s, see Leon Poliakov, *Harvest of Hate* (London: Elek Books, 1956), 281–311.
14. Arendt, "Introduction," in Naumann, *Auschwitz*, xvii.
15. Gerald Reitlinger, *The SS: Alibi of a Nation, 1922–1945* (1956; Englewood Cliffs, N.J.: Prentice-Hall, 1981), 451–52.
16. Ibid.
17. Wittmann, "Wheels," 346.
18. Jeffrey Herf, *Divided Memory: The Nazi Past in the Two Germanys* (Cambridge: Harvard University Press, 1997), 335.
19. For a synthesis of Langbein's lifelong contributions, see "Herman Langbein, 83, Aided Holocaust Victims," *New York Times*, November 1, 1995.
20. Akiba A. Cohen, Tamar Zemach-Marom, Jürgen Wilke, and Birgit Schenk, *The Holocaust and the Press: Nazi War Crimes Trials in Germany and Israel* (Cresskill, N.J.: Hampton Press, 2002), 18.
21. Arendt, "Introduction," xiii. Arendt is quoting a reporter by the name of Sybille Bedford when she mentions the "outcast" comment.
22. Friedlander, "Judiciary," 32–33.
23. Ibid.
24. Adalbert Rückerl, *The Investigation of Nazi Crimes 1945–1978*, trans. Derek Rutter (Hamden, Conn.: Archon Books, 1980), 34–35.
25. See "Bonn Aide Opposes War-Crime Amnesty," *New York Times*, March 9, 1964.
26. Arthur J. Olsen, "The Auschwitz Trial," *New York Times*, April 3, 1964.
27. Osiel, *Mass Atrocity*, 192. See Anna J. Merritt and Richard L. Merritt, *Public Opinion in Occupied Germany: The OMGUS Surveys 1945–1949* (Urbana: University of Illinois Press, 1970).
28. Osiel, *Mass Atrocity*, 192. For some of the most insightful commentaries on these Auschwitz proceedings, see Yisrael Gutman and Michael Berenbaum, eds., *Anatomy of the Auschwitz Death Camp* (Bloomington: Indiana University Press, 1998); Hermann Langbein, *Der Auschwitz Prozess: Eine Documention* (Frankfurt on Main: Europaische Verlagsanstalt, 1965); Devin O. Pendas, "Displaying Justice: Nazis on Trial in Postwar Germany" (Ph.D. diss., University of Chicago, 2000); Wittmann, "Wheels," 345–378; Rebecca Elizabeth Wittmann, "Indicting Auschwitz?: The Paradox of the Frankfurt Trial," *German History* 21 (2003): 505–531.
29. Hans Buchheim, "The SS-Instrument of Domination," in Helmut Krausnick, Hans Buchheim, Martin Broszat, and Hans-Adolf

Jacobsen, *Anatomy of the SS State*, trans. Richard Barry, Marian Jackson, and Dorothy Long (New York: Walker, 1968), 224.

30. See "Dr. Fritz Bauer; Prosecuting Nazis," *New York Times*, July 2, 1968.
31. Fritz Bauer, quoted in Wittmann, "Indicting," 505.
32. Buruma, *Wages of Guilt*, 148.
33. Devin O. Pendas, "'I Didn't Know What Auschwitz Was': The Frankfurter Auschwitz Trial and the German Press, 1963—1965," *Yale Journal of Law and Humanities* 12 (2000): 399.
34. Emmi Bonhoeffer, *Auschwitz Trials: Letters from an Eyewitness*, trans. Ursula Stechnow (Richmond, Va.: John Knox Press, 1967), 15.
35. Cohen et al., *Holocaust*, 19.
36. Helge Grabitz, "Problems of Nazi Trials in the Federal Republic of Germany," *Holocaust and Genocide Studies* 3 (1988): 212.
37. Arendt, "Introduction," xi.
38. Friedlander, "Judiciary," 34–35.
39. Grabitz, "Problems," 212.
40. Ibid., 213.
41. Pendas, *Displaying*, 195.
42. Grabitz, "Problems," 213.
43. Ibid., 214.
44. Friedlander, "Judiciary," 34, 35.
45. Wittmann, "Wheels," 350–352.
46. Wilcke, "Auschwitz Trial," 1.
47. Arendt, "Introduction," xiii.
48. Ibid., xix.
49. See Friedrich Karl Kaul, *Auschwitz Trial in Frankfurt-on-Main* (Dresden: Verlag Zeit im Bild, 1965).
50. Jean Steinberg, "Translator's Preface," in Naumann, *Auschwitz*, v.
51. Pendas, *Displaying*, 192.
52. Ibid.
53. Ibid., 189.
54. Naumann, *Auschwitz*, 33–34.
55. Ibid., 35.
56. Ibid.
57. Ibid., 39.
58. Ibid., 40.
59. Ibid., 32.
60. Ibid., 84.

61. For an American critique of the work of the four German historians, see George L. Mosse, "Anatomy of the SS State," *New York Times*, December 22, 1968.
62. Krausnick et al., xv.
63. Ibid., xiii.
64. Ibid., xiv.
65. Mosse, "Anatomy."
66. Wolken, quoted in Naumann, *Auschwitz*, 85.
67. Naumann, *Auschwitz*, 122.
68. Ibid., 108–109.
69. See some of the corroborating testimony of Eugeniusc Motz of Warsaw, who was twenty years old when he worked under Arthur Breitwieser. Naumann, *Auschwitz*, 310.
70. Naumann, *Auschwitz*, 112–113.
71. Ibid., 124–125.
72. Ibid., 136.
73. Arendt, "Introduction," xiii.
74. Naumann, *Auschwitz*, 255–256.
75. Cohen et al., *Holocaust*, 18–19.
76. Naumann, *Auschwitz*, 325.
77. Ibid., 336.
78. Arendt, "Introduction," xiii.
79. Pendas, *Displaying*, 216.
80. Arendt, "Introduction," xiv.
81. Eggert, Schallock, Staiger, Steinacker, Joschoko, Burger, Erhard, Gerhardt, Zarnack, Gollner, Knogel, Reiners, and Naumann.
82. Robert K. Woetzel, "Review: *Auschwitz: A Report on the Proceedings against Robert Karl Ludwig Mulka and Others before the Court at Frankfurt*," *American Journal of International Law* 62 (1968): 234.
83. Eggert, quoted in Naumann, *Auschwitz*, 388.
84. Mulka, quoted in Pendas, *Displaying*, 200.
85. Pendas, *Displaying*, 205–206.
86. Hofmeyer, quoted in Naumann, *Auschwitz*, 48.
87. Naumann, *Auschwitz*, 315.
88. Arendt, "Introduction," xv.
89. Buchheim, "SS," 161.
90. Mark J. Osiel, *Obeying Orders: Atrocity, Military Discipline, and the Rule of Law* (New Brunswick, N.J.: Transaction, 1999), 148.
91. Arendt, "Introduction," xviii.

92. As early as 1953, Gerald Reitlinger made the insightful claim that he was living at a time when "this unspeakable tragedy may come to be regarded as no more than an accumulation of accidents." Reitlinger, *Final Solution*, 465.
93. Pendas, *Displaying*, 199. For more on Hans Stark's work at Auschwitz, see "Defendant Detained at Auschwitz Trial," *New York Times*, May 16, 1964.
94. Langbein, *Auschwitz*, 600; Pendas, *Displaying*, 201.
95. "Ex-inmate Defends Auschwitz Doctor," *New York Times*, February 2, 1964.
96. Naumann, *Auschwitz*, 71.
97. Grabitz, "Problems," 215.
98. Ibid.
99. Arendt, "Introduction," xxiv.
100. Ormond, quoted in Grabitz, "Problems," 219.
101. Arendt, "Introduction," xxiii.
102. Mulka, quoted in Naumann, *Auschwitz*, 31.
103. Frank, quoted in Naumann, *Auschwitz*, 63.
104. Kaduk, quoted in Naumann, *Auschwitz*, 389.
105. Rudolf Hoess, *Commandant of Auschwitz* (New York: Popular Library, 1961), 135–146.
106. Aleksander Lasik, "Postwar Prosecution of the Auschwitz SS," 597.
107. Pendas, *Displaying*, 356–360.
108. Pendas, "I Didn't Know," 433.
109. See Frank Biess, "Book Review: *Genocide on Trial*," *Totalitarian Movements and Political Religions* 3 (2002): 122.
110. Pendas, *Displaying*, 360–364.
111. Hofmeyer, quoted in Bonhoeffer, *Auschwitz Trials*, 60.
112. Rückerl, *Investigation*, 39.
113. Some polls taken during the Auschwitz trial showed that 20 percent of Germans opposed war crimes hearings. "Germans Cool to Nazi Trials," *New York Times*, August 23, 1964.
114. Arendt, "Introduction," xi. For more on the politics of these memories, see Norbert Frei, *Vergangenheitspolitik: Die Anfange der Bundesrepublik und die NS-Vergangenheit* (Munich: C. H. Beck, 1996); Jonathan Wiesen, *West German Industry and the Challenge of the Nazi Past* (Chapel Hill: University of North Carolina Press, 2001).
115. Naumann, *Auschwitz*, vii.
116. Pendas, "I Didn't Know," 434.
117. Bonhoeffer, *Auschwitz Trials*, 30–31.

118. Jeffrey Herf, for example, contends that the "essential truth" is that since the 1960s, the "Social Democrats and the New Left argued that more democracy required more memory and more justice." Herf, *Divided Memory*, 334.
119. Naumann, *Auschwitz*, vii.
120. Krausnick et al., *Anatomy*, xiii.
121. Ibid., xiii–xiv.
122. Buruma, *Wages of Guilt*, 152–153.
123. Krausnick et al., *Anatomy*, xiii.
124. Poliakov, *Harvest*, 209.
125. Arendt, "Introduction," xvi.
126. Grabitz, "Problems," 209.
127. Ibid., 210.
128. Ibid., 211.
129. Gordon Craig, "An Inability to Mourn," *New York Review of Books*, July 14, 1994, 43–44.
130. Bass, *Stay the Hand*, 278.
131. For a more detailed discussion of these pro-Nuremberg numbers, see Robert L. Merritt, *Democracy Imposed: U.S. Occupation Policy and the German Public, 1945–1949* (New Haven, Conn.: Yale University Press, 1995), 157, 160–161.
132. See Thomas Alan Schwartz, *America's Germany: John J. McCloy and the Federal Republic of Germany* (Cambridge, Mass.: Harvard University Press, 1991), 159–165.
133. Bass, *Stay the Hand*, 296.
134. Langer, "The Literature of Auschwitz," in Gutman and Berenbaum, *Anatomy*, 601.
135. Naumann, *Auschwitz*, 85.
136. Arendt, "Introduction," xvii.
137. Buchheim, "Command and Compliance," in Gutman and Berenbaum, *Anatomy*, 357.
138. Naumann, *Auschwitz*, viii.
139. Arendt, "Introduction," xxvi, xi.
140. Grabitz, "Problems," 212.
141. Ibid., 220.

Chapter Four. Israeli Judicial Proceedings and Changing Remembrances of the Holocaust

1. Felman, *Juridical Unconscious*, 127.
2. Rousso, *Vichy Syndrome*, 219–221.

3. One of the most intriguing discussions of the Eichmann show trial came from the pen of Clarence L. Coleman Jr., the president of the American Council for Judaism, who argued that the Israelis were trying to promote the "Zionist" idea that there was some "separate body politic" that spoke for all Jews. Coleman argued that this left out the opinions of some 5,500,000 American Jews who decided to stay in their "homeland." "Letters," *New York Times*, January 8, 1961.
4. George F. Will, "Lessons from Nuremberg," *Washington Post*, December 15, 2003, http://web.lexis-nexis.com/universe (December 25, 2004).
5. Eviatar, "Show Trial."
6. Ibid.
7. Marie-Bénédicte Dembour and Emily Haslam, "Silencing Hearings? Victim-Witnesses at War Crimes Trials," *European Journal of International Law* (2004): 176.
8. Dina Porat, *The Blue and the Yellow Stars of David: The Zionist Leadership in Palestine and the Holocaust 1939–1945* (Cambridge, Mass.: Harvard University Press, 1990), 13.
9. Ibid., 2.
10. Dina Porat, "Palestinian Jewry and the Jewish Agency: Public Response to the Holocaust," in *Vision and Conflict in the Holy Land*, ed. Richard Cohen (New York: St. Martin's Press, 1985), 246.
11. For the panic that was caused in the Yishuv during Germany's North African campaign, see Tom Segev, *The Seventh Million: Israelis and the Holocaust*, trans. Haim Watzman (New York: Hill and Wang, 1993), 69.
12. Porat, *Blue*, 1.
13. Obviously, there had also been a great deal of illegal immigration that had taken place during the war years. See Dalia Ofer, *Escaping the Holocaust: Illegal Immigration to the Land of Israel, 1939–1944* (New York: Oxford University Press, 1990).
14. For a long time the Kastner case has been overshadowed by the Eichmann trial, but this is slowly changing. See, for example, Yehuda Bauer, *Jews for Sale? Jewish Negotiations, 1933–1945* (New Haven, Conn.: Yale University Press, 1994); Leora Bilsky, "Judging Evil in the Trial of Kastner," *Law and History Review* 19 (Spring 2001): 117–160; Segev, *Seventh Million*, 255–320.
15. Bilsky, "Judging Evil," 119.
16. Walter Z. Laqueur, "The *Kastner* Case: Aftermath of the Catastrophe," *Commentary* 20 (December 1955): 500. In many of the academic chronicles of the Holocaust, Kastner was considered to be a special character because he was one of the few Jews who had engaged in

conversations with Eichmann and still lived. Reitlinger, *Final Solution*, 391.

17. David Morrison, "Introduction to the New Edition," in Ben Hecht, *Perfidy* (1961; Jerusalem: Milah Press, 1997), i. I have to disagree with Morrison's last statement, because Yechiam Wietz has provided us with a wealth of path-breaking work over the years on Kastner.
18. Bilsky, "Judging Evil," 121.
19. Isaiah Trunk, *Judenrat: The Jewish Councils in Eastern Europe under Nazi Occupation* (New York: Macmillan, 1972), 561.
20. Ibid., 562.
21. Ibid., 567.
22. Ibid.
23. "Kastner Cleared by Israeli Court," *New York Times*, January 16, 1958.
24. Bauer, *Jews for Sale*, 260.
25. "Zionist Ex-Leader Accused of Perjury," *New York Times*, July 8, 1955.
26. "Israeli 'Quisling' Dead of Wounds," *New York Times*, March 16, 1957.
27. Pnina Lahav, *Judgment in Jerusalem: Chief Justice Simon Agranat and the Zionist Century* (Berkeley: University of California Press, 1997), 122.
28. Hanna Yablonka has recently concluded that the Basel committee "never reached any conclusions" about the accusations against Kastner, and that the "matter appeared to recede gradually from public consciousness." Hanna Yablonka, *The State of Israel vs. Adolf Eichmann*, trans. Ora Cummings and David Herman (New York: Schocken Books, 2004), 27.
29. Kastner, quoted in Leora Bilsky, "Judging and Understanding," *Law and History Review* 19 (2001): 183.
30. Devin O. Pendas, "Book Review: *The Case for Auschwitz*," *Holocaust and Genocide Studies* 17 (2003): 377.
31. "Quisling Charge Stirs All Israel," *New York Times*, July 3, 1955.
32. Akiva Orr, "The Kastner Case, Jerusalem, 1955," in *Israel, Politics, Myths, and Identity Crises* (Boulder, Colo.: Pluto Press, 1994), 81–116.
33. Lahav, *Judgment*, 123.
34. Hecht, *Perfidy*, 5.
35. Bilsky, "Judging Evil," 120.
36. See Harry Gilroy, "Kastner Case Embitters Israel's Party Struggles," *New York Times*, July 3, 1955.
37. Lahav, *Judgment*, 121.
38. Lawrence Douglas, "Language, Judgment, and the Holocaust," *Law and History Review* 19 (2001): 177.

39. Nora Levin, *The Holocaust: The Destruction of European Jewry, 1933–1945* (New York: Thomas Y. Crowell, 1968), 597.
40. Ibid.
41. Lahav, *Judgment*, 121.
42. Reitlinger, *Final Solution*, 275.
43. Ibid., 437.
44. John R. Fischel, *The Holocaust* (Westport, Conn.: Greenwood Press, 1998), 76.
45. Bauer, *Jews for Sale*, 258.
46. Ibid.
47. Fisher, *Holocaust*, 77.
48. Lahav, *Judgment*, 123–124.
49. Bilsky, "Judging Evil," 120.
50. Osiel, *Mass Atrocity*, 3.
51. See Martin Edelman, "Book Review: *Judgment in Jerusalem: Chief Justice Simon Agranat and the Zionist Century*," *American Journal of Legal History* 42 (1998): 303.
52. Segev, *Seventh Million*, 272.
53. Osiel, *Mass Atrocity*, 3.
54. Segev, *Seventh Million*, 282–283.
55. Lahav, *Judgment*, 125.
56. As one reporter told American readers, "'Kastnerism' became a term denoting wickedness" in Israel after a district court judge, Benjamin Halevy, branded Kastner as a man who had "sold his soul to the devil." "Accuser Found Guilty of Libel as Israeli Court Clears Kastner," *New York Times*, January 18, 1958.
57. Lahav, *Judgment*, 127.
58. Simpson, "Didactic," 803.
59. Lahav, *Judgment*, 128.
60. Ibid., 131.
61. "Accuser," 3.
62. Lahav, *Judgment*, 132.
63. Ibid., 121.
64. Ibid.
65. Orr, "*Kastner* Case," 81.
66. Adolf Eichmann, "Eichmann Tells His Own Damning Story," *Life*, November 28, 1960, 19–24, 101–112; Adolf Eichmann, "Eichmann's Own Story: Part II: 'To Sum It All Up, I Regret Nothing,'" *Life*, December 5, 1960, 146–160.
67. Reitlinger, *Final Solution*, 429.

68. Bauer, *Jews for Sale*, 258.
69. Ibid.
70. Ibid., 259.
71. Moshe Pearlman, *The Capture and Trial of Adolf Eichmann* (New York: Simon and Schuster, 1963), 60; Matthew Lippman, "The Trial of Adolf Eichmann and the Protection of Universal Human Rights under International Law," *Houston Journal of International Law* 5 (1982): 1.
72. Lawrence Fellows, "Israel Prepares for *Eichmann* Trial," *New York Times*, February 2, 1961.
73. See "Duty Bound," *New York Times*, January 22, 1961.
74. Persico, *Nuremberg*, 47.
75. For example, the Israeli Trade Union newspaper *Davar* had a writer who alleged that the "Jewish people were not summoned to sit among those sitting in judgment [at Nuremberg]," and this meant that "the greatest of the crimes of nazism was relegated to oblivion." "Trial Dominates European Press," *New York Times*, April 12, 1961.
76. For some of the most intriguing discussions of the Eichmann trial, see Arendt, *Eichmann*; Pnina Lahav, "The *Eichmann* Trial, the Jewish Question, and the American-Jewish Intelligentsia," *Boston University Law Review* 72 (1992): 555–575; Lippman, "Trial," 1–34; Michael A. Musmanno, "The Objections in Limine to the *Eichmann* Trial," *Temple Law Quarterly* 35 (1961): 1–22; Helen Silving, "*In Re Eichmann*: A Dilemma of Law and Morality," *American Journal of International Law* 55 (1961): 307–358.
77. Douglas, *Memory of Judgment*, 104, 97–182.
78. "The *Eichmann* Trial," *New York Times*, April 11, 1961.
79. Lawrence Fellows, "Impact on Israel," *New York Times*, April 16, 1961.
80. Lawrence Fellows, "Israeli Emotions on Trial Diverse," *New York Times*, April 8, 1961.
81. Telford Taylor, "Large Questions in the Eichmann Case," *New York Times*, January 22, 1961.
82. Lord Russell, *The Record: The Trial of Adolph Eichmann for His Crimes against the Jewish People and against Humanity* (New York: Alfred A. Knopf, 1963), xxviii.
83. Gideon Hausner, *Justice in Jerusalem* (New York: Harper and Row, 1966), 291.
84. Arendt, *Eichmann*, 44; Lippman, "Trial," 2.
85. Yablonka, *State of Israel*, 25.
86. See Jack Gould, "TV: The *Eichmann* Trial," *New York Times*, April 10, 1961.

87. Landau, quoted in Russell, *Record,* 3–4.
88. Ibid., 5–7.
89. Jacob Robinson, *And the Crooked Shall Be Made Straight: A New Look at the Eichmann Trial* (New York: Macmillan, 1965), 120.
90. Yablonka, *State of Israel,* 135, 134.
91. Segev, *Seventh Million,* 337.
92. Ibid., 339.
93. Ibid., 349.
94. Hausner, *Justice,* 266.
95. Homer Bigart, "Eichmann Loses Plea to Bar Trial; Denies His Guilt," *New York Times,* April 17, 1961.
96. Segev, *Seventh Million,* 350.
97. Ibid., 351.
98. Russell, *Record,* 131–133.
99. "Could Not Rebel, Nazi Victims Says," *New York Times,* May 2, 1961.
100. Ibid.
101. Segev, *Seventh Million,* 351.
102. Douglas, *Memory,* 107.
103. Freudiger, quoted in Russell, *Record,* 169.
104. Hausner, *Justice,* 336.
105. Russell, *Record,* 190–193.
106. Hausner, *Justice,* 6.
107. Lippman, "Trial," 2.
108. Hausner, *Justice,* 5.
109. Arendt, *Eichmann,* 46; Lippman, "Trial," 2–3.
110. For an intriguing commentary on just why this historical trial shouldn't be viewed as a show trial, see Yablonka, *State of Israel,* 238–249.
111. Arendt, *Eichmann,* 9–10.
112. David Ben-Gurion, "The *Eichmann* Case as Seen by Ben-Gurion," *New York Times Magazine,* December 18, 1960, 62. For one of the best analyses of British immigration policies during World War II, see Bernard Wasserstein, *Britain and the Jews of Europe, 1939–1945* (Oxford: Oxford University Press, 1988).
113. Gideon Hausner, "Eichmann and His Trial," *Saturday Evening Post,* November 19, 1962, 86.
114. Ben-Gurion, "*Eichmann* Case," 7.
115. Ibid.
116. Arendt, *Eichmann,* 19.
117. Ibid.

118. Ibid., 125.
119. For an overview of her discussion of how modernity and Nazi totalitarianism brought about the degeneration of the masses, see Hannah Arendt, *Totalitarianism* (1951; New York: Harcourt, Brace and World, 1968), esp. 50–62.
120. Adi Ophir, "Between Eichmann and Kant: Thinking on Evil after Arendt," *History and Memory* (1996): 109.
121. The American Institute of Public Opinion, survey 643-K, April 1961, quoted in Irving Crespi, "Public Reaction to the *Eichmann* Trial," *Public Opinion Quarterly* 28, no. 1 (Spring 1964): 90.
122. Christopher R. Browning, "German Memory, Judicial Interrogation, and Historical Reconstruction: Writing Perpetrator History from Postwar Testimony," in Friedlander, *Probing the Limits*, 27. For an insightful discussion of some of the obstacles that confronted some of these earlier writers who commented on the Holocaust, see Raul Hilberg, *The Politics of Memory: The Journey of a Holocaust Historian* (Chicago: Ivan R. Dee, 1996).
123. Browning, "German Memory," 31.
124. Segev, *Seventh Million*, 412.
125. For some of the best discussions of the Demjanjuk affair, see Asher Felix Landau and David Levinson, *The Demjanjuk Trial* (Tel Aviv: Israel Bar, 1991); Gitta Sereny, "John Demjanjuk and the Failure of Justice," *New York Review of Books*, October 8, 1992, 32–34; Amir Shaviv, *Ivan the Terrible: The Demjanjuk Trial* (New York: Adama Books, 1988); Yoram Sheftel, *Defending "Ivan the Terrible": The Conspiracy to Convict John Demjanjuk* (Washington, D.C.: Regnery, 1996); Alfred de Zayas, "Impunity for War Crimes, or Mistaken Identity?," *Criminal Law Forum* 6 (1995): 547–555.
126. On Demjanjuk's denaturalization, see *United States v. Demjanjuk*, 518 F. Supp. 1362 (N.D. Ohio 1981), affirmed 680 F.2d 32 (6th Cir. 1982) (per curiam), certiorari denied, 459 U.S. 1036 (1982).
127. Zayas, "Impunity," 548.
128. Douglas, *Memory*, 196.
129. Pazner, quoted in Thomas L. Friedman, "Treblinka Trial Becomes an Israeli Obsession," *New York Times*, March 13, 1987.
130. Gol, quoted in Friedman, "Treblinka."
131. Sereny, "John Demjanjuk," 32.
132. Ibid.
133. Ibid.
134. Ibid.

135. Ibid.
136. Ibid.
137. U.S. Immigration and Naturalization Act of October 30, 1978, Public Law No. 95–549, sections 101–105, 92 Statute 2065 (1978).
138. Zayas, "Impunity," 550.
139. Sher, quoted in Kenneth B. Noble, "Lobbying the Office That Hunts Nazi Suspects," *New York Times,* March 3, 1987.
140. The members of both the Northern District Court of Ohio and the Israeli Supreme Court believed in the authenticity of the "Trawniki card" that linked Demjanjuk to Nazi auxiliary forces. See *United States v. Demjanjuk,* 518 F. Supp. 1368; *Demjanjuk v. Israel* (July 29, 1993).
141. Sereny, "John Demjanjuk," 33.
142. See *In re Extradition of Demjanjuk,* 612 F. Supp. 544 (N.D. Ohio 1985). On the habeas corpus proceedings that were initiated after the extradition order, see *Demjanjuk v. Petrovsky,* 612 F. Supp. 571 (N.D. Ohio 1985), affirmed 776 F.2d 571 (6th Cir 1985), certiorari denied 475 U.S. 1016 (1986).
143. Zayas, "Impunity," 549.
144. This included the potential exculpatory information that came from Danilchenko's testimony and the "Trawniki card" itself.
145. Sereny, "John Demjanjuk," 33.
146. Statement of Ignat Danilchenko, November 21, 1979, quoted in Sereny, "John Demjanjuk," 34.
147. Segev, *Seventh Million,* 414.
148. Ibid.
149. Sereny, "John Demjanjuk," 34.
150. Ibid.
151. Friedman, "Treblinka."
152. Zayas, "Impunity," 550.
153. *Demjanjuk v. Israel* (July 29, 1993), quoted in Zayas, "Impunity," 555.
154. *Demjanjuk v. Petrovsky,* 10 F.3d 354.
155. Sereny, "John Demjanjuk," 32.
156. Zayas, "Impunity," 549.
157. Sereny, "John Demjanjuk," 32.
158. Novick, quoted in Osiel, *Mass Atrocity,* 104–105.
159. See Mark Gillispie, "Demjanjuk Faces Charges Again," *Cleveland Plain Dealer,* May 20, 1999.
160. Edward Walsh, "Demjanjuk Again Stripped of Citizenship," *Washington Post,* February 22, 2002.

161. John Caniglia, "Demjanjuk Loses Bid to Retain Citizenship," *Cleveland Plain Dealer,* November 18, 2004. More than a year later, U.S. Judge Michael Creppy ordered John Demjanjuk to leave the country. Demanjuk was said to have lied about his past, and Creppy argued that Demjanjuk had served as a security guard at three World War II camps. John Caniglia and Joe Guillen, "Judge Orders Demajanjuk Deported," *Cleveland Plain Dealer,* December 29, 2005.
162. Yablonka, *State of Israel,* 219.

Chapter Five. Canada's Experiences with Holocaust Trials

1. Kenneth Freed, "'Hate Law' Trial—Painful Reminder for Canada," *Los Angeles Times,* February 24, 1985.
2. Clyde H. Farnsworth, "Canada Says It Will Punish War Criminals," *New York Times,* April 9, 1995.
3. John-Paul Himka, "Ukrainians Who Resisted," *New York Times,* December 23, 1984.
4. Ibid.
5. Stanley R. Barrett, *Is God a Racist?: The Right Wing in Canada* (Toronto: University of Toronto Press, 1989), 25.
6. Franklyn Bialystok, "The Politicalization of Holocaust Survivors in Canada 1945–1985," in *Confronting the Holocaust: A Mandate for the 21st Century, Part Two,* ed. Stephen C. Feinstein, Karen Schierman, and Marcia Sachs Littell (Lanham, Md.: University Press of America, 1998), 193.
7. See, for example, Theodor Adorno, *Prisms,* trans. Samuel Weber and Sherry Weber (London: Spearman, 1955); Caruth, *Unclaimed Experience;* Felman and Laub, *Testimony;* Dominick LaCapra, *Representing the Holocaust* (Ithaca, N.Y.: Cornell University Press, 1994).
8. Freed, "'Hate Law.'"
9. For some interesting explanations for this belated interest in judicial activism in this area, see Howard Margolian, *Unauthorized Entry: The Truth about Nazi War Criminals in Canada, 1946–1956* (Toronto: University of Toronto Press, 2000); David Matas and Susan Charendoff, *Justice Delayed: Nazi War Criminals in Canada* (Toronto: Summerhill Press, 1987); Harold Tropper, *Old Wounds: Jews, Ukrainians and the Hunt for Nazi War Criminals in Canada* (Markham, Ontario: Viking, 1988).
10. Cyril Levitt, quoted in Bialystok, "Politicalization," 193.

11. See Freed, "'Hate Law.'"
12. Special Committee on Hate Propaganda, *Report of the Special Committee on Hate Propaganda* (Ottawa: Queen's Printer, 1966), quoted with approval in *Regina v. Keegstra* (1990) 3 S.C.R. 697, 725 (Can.); Mayo Moran, "Talking about Hate Speech: American and Canadian Approaches to the Regulation of Hate Speech," *Wisconsin Law Review* 1994 (1994): 1481.
13. Dino Bottos, "*Keegstra* and *Andrews*: A Commentary on Hate Propaganda and the Freedom of Expression," *Alberta Law Review* 27 (1989): 461–462.
14. Criminal Code, R.S.C. 1985, ch. C46, section 318.
15. Criminal Code, R.S.C. 1985, ch. C46, section 319 (1).
16. Criminal Code, R.S.C. 1985, ch. C46, section 319 (2).
17. Moran, "Talking," 1482.
18. For example, both the *Regina v. Keegstra* case ([1990], 3 S.C.R. 697 [Can.]) and the *Regina v. Andrews* decision ([1990], 3 S.C.R. 870 [Can.]) involved challenges to the Criminal Code sections that criminalized the willful promotion of hatred (Criminal Code, R.S.C. 1985, ch. C46, section 319 [2]).
19. See Moran, "Talking," 1464–1467.
20. Ibid., 1464.
21. Ibid., 1464–1467.
22. *Regina v. Keegstra* (1985) 19 C.C.C. (3d) 254 (Alta. Q.B.), (1988) 60 Alta. L. R. (2d) 1 (Alta. C.A.).
23. David Bercuson and Douglas Wertheimer, *A Trust Betrayed: The Keegstra Affair* (Toronto: Doubleday Canada, 1985), x–xi.
24. Alan Davies, "A Tale of Two Trials, Anti-Semitism in Canada 1985," *Holocaust and Genocide* 4 (1989): 77. For a devastating critique of such restrictions as protection for free expression values, see Terry Heinrichs, "Censorship as Free Speech! Free Expression Values and the Logic of Silencing in *R. v. Keegstra*," *Alberta Law Review* 36 (1998): 835–904.
25. Alan Davies, "The *Queen versus James Keegstra*: Reflections on Christian Anti-Semitism in Canada," *American Journal of Theology and Philosophy* 9 (1988): 99.
26. Bottos, "*Keegstra*," 462.
27. For some of the most interesting interpretations of the Keegstra cases, see Steve Mertl and John Ward, *Keegstra: The Issues, the Trial, the Consequences* (Calgary: Western Producer Prairie Books, 1986); Richard Moon, "Drawing Lines in a Culture of Prejudice: *R. v. Keegstra* and the

Restriction of Hate Propaganda," *University of British Columbia Law Review* 26 (1992): 99–143.

28. Douglas Martin, "Hate-Mongering: Teacher Tests Canada's Patience," *New York Times* May 26, 1983.
29. Bercuson and Wertheimer, *Trust,* 57.
30. Ibid., 179.
31. Ibid., 181.
32. Ibid., 181–182.
33. Davies, "*Queen,*" 99.
34. Ibid., 100–101.
35. For a typical legal discussion that justified the limitation of freedom of speech in the name of halting "hate propaganda," see Alan R. Regel, "Hate Propaganda: A Reason to Limit Freedom of Speech," *Saskatchewan Law Review* 2 (1984–85): 303–318.
36. Bercuson and Wertheimer, *Trust,* 129.
37. Ibid.
38. Davies, "*Queen,*" 104–105.
39. *Regina v. Keegstra* (1990), 61 C.C.C. 1; Moon, "Drawing Lines," 99.
40. Moon, "Drawing Lines," 106.
41. Alex Frazer-Harrison and David Jala, "Keegstra Hate Case Finally Closed," *Toronto Sun,* February 29, 1996, http://web.lexis-nexis.com/universe (December 24, 2004).
42. Ibid.
43. Ibid.
44. Peeter Kopvillem, "Guilty as Charged," *Maclean's,* March 11, 1996, 24.
45. Leonidas E. Hill, "The Trial of Ernst Zündel: Revisionism and the Law in Canada," *Simon Wiesenthal Center Annual* 6 (1989): 165–166.
46. Lipstadt, *Denying the Holocaust,* 59.
47. Freed, "'Hate Law.'"
48. Credence Fogo-Schensul, "More Than a River in Egypt: Holocaust Denial, The Internet, and International Freedom of Expression," *Gonzaga Law Review* 33 (1997-1998): 244.
49. Lipstadt, *Denying the Holocaust,* 158.
50. Ibid.
51. "Profile: Who Says It Never Happened? Ernst Zündel and Other 'Holocaust Deniers' Promote Their Message That the Extermination of the Jews during World War II Never Happened," *60 Minutes* (CBS television broadcast, March 20, 1994).
52. Manuel Prutschi, "The Zündel Affair," in *Anti-Semitism in Canada: History and Interpretation,* ed. Alan Davies (Waterloo, Ontario: Wilfrid

Laurier University Press, 1992), 249. See Terry Heinrichs, "Free Speech and the Zündel Trial," *Queen's Quarterly* 95 (1988): 854.

53. Freed, "'Hate Law.'"
54. Vera Ranke, "Holocaust History and the Law: Recent Trials Emerging Theories," *Cardozo Studies in Law and Literature* 9 (1997): 23.
55. Prutschi, "Zündel Affair," 249.
56. Hill, "Trial," 165. See Prutschi, "Zündel Affair," 272.
57. For a chronological summary of the early Zündel cases, see John F. Burns, "Canada Puts Neo-Nazi's Ideas on Trial, Again," *New York Times*, March 30, 1988.
58. Davies, "Tale of Two Trials," 78.
59. Zündel's literature was being circulated in at least forty-two countries. Alan Davies, "After the Holocaust: National Attitudes to [sic] Jews': A Tale of Two Trials—Antisemitism in Canada 1985," *Holocaust and Genocide Studies* 4 (1989): 77.
60. Ibid.
61. Douglas, "Memory of Judgment," 100.
62. Ibid.
63. Hill, "Trial," 181.
64. Prutschi, "Zündel Affair," 272.
65. Heinrichs, "Free Speech," 837.
66. Claude Adams, "Through the Fingers," *Canadian Lawyer* (April 1985): 18.
67. Ibid.
68. Therese O'Donnell, "The Trial of Maurice Papon: The Night and Fog of France's Vichy Past," *Contemporary Issues in Law* 6 (2002–2003): 154.
69. Douglas, "Memory of Judgment," 112.
70. Prutschi, "Zündel Affair," 251–252.
71. Ibid., 252.
72. Adams, "Through the Fingers," 17.
73. Ibid.
74. Ibid., 18.
75. Ibid.
76. Hal Quinn, "The Holocaust Trial," *Maclean's*, March 11, 1985, 43.
77. Nadine Fresco provides an insightful discussion of Faurisson's troubles in France. See Fresco, "Denial of the Dead," 467–483.
78. Adams, "Through the Fingers," 18.
79. On the other hand, part 1, section 7, of the Canadian Constitutional Act allows for "such reasonable limits prescribed by law as can be

demonstrably justified in a free and democratic society." Fogo-Schensul, "More Than a River," 265.

80. Hill, "Trial," 178.
81. Ibid., 171.
82. For an excellent discussion of some of the dangers that attend the policing of many different types of "socio-political falsehoods," see Stefan Braun, "Social and Racial Tolerance and Freedom of Expression in a Democratic Society: Friends or Foes? *Regina v. Zündel,*" *Dalhousie Law Journal* 11 (1988): 471–513.
83. Hill, "Trial," 194.
84. Douglas, *Memory of Judgment,* 2.
85. Douglas, "Memory," 101.
86. Lipstadt, *Denying the Holocaust,* 159.
87. Prutschi, "Zündel Affair," 251. See also *Regina v. Zündel,* 56 S.C.R. (1987) 55.
88. Quinn, "Holocaust," 43.
89. Ibid., 42. See also Gabriel Weimann and Conrad Winn, *Hate on Trial: The Zündel Affair, the Media, and Public Opinion in Canada* (Oakville, Ontario: Mosaic Press, 1986).
90. Adams, "Through the Fingers," 19.
91. Douglas, *Memory of Judgment,* 255.
92. Adams, "Through the Fingers," 17.
93. See, for example, Evelyn Kallen, "Never Again: Target Group Responses to the Debate Concerning Anti-Hate Propaganda Legislation," *Windsor Yearbook of Access to Justice* 11 (1991): 46–73.
94. Lipstadt, *Denying the Holocaust,* 161.
95. Heinrichs, "Free Speech," 854, n.2.
96. Lipstadt, *Denying the Holocaust,* 163.
97. Heinrichs, "Free Speech," 837.
98. In April 1988, a Canadian jury concluded that Zündel should again be found guilty, and he was sentenced in May to nine months in jail. Heinrichs, "Free Speech," 837; Lipstadt, *Denying the Holocaust,* 170. As I note in the text, the case would be overturned in part in *Regina v. Zündel* (1992) 2 S.C.R. (Can.) 731.
99. *Regina v. Zündel,* 732.
100. Ibid., 733, 744.
101. Ibid., 733.
102. Ibid., 743.
103. Ibid., 751.
104. Ibid., 769.

105. Ibid., 778.
106. Ibid., 780.
107. Ibid., 787.
108. Quinn, "Holocaust," 43.
109. *Regina v. Zündel,* 787.
110. Fogo-Schensul, "More Than a River," 275.
111. Stern, *Holocaust Denial,* xii.
112. Prutschi, "Zündel Affair," 251.
113. Hill, "Trial," 205.
114. Hellmut W. Schade, "Zündel's Ideas Threaten Democracy," *Ottawa Citizen,* January 29, 1999, http:web.lexis-nexis.com/universe (January 10, 2003).
115. Sionaidh Douglas-Scott, "The Hatefulness of Protected Speech: A Comparison of American and European Approaches," *William and Mary Bill of Rights Journal* 7 (1999), 345.
116. Lasson, "Holocaust Denial," 81.
117. Ranke, "Holocaust History," 15–44.
118. Quinn, "Holocaust," 43.
119. Heinrichs, "Free Speech," 849.
120. Douglas Martin, "Anti-Semite on Trial, but Did Ontario Blunder?" *New York Times,* February 15, 1985.
121. See David E. Weiss, "Striking a Difficult Balance: Combating the Threat of Neo-Nazism in Germany While Preserving Individual Liberties," *Vanderbilt Journal of Transnational Law* 27 (1994): 899–939.
122. "Holocaust Denier's Appeal Rejected," *Jerusalem Post,* October 24, 2004.
123. For an excellent discussion of the power of this institution's publications, see Stern, *Holocaust Denial.*
124. Fogo-Schensul, "More Than a River," 245.
125. Heinrichs, "Free Speech," 838.
126. "New Platform for Hate," *The Toronto Star,* January 24, 1987.
127. Douglas, *Memory of Judgment,* 255.
128. See Ken McVay, OBC, *Kenneth McVay's Home Page,* http://www1.us.nizkor.org/~kmcvay.
129. See the Simon Wiesenthal Center, *CyberWatch Perspective,* http://www.wiesenthal.com/watch/wpers.htm.
130. Fogo-Schensul, "More Than a River," 245.
131. For an excellent overview of some of freedom of expression issues in Canadian contexts, see Chris Gosnell, "Hate Speech on the Internet: A Question of Context," *Queen's Law Journal* 23 (1998): 369–439.

132. Malcolm Gray and Heather Kneen, "Accusations of War Crimes," *Maclean's*, December 21, 1987, 31.
133. David Matas and Paul Marcus, "Two Views: Prosecuting War Criminals," *Ottawa Citizen*, May 13, 1992, http:web.lexis-nexis.com/universe (January 16, 2003).
134. Bergman and Van Dusen, "Race," 16.
135. See R.S.C., ch. 30, section 1 (3rd Supp. 1985) (Canada).
136. Gray and Kneen, "Accusations," 31.
137. Ibid.
138. Ibid.
139. Irwin Cotler, "*Regina v. Finta*," *American Journal of International Law* 90 (1996): 461.
140. Martin Broszat, "A Controversy about the Historicization of National Socialism," *New German Critique* 44 (Spring/Summer, 1988): 90, 118.
141. Barbara Wickens, "The Case of Imre Finta," *Maclean's*, November 27, 1989, 70.
142. Ibid.
143. The four charges that Finta faced in the Ontario Supreme Court were unlawful confinement, kidnapping, robbery, and manslaughter. "War-Crimes Trial," *Maclean's*, December 4, 1989, 15.
144. Wickens, "Case," 70.
145. Bergman and Van Dusen, "Race," 16.
146. Patricia Chisholm, "Verdict on the Past," *Maclean's*, June 4, 1990, 58.
147. Ibid.
148. Stephen Ward, "Law Page," *London Independent*, May 10, 1991.
149. Ibid.
150. Ibid.
151. Ibid.
152. Ibid.
153. See, for example, Ted Morgan, *An Uncertain Hour: The French, the Germans, the Jews, and the Klaus Barbie Trial, and the City of Lyon, 1940–1945* (New York: Arbor House, 1990).
154. Chisholm, "Verdict," 58.
155. Paul Moloney, "Judge 'Interfered,' Finta Appeal Told," *Toronto Star*, January 22, 1991, http:web.lexis-nexis.com/universe (January 16, 2003).
156. Ibid.
157. Chisholm, "Verdict," 58.
158. Christie's remarks about the Japanese in Canada would be echoed in the popular press for weeks after the trial. See, for example, Barbara

Amiel, "The Trouble with War-Crimes Trials," *Maclean's*, June 11, 1990, 15.

159. Chisholm, "Verdict," 58.
160. Paul Moloney, "Finta's Defence Appealed to Prejudice, Court Told," *Toronto Star*, January 23, 1991, http:web.lexis-nexis.com/universe (January 16, 2003).
161. David Vienneau, "Supreme Court Wrestles with Fate of War Crimes Law," *Toronto Star*, June 3, 1993, http:web.lexis-nexis.com/universe (January 16, 2003).
162. Chisholm, "Verdict," 58.
163. Ibid.
164. "Canada Jury Clears Man Accused of Nazi Crimes," *Boston Globe*, May 26, 1990, http:web.lexis-nexis.com/universe (January 16, 2003).
165. Chisholm, "Verdict," 58.
166. Alan Ferguson, "Finta Verdict Shocks Witnesses," *Toronto Star*, May 29, 1990, http:web.lexis-nexis.com/universe (January 16, 2003).
167. Chisholm, "Verdict," 58.
168. Ferguson, "Finta Verdict."
169. Ibid.
170. Chisholm, "Verdict," 58.
171. Ibid.
172. Ibid.
173. Ibid.
174. Ibid., 15.
175. David Vienneau, "Justice Minister to Review Transcripts of *Finta* Trial," *Toronto Star*, June 5, 1990, http:web.lexis-nexis.com/universe (January 16, 2003).
176. "Passages; Appealed," *Maclean's*, June 25, 1990, 6.
177. Moloney, "Judge."
178. Moloney, "Finta's Defence."
179. Ibid.
180. Ibid.
181. Stephen Bindman, "Divided Court Lets Finta's Acquittal Stand in War-Crimes Trial," *Montreal Gazette*, April 30, 1992, http:web.lexis-nexis.com/universe (January 16, 2003).
182. Matas and Marcus, "Two Views."
183. David Vienneau, "Acquittal of Finta Appealed by Ottawa," *Toronto Star*, May 27, 1992, http:web.lexis-nexis.com/universe (January 16, 2003).

184. Amerasinghe, quoted in David Vienneau, "War Crimes Law on Trial," *Toronto Star*, June 2, 1993, http:web.lexis-nexis.com/universe (January 16, 2003).
185. David Vienneau, "Finta Just Following Orders, Lawyer Says," *Toronto Star*, June 3, 1993, http:web.lexis-nexis.com/universe (January 16, 2003).
186. David Vienneau, "Supreme Court Deliberates on New *Finta* Trial," *Toronto Star*, June 4, 1993, http:web.lexis-nexis.com/universe (January 16, 2003).
187. Ibid.
188. Ibid.
189. Ibid.
190. *Regina v. Finta* (1994), 1 S.C.R. 701.
191. Stephen Bindman, "War-Crimes Law Valid, Court Rules; Rulings Free Finta, Complicate Future Prosecutions," *Ottawa Citizen*, March 24, 1994, http:web.lexis-nexis.com/universe (January 16, 2003).
192. Ibid.
193. David Vienneau, "War Crimes Ruling Questioned; Jewish Congress Fears Convictions May Be Impossible," *Toronto Star*, April 3, 1994, http:web.lexis-nexis.com/universe (January 16, 2003).
194. David Vienneau, "Supreme Court Won't Reopen War Crimes Case," *Toronto Star*, June 24, 1994, http:web.lexis-nexis.com/universe (January 16, 2003).
195. Bindman, "War-crimes Law Valid."
196. Vienneau, "War Crimes Ruling."
197. Bergman and Van Dusen, "Race," 16.
198. Curran, "Legalization of Racism," 88.

Chapter Six. Understanding England's Holocaust Memories

1. Tony Kushner, "Too Little, Too Late? Reflections on Britain's Holocaust Memorial Day," *Journal of Israeli History* 23 (2004): 116.
2. Louise London, for example, observed that during "the Holocaust, Britain's policy—much of it made in conjunction with the United States government—continued to put self-interest first, leaving minimal scope for humanitarian action." Louise London, *Whitehall and the Jews, 1933–1948: British Immigration Policy and the Holocaust* (New York: Cambridge University Press, 2000), 1.

3. In April 1999, Sawoniuk was convicted of murder by the Crown Court on two counts. See *R. v. Sawoniuk*, Court of Appeal, Criminal Division, February 10, 2000, Lexis U.K. CD M365; 2 Cr. App. Rep. 220, Crim. L. R. 506.
4. *Irving v. Penguin Books Ltd. and Another*, No. 1996-I–1113, 2000 WL 362478 (Q.B. April 11, 2000).
5. "Nazi Crimes: M.P.s to See Prison Camps," *London Times*, April 20, 1945.
6. Raymond Phillips, ed., *Trial of Joseph Kramer and Forty-four Others: (The Belsen Trial)* (London: William Hodge, 1949), xxiii–xxiv.
7. "Prior to the *Sawoniuk* proceedings," argues Donald Bloxham, "the last war crimes trial held before an English bench was in the German city of Hamburg in 1949." Donald Bloxham, "Punishing German Soldiers during the Cold War: The Case of Erich von Manstein," *Patterns of Prejudice* 33 (1999): 25.
8. See Donald Bloxham, "'The Trial That Never Was': Why There Was No Second International Trial of Major War Criminals at Nuremberg," *History* 87 (2002): 41–67.
9. John Silverman, "War on the Wanted," *Manchester Guardian* November 17, 1998, http:web.lexis-nexis.com/universe (January 24, 2003).
10. Robert Verkaik,"Why the Law Finds It So Difficult to Deal with the Crimes of History," *London Independent*, January 4, 2000, http:web.lexis-nexis.com/universe (January 24, 2003).
11. Geoffrey Howe, *Conflicts of Loyalty* (New York: St. Martin's Press, 1994), 625. See Thomas Hetherington and William Chalmers, *War Crimes Report of the War Crimes Inquiry* (London: H.M.S.O., 1989).
12. Howe, *Conflicts*, 625.
13. Theodor Meron, "International Criminalization of Internal Atrocities," *American Journal of International Law* 89 (1995): 572.
14. Ibid., 573.
15. Howe, *Conflicts*, 625.
16. James Heartfield, "Frail Old Men with Thick, Foreign Accents Are Tried for Crimes Committed Half a Century Earlier," *London Times*, February 16, 1999, http:web.lexis-nexis.com/universe (January 24, 2003).
17. For an excellent overview of the 1980s and early 1990s British debates on war crimes, see David Cesarani, *Justice Delayed: How Britain Became a Refuge for Nazi War Criminals* (London: Heinemann, 1992).
18. Howe, *Conflicts*, 625.
19. Heartfield, "Frail Old Men," 20.

20. See A. P. V. Rogers, "War Crimes Trials under the Royal Warrant: British Practice 1945–1949," *International and Comparative Law Quarterly* 39 (1990): 780–800.
21. Anne Applebaum, "The Nightmarish World That Awaits a British Jury," *London Sunday Telegraph*, February 14, 1999, http:web.lexis-nexis.com/universe (January 24, 2003).
22. Barrie Penrose, "Londoner, 76, in Nazi War Trial," *London Times*, August 31, 1997, http:proquest.umi.com (January 17, 2005).
23. David Hirsh, "The Trial of Andrei Sawoniuk: Holocaust Testimony under Cross-Examination," *Social and Legal Studies* 10 (2001): 531.
24. Ibid., 533.
25. Silverman, "War."
26. Penrose, "Londoner."
27. Vivian Grosswald Curran, "Politicizing the Crime against Humanity: The French Example," *University of Notre Dame Law Review* 78 (2003): 678.
28. Hirsh, "Trial," 535–539.
29. Christopher Elliott, "Briton Held Over Nazi War Crimes," *Manchester Guardian*, September 27, 1997, http:proquest.umi.com (January 24, 2003).
30. Nick Hopkins, "Briton 'Was Nazi Crimes Enthusiast': Elderly Accused Helped Murder Belarus Jews, Old Bailey Told," *Manchester Guardian*, February 10, 1999, http:proquest.umi.com (January 24, 2003).
31. Patrick McGowan and Stewart Payne, "The Man Accused of War Crimes in 1942," *London Evening Standard*, February 8, 1999, http: proquest.umi.com (January 17, 2005).
32. Hirsh, "Trial," 534.
33. Ibid., 542.
34. Sturken, *Tangled Memories*, 5.
35. Matt Wells, "History Made as War Trial Begins," *Edinburgh Scotsman*, February 9, 1999, http:proquest.umi.com (January 24, 2003).
36. Tim Jones, "War Crimes Defendant 'Embraced the Final Solution with Enthusiasm,'" *London Times*, February 10, 1999, http:proquest.umi.com (January 24, 2003).
37. Ibid.
38. Ibid.
39. For an excellent commentary on the lack of national identities in this region, see Applebaum, "Nightmarish," 35.
40. Jones, "War Crimes Defendant."
41. Hopkins, "Briton."

42. Sue Clough, "Volunteer 'Aided Nazi Genocide with Enthusiasm,'" *Daily Telegraph,* February 10, 1999, http:proquest.umi.com (January 24, 2003).
43. Andrew Buncombe, "Jury Sees Pictures of Death Road," *Independent,* February 11, 1999, http:proquest.umi.com (January 24, 2003).
44. Ibid.
45. Alan Hamilton and Tim Jones, "Court Will Visit Death Site in War Crime Trial," *London Times,* February 9, 1999, http:web.lexis-nexis.com/universe (January 24, 2003).
46. See, for example, "World Watch: Domachevo," *Time International,* March 1, 1999, 14.
47. Alan Hamilton, "Trail Deep in Snow and Past Dread," *London Times,* February 17, 1999, http:proquest.umi.com (January 24, 2003).
48. Nick Hopkins, "Grim Memories on Road of Death," *Manchester Guardian,* February 17, 1999, http:proquest.umi.com (January 24, 2003).
49. Maureen Messent, "Dangers Lurking in this Trial," *Birmingham Evening Mail,* February 19, 1999, http:proquest.umi.com (January 24, 2003).
50. Nick Hopkins, "Sawoniuk 'Turned Cruel,'" *Manchester Guardian,* February 24, 1999, http:proquest.umi.com (January 24, 2003).
51. Hirsh, "Trial," 535.
52. Ibid.
53. Galina Puchkina, quoted in "Jury Told of Nazi Massacre Horror," *Manchester Guardian,* March 3, 1999, http:proquest.umi.com (January 24, 2003).
54. Ibid.
55. Stewart Payne, "I Saw Woman Shot in Head by Sawoniuk," *London Evening Standard,* March 5, 1999, http:proquest.umi.com (January 24, 2003). See Sue Clough, "War Crime Suspect Attacks Accusers," *Daily Telegraph,* March 11, 1999, http:proquest.umi.com (January 24, 2003); Tim Jones, "I Buried Jews for Sawoniuk, Old Bailey Told," *London Times,* March 6, 1999, http:proquest.umi.com (January 24, 2003).
56. Tim Jones, "War Crimes Trial Is Told of Deaths of 15 Jewish Women," *London Times,* March 16, 1999, http:proquest.umi.com (January 24, 2003).
57. Nick Hopkins, "Sawoniuk 'May Have Joined Police to Avoid Slave Camp,'" *Manchester Guardian,* February 13, 1999, http:proquest.umi.com (January 24, 2003).
58. Jones, "I Buried."

59. William Clegg, "Frail Sawoniuk Tells Court: I Did Not Murder Jews," *London Evening Standard,* March 19, 1999, http:proquest.umi.com (January 24, 2003).
60. Ibid.
61. Ibid.
62. Tim Jones, "War Crimes Accused Attacks Witness 'Lies,'" *London Times,* March 20, 1999, http:proquest.umi.com (January 24, 2003).
63. Audrey Gillan and Libby Brooks, "'I Did Not Kill My Friends the Jews,': Alleged War Criminal Cleared of Two Murders," *Manchester Guardian,* March 20, 1999, http:proquest.umi.com (January 24, 2003).
64. See Andrew Buncombe, "War Crime Witnesses Branded Liars," *London Independent,* March 11, 1999, http:proquest.umi.com (January 24, 2003).
65. Jones, "War Crimes Accused."
66. Ibid.
67. "'I Am Not a Monster,' Claims War Crimes Defendant," *Manchester Guardian,* March 23, 1999, http:proquest.umi.com (January 24, 2003).
68. Ibid.
69. Hirsh, "Trial," 541.
70. "'I Am Not a Monster.'"
71. Ibid.
72. Tim Jones, "Sawoniuk Threatens Walkout," *London Times,* March 24, 1999, http:proquest.umi.com (January 24, 2003).
73. Ibid.
74. Tim Jones, "The Outsider Driven by a Hatred of Jews," *London Times,* April 2, 1999, http:proquest.umi.com (January 24, 2003).
75. "Killer Gets Life Term in Britain's First War Crimes Trial," *Los Angeles Times,* April 2, 1999, http:web.lexis-nexis.com/universe (January 24, 2003).
76. Sue Clough, "Retiree Jailed for War Crimes," *Montreal Gazette,* April 2, 1999, http:proquest.umi.com (January 24, 2003).
77. Tim Jones, "The Only Trial Out of 393 Suspects," *London Times,* April 2, 1999, http:web.lexis-nexis.com/universe (January 24, 2003).
78. Ibid.
79. Hugh Muir, "Plan for New Met War Crimes Unit Falls Foul of Funding Problems," *London Guardian,* January 5, 2004, http:web.lexis-nexis.com/universe (January 16, 2005).
80. "Killer Gets Life," 27.

81. Nick Hopkins, "Verdict Encourages Those Seeking Belated Justice," *Manchester Guardian*, April 2, 1999, http:proquest.umi.com (January 24, 2003).
82. Ibid.
83. "The Roll of Dishonour," *Birmingham Post*, April 2, 1999, http: proquest.umi.com (January 24, 2003).
84. Fergal Keane, "The Importance of Convicting This Elderly Man of Murder," *London Independent*, April 3, 1999, http://web.lexis-nexis.com (January 24, 2003).
85. Alasdair Palmer, "Comment: New Echoes of the Holocaust," *The Sunday Telegraph*, April 4, 1999, 35.
86. Jay Rayner, "News: Nazi War Crimes Trial," *London Observer*, April 4, 1999, http://web.lexis-nexis.com (January 24, 2003).
87. David Cesarani, "At Home with Hatred," *Sunday Times*, April 4, 1999, http:proquest.umi.com (January 24, 2003).
88. Dr. C. O. Lister, "Letter to the Editor: War Crimes Sentence: The Case For and Against," *London Daily Telegraph*, April 5, 1999, http://web.lexis-nexis.com (January 24, 2003).
89. Matt Wells, "A Triumph for Human Rights, or a 10m Pound Waste of Time?" *Scotsman*, April 2, 1999, 3, http://web.lexis-nexis.com (January 24, 2003).
90. Applebaum, "Nightmarish."
91. Heartfield, "Frail Old Men," 20.
92. Ibid.
93. "Sawoniuk Condemned," *London Daily Telegraph*, April 2, 1999.
94. See http://web.lexis-nexis.com (January 24, 2003).
95. McNamara, "History," 364.
96. See Richard J. Evans, *Lying about Hitler: History, Holocaust, and the David Irving Trial* (New York: Basic Books, 2001); D. D. Guttenplan, *The Holocaust on Trial* (New York: Norton, 2001); Robert Jan van Pelt, *The Case for Auschwitz: Evidence from the Irving Trial* (Bloomington: Indiana University Press, 2002).
97. See *David John Cawdell Irving v. Penguin Books Limited & Deborah E. Lipstadt* (London: Harry Counsell, 2000) [32 days] (hereafter cited as "Trial transcript").
98. Douglas, *Memory of Judgment*, 3.
99. Australia and Canada have already barred Irving's entry, and he is currently fighting a legal battle with New Zealand's Immigration Service. See Tracy Watkins, "Holocaust Denier Is Likely to Test Ruling,"

Wellington Dominion Post, August 2, 2004, http://web.lexis-nexis.com (January 6, 2005).

100. See Lasson, "Holocaust Denial," 35–40.
101. McNamara, "History," 391.
102. Dan Jacobson, "The Downfall of David Irving," *Times Literary Supplement*, April 21, 2001, 12.
103. Dennise Mulvihill, "*Irving v. Penguin*: Historians on Trial and the Determination of Truth under English Libel Law," *Fordham Intellectual Property, Media and Entertainment Law Journal* 11 (2000): 218–219.
104. See Charles Gray, *The Irving Judgment: David Irving v. Penguin Books and Professor Deborah Lipstadt* (London: Penguin, 2000).
105. Guttenplan, *Holocaust*, 287–289.
106. For example, Gordon A. Craig, "The Devil Is in the Details," *New York Review of Books*, September 19, 1996, 8–12; Christopher Hitchens, "Hitler's Ghost," *Vanity Fair*, June 1996, 74.
107. Jay Tolson and Thomas K. Grose, "Wresting with the Past," *U.S. News and World Report*, February 14, 2000, 44.
108. Note here, for example, Deborah Lipstadt, *Beyond Belief: The American Press and the Coming of the Holocaust 1933–1945* (New York: Free Press, 1986).
109. See Lipstadt, *Denying the Holocaust*; Jacobson, "Downfall," 13; Guttenplan, "Holocaust," 45.
110. Trial transcript, 11 January 2000, 8.
111. See Anthony Julius and James Libson, "Losing Was Unthinkable, the Rest Is History," *London Independent*, April 18, 2000, http://web.lexis.nexis.com/universe/document (July 7, 2001).
112. Guttenplan, *Holocaust*, 2.
113. Gray, *Irving Judgment*, 1.
114. Bert Roughton Jr., "Historians' Views Clash in Court," *Atlanta Journal and Constitution*, January 12, 2000, http://web.lexis-nexis.com (January 24, 2003).
115. Lawrence Douglas, "Policing the Past: Holocaust Denial and the Law," in *Censorship and Silencing: Practices of Cultural Regulation*, ed. Robert C. Post (Los Angeles: Getty Research Institute, 1998), 83–84.
116. Douglas W. Vick and Linda MacPherson, "Anglicizing Defamation Law in the European Union," *Virginia Journal of International Law* 36 (1996): 933.
117. For an overview of British libel laws, see Marlene Arnold Nicholson, "McLibel: A Case Study in English Defamation Law," *Wisconsin International Law Journal* 18 (2000): 1–144.

118. Derek Devgun, "United States Enforcement of English Defamation Judgments: Exporting the First Amendment?" *Anglo- American Law Review* 23 (1994): 196–197.
119. Mulvihill, *"Irving,"* 223.
120. Douglas W. Vick and Linda MacPherson, "An Opportunity Lost: The United Kingdom's Failed Reform of Defamation Law," *Federal Communications Law Journal* 49 (1997): 647.
121. Mulvihill, *"Irving,"* 222.
122. Ibid.
123. Ibid., 305.
124. See "Fighting the Deniers," *Jerusalem Post,* January 26, 2000, http://web.lexis-nexis.com (January 24, 2003).
125. D. D. Guttenplan, "The Holocaust on Trial," *Atlantic Monthly,* February 2000, 47.
126. Deborah Lipstadt, quoted in Walter Reich, "The Stakes in a Holocaust Trial," *New York Times* January 19, 2000.
127. McNamara, "History," 379.
128. Trial transcript, 11 January 2000, 17.
129. Ibid., 47.
130. Trial transcript, 11 January 2000, 12.
131. Ibid.
132. Ibid.
133. Ibid., 13.
134. Guttenplan, "Holocaust," 49–50.
135. Trial transcript, 11 January 2000, 15.
136. Trial transcript, 11 January 2000, 20.
137. Ibid., 15.
138. Ibid., 23.
139. Ibid., 24.
140. Ibid., 24–25.
141. Ibid., 28.
142. Trial transcript, 11 January 2000, 88–89.
143. Ibid., 89.
144. Van Pelt, *Case,* ix.
145. Trial transcript, 11 January 2000, 89.
146. Ibid., 90–91. Heydrich was once the second most important leader of the Nazi SS. He was assassinated by Czech partisians in 1942.
147. Ibid., 94–95.
148. Ibid., 97.
149. Gray, *Irving Judgment,* 348.

150. See *Irving v. Penguin Books Limited and Another*, [2001] EWCA Civ. 935, June 15, 2001.
151. Elli Wohlgelernter, "Shoah Showdown," *Jerusalem Post*, September 24, 1999, http://web.lexis-nexis.com/universe (January 16, 2005).
152. James Dalrymple, "The Curse of Revisionism," *London Independent*, January 21, 2000, http://web.lexis-nexis.com/universe/document (February 20, 2001).
153. Jonathan Freedland, "Irving Libel Trial: Court 73 Where History Is on Trial," *Manchester Guardian*, February 5, 2000, http://web.lexis-nexis.com/universe/document (February 20, 2000).
154. Lipstadt, *Denying the Holocaust*, 1–30.
155. R. E. Boustred, "Letter to the Editor: Would Our Hands Ever Have Been Clean?" *London Daily Telegraph*, February 20, 1999, http://web.lexis-nexis.com (January 24, 2003).
156. Ibid.
157. Heartfield, "Frail Old Men," 20.
158. Applebaum, "Nightmarish."
159. Heartfield, "Frail Old Men," 20.
160. Robert Verkaik, "Judges Clash on Jailing of War Criminal," *London Independent*, June 25, 1999, http://web.lexis-nexis.com (January 24, 2003).
161. Nick Hopkins, "National Roundup: War Crimes Conviction Upheld," *Manchester Guardian*, February 11, 2000, http://web.lexis-nexis.com (January 24, 2003).
162. Ibid.
163. Ibid.
164. "Efforts to Bring Kalejs to Trial Are Stepped Up," *Glasgow Herald*, January 27, 2000, http://web.lexis-nexis.com (January 24, 2003).
165. Bernard Wasserstein, "Britain's Role in the Holocaust," *Jerusalem Post*, May 29, 2000, 8.

Chapter Seven. The Future of Legal Involvement in Holocaust Memories

1. David Cesarani, "Holocaust Controversies in the 1990s: The Revenge of History or the History of Revenge?" *Journal of Israeli History* 23 (2004): 82.
2. Jackson, quoted in Taylor, "Large Questions."

3. See John Caniglia, "U.S. Nazi-Hunters Have Fewer Cases as Suspects Grow Older," *Cleveland Plain Dealer*, January 4, 2004, http://web.lexis-nexis.com (January 26, 2003).
4. Hilary Leila Krieger, "Nazi War Criminal Investigations Up 20%," *Jerusalem Post*, April 20, 2004, http://web.lexis-nexis.com (January 26, 2003).
5. See Tom Buckham, "Lawyer Criticizes Revoking Demjanjuk's Citizenship," *Buffalo News*, February 24, 2002, http://web.lexis-nexis.com (January 26, 2003).
6. Eviatar, "Show Trial."
7. Taylor, "Large Questions."
8. For a perceptive look at the role that "revenge" plays in Holocaust memory work in general and legal cases like Demjanjuk's in particular, see Berel Lang, "Holocaust Memory and Revenge: The Presence of the Past," *Jewish Social Studies* 2 (Winter 1996): 1–20.
9. See Marianne Hirsch, "Surviving Images: Holocaust Photographs and the Work of Postmemory," in *Visual Culture and the Holocaust*, ed. Barbie Zelizer (New Brunswick, N.J.: Rutgers University Press, 2001), 215–246.
10. Lawrence Douglas, for example, argues that "it is the memory of these earlier trials that creates the hope, if not the expectation, that today's perpetrators will be forced to answer to the law." Douglas, *Memory of Judgment*, 1. I understand these sentiments, but this type of argument makes some huge assumptions about the interrelationship that exists between law, memory, and judgment. For one, it assumes that there is some unitary or consensual "law" that exists and that can be identified as a constraint on state power.
11. Michael Schudson, "Dynamics of Distortion in Collective Memory," in *Memory Distortion: How Minds, Brains, and Societies Reconstruct the Past*, ed. Daniel L. Schacter (Cambridge, Mass.: Harvard University Press, 1997), 348.
12. For a critique of these apparently "neutral" frameworks, see Hariman, *Popular Trials*.
13. Dembour and Haslam, "Silencing," 169.
14. Curran, "Politicizing," 679.
15. Arendt, *Eichmann*, 253.
16. Curran, "Politicizing," 708.
17. Dembour and Haslam, "Silencing," 153.
18. Curran, "Politicizing," 706.

19. Arno J. Mayer, "Response," *French Historical Studies* 24 (Fall 2001): 593–594.
20. Dembour and Haslam, "Silencing," 169.
21. Osiel, *Mass Atrocity*, 105. For an interesting example of how historians worry about the polysemic nature of rhetoric and the existence of historical relativism, see Richard J. Evans's recent attack on "postmodernist hyper-relativism." Evans, *Lying*, 1.
22. See John C. Zimmerman, *Holocaust Denial: Demographics, Testimonies, and Ideologies* (Landham, Md.: University Press of America, 2000).
23. Osiel is insightful when he remarks that "all antagonists" need to feel that they "have had a fair hearing" and that the courts needed to weave "their strictly legal conclusions into a plausible and relatively capacious narrative about the country's recent conflagration." Osiel, *Mass Atrocity*, 298.
24. For an overview of the conceptual and legal problems with the *tu quoque* defense, see Osiel, *Mass Atrocity*, 123–124.
25. Ben-Gurion, "*Eichmann* Case," 62.
26. In 1986, Morton Weinfeld and John Sigal suggested that some children are more likely to learn about the Holocaust from "books or other media than college courses." Morton Weinfeld and John J. Sigal, "The Effect of the Holocaust on Selected Socio-Political Attitudes of Adult Children of Survivors," *Canadian Review of Sociology and Anthropology* 23 (1986): 378.
27. John C. Zimmerman, "Holocaust Denial," *Los Angeles Times*, January 16, 2000, http://web.lexis-nexis.com (January 24, 2003).
28. Samantha Power, "To Suffer by Comparison," *Daedalus* 128 (Spring 1999): 41–42.
29. Segev, *Seventh Million*, 415.
30. Heartfield, "Frail Old Men."
31. "'Hate Speech' Again, Abroad," September 9, 1995, *Washington Post*, http://web.lexis-nexis.com (January 24, 2003).
32. See, for example, the arguments presented in Ward Churchill, *A Little Matter of Genocide: Holocaust Denial in the Americas, 1492 to the Present* (San Francisco: City Light Books, 1997).
33. Amos Funkenstein, "History, Counterhistory, and Narrative," in Friedlander, *Probing the Limits*, 80–81.
34. Power, "Suffer," 32.
35. Priscilla Hayner, paraphrased in D. W. Miller, "Truth and Consequence," *Chronicle of Higher Education*, September 8, 2000, A–24.

36. Dembour and Haslam are leading the way in one area as they reassess the ways that "victim-witnesses" think about the benefits of war crimes trials. Dembour and Haslam, "Silencing," 151–177.
37. Amiel, "Trouble," 15.
38. Siegel, "Comment," 397.
39. *Reno v. ACLU* 117 S.Ct. 2329 (1997). This was a 1997 decision where the U.S. Supreme Court found that parts of the Communication Decency Act needed to be struck down because they were an unconstitutional regulation of the internet.
40. Craig, "Devil," 8.
41. Countryman, "Letter to the Editor."
42. Dershowitz, "Academic Freedom," 72.
43. Curran, "Legitimation of Racism," 96.
44. Taylor, "Large Questions."
45. For some insightful commentaries on these tribunals, see Richard J. Gladstone, *For Humanity: Reflections of a War Crimes Investigator* (New Haven, Conn.: Yale University Press, 2000).
46. Audrey R. Chapman and Patrick Ball, "The Truth of Truth Commissions: Comparative Lessons from Haiti, South Africa, and Guatemala," *Human Rights Quarterly* 23 (February 2001): 2.

Selected Bibliography

Adams, Claude. "Through the Fingers." *Canadian Lawyer* (April 1985).

Arendt, Hannah. *Eichmann in Jerusalem: A Report on the Banality of Evil*. New York: Viking Press, 1966.

Ashplant, T. G., Graham Dawson, and Michael Roper. *The Politics of War, Memory and Commemoration*. New York: Routledge, 2000.

Ball, Howard. *Prosecuting War Criminals and Genocide: The Twentieth-Century Experience*. Lawrence: University Press of Kansas, 1999.

Barrett, Stanley R. *Is God a Racist?: The Right Wing in Canada*. Toronto: University of Toronto Press, 1989.

Bass, Gary Jonathan. *Stay the Hand of Vengeance: The Politics of War Crimes Tribunals*. Princeton, N.J.: Princeton University Press, 2000.

Bauer, Yehuda. *American Jewry and the Holocaust: The American Jewish Joint Distribution Committee, 1939–1945*. Detroit: Wayne State University Press, 1981.

_____. *Jews for Sale? Jewish Negotiations, 1933–1945*. New Haven, Conn.: Yale University Press, 1994.

Benton, William E., and Georg Grimm, eds. *Nuremberg: German Views of the War Trials*. Dallas: Southern Methodist University Press, 1955.

Bercovitch, Sacvan. *The Rites of Assent: Transformation in the Symbolic Construction of America*. New York: Routledge, 1993.

Biddle, Francis. *In Brief Authority*. Garden City, N.J.: Doubleday, 1962.

Bilsky, Leora. "Judging Evil in the Trial of Kastner." *Law and History Review* 19 (2001): 117–160.

Binder, Guyora, and Robert Weisberg. *Literary Criticisms of Law*. Princeton, N.J.: Princeton University Press, 2000.

Bloxham, Donald. *Genocide on Trial*. New York: Oxford University Press, 2001.

Bodnar, John. *Remaking America: Public Memory, Commemoration, and Patriotism in the Twentieth Century*. Princeton, N.J.: Princeton University Press, 1992.

Bonhoeffer, Emmi. *Auschwitz Trials: Letters from an Eyewitness*. Trans. Ursula Stechnow. Richmond, Va.: John Knox Press, 1967.

Bosch, William J. *Judgment on Nuremberg: American Attitudes toward the Major German War-Crimes Trials*. Chapel Hill: University of North Carolina Press, 1970.

Braun, Stefan. "Social and Racial Tolerance and Freedom of Expression in a Democratic Society: Friends or Foes? *Regina v. Zündel*." *Dalhousie Law Journal* 11 (1988): 471–513.

Brennan, Bonnie, and Hanno Hardt. eds. *Picturing the Past: Media, History and Photography*. Urbana: University of Illinois Press, 1999.

Brooks, Peter, and Paul Gewirtz, eds. *Law's Stories: Narrative and Rhetoric in the Law*. New Haven, Conn.: Yale University Press, 1996.

Browne, Stephen H. "Reading, Rhetoric, and the Texture of Public Memory." *Quarterly Journal of Speech* 81 (1993): 237–250.

Buruma, Ian. *The Wages of Guilt: Memories of War in German and Japan*. New York: Penguin Books, 1995.

Butler, Thomas, ed. *Memory, History, Culture, and the Mind*. Oxford: Blackwell, 1989.

Caruth, Cathy. *Unclaimed Experience: Trauma, Narrative, and History*. Baltimore, Md.: Johns Hopkins University Press, 1995.

———, ed. *Trauma: Explorations in Memory*. Baltimore: Johns Hopkins University Press, 1995.

Cesarani, David. *Justice Delayed: How Britain Became a Refuge for Nazi War Criminals*. London: Heinemann, 1992.

Cohen, Akiba A., Tamar Zemach-Marom, Jürgen Wilke, and Birgit Schenk. *The Holocaust and the Press: Nazi War Crimes Trials in Germany and Israel*. Cresskill, N.J.: Hampton Press, 2002.

Cole, Tim. *Selling the Holocaust*. New York: Routledge, 1999.

Conan, Éric, and Henry Rousso. *Vichy: An Ever-Present Past*. Hanover, N.H.: University Press of New England, 1998.

Condit, Celeste M., and John L. Lucaites. *Crafting Equality: America's Anglo-African Word*. Chicago: University of Chicago Press, 1993.

Conway, John S. "The First Report about Auschwitz." *Simon Wiesenthal Center* 1 (1984): 133–151.

Cotler, Irwin. "When Academic Freedom and Free Speech Confront Holocaust Denial and Group Libel: Comparative Perspectives." *Boston College Third World Law Journal* 8 (1988): 65–90.

Curran, Vivian G. "Deconstruction, Structuralism, Antisemitism and the Law." *Boston College Law Review* 36 (1994): 1–52.

———. "The Legalization of Racism in a Constitutional State: Democracy's Suicide in Vichy France." *Hastings Law Journal* 50 (1998): 1–96.

Davidson, Eugene. *The Trial of the Germans: An Account of the Twenty-two Defendants before the International Military Tribunal at Nuremberg*. New York: Macmillan, 1966.

Davies, Alan, ed. *Anti-Semitism in Canada: History and Interpretation*. Waterloo, Ontario: Wilfrid Laurier University Press, 1992.

Deák, István, Jan T. Gross, and Tony Judt. *The Politics of Retribution in Europe: World War II and Its Aftermath*. Princeton, N.J.: Princeton University Press, 2000.

Dembour, Marie-Bénédicte, and Emily Haslam. "Silencing Hearings: Victim-Witnesses at War Crimes Trials." *European Journal of International Law* 15 (2004): 151–177.

De Mildt, Dick. *In the Name of the People: Perpetrators of Genocide in the Reflections of Their Post-War Prosecution in West Germany: The "Euthanasia" and "Aktion Reinhard" Trial Cases*. The Hague: Martinus Nijhoff, 1996.

Doneson, Judith E. "Holocaust Revisited: A Catalyst for Memory or Trivialization?" *Annals of the American Academy of Political and Social Science* 548 (1996): 70–77.

Douglas, Lawrence. *The Memory of Judgment: Making Law and History in the Trials of the Holocaust*. New Haven, Conn.: Yale University Press, 2001.

Enholm, Donald K. "Robert Taft and Nuremberg: The Verdict of Time." *Communication Studies* 51 (2000): 35–54.

Evans, Richard J. *Lying about Hitler: History, Holocaust, and the David Irving Trial*. New York: Basic Books, 2001.

Feingold, Henry L. *Bearing Witness: How America and Its Jews Responded to the Holocaust*. Syracuse, N.Y.: Syracuse University Press, 1995.

_____. *The Politics of Rescue: The Roosevelt Administration and the Holocaust, 1938–1945*. New Brunswick, N.J.: Rutgers University Press, 1970.

Feinstein, Stephen C., Karen Schierman, and Marcia Littell, eds. *Confronting the Holocaust: A Mandate for the 21st Century, Part Two*. Lanham, Md.: University Press of America, 1988.

Felman, Shoshana. *The Juridical Unconscious: Trials and Traumas in the Twentieth Century*. Cambridge, Mass.: Harvard University Press, 2002.

Felman, Shoshana, and Doris Laub, eds. *Testimony: Crises of Witnessing in Literature, Psycho-analysis, and History*. New York: Routledge, 1992.

Feltman, Brian K. "Legitimizing Justice: The American Press and the International Military Tribunal, 1945–1946." *Historian* 66 (2004): 300–319.

Finkelstein, Norman G. *The Holocaust Industry: Reflections on the Exploitation of Jewish Suffering*. London: Verso, 2000.

Finkielkraut, Alain. *The Imaginary Jew*. Trans. K. O'Neill and D. Suchoff. Lincoln: University of Nebraska Press, 1994.

Fish, Stanley. *Doing What Comes Naturally*. Durham, N.C.: Duke University Press, 1989.

Fresco, Nadine. "The Denial of the Dead." *Dissent* 28 (1981): 467–483.

Friedlander, Saul, ed. *Probing the Limits of Representation: Nazism and the "Final Solution."* Cambridge, Mass.: Harvard University Press, 1992.

Fussell, Paul. *The Great War and Modern Memory*. New York: Oxford University Press, 1975.

Gilbert, Martin. *Auschwitz and the Allies*. New York: Holt, Rinehart and Winston, 1981.

Gillis, J. R., ed. *Commemorations: The Politics of National Identity*. Princeton, N.J.: Princeton University Press, 1994.

Goodell, Stephen, Kevin A. Mahoney, and Sybil Milton. *1945: The Year of Liberation*. Washington, D.C.: U.S. Holocaust Memorial Museum, 1995.

Gordon, Robert W. "The Politics of Legal History and the Search for a Usable Past." *Benchmark* 4 (1990): 269–281.

Gutman, Yisrael, and Michael Berenbaum, eds. *Anatomy of the Auschwitz Death Camp*. Bloomington: Indiana University Press, 1998.

Halbwachs, Maurice. *On Collective Memory*. Chicago: University of Chicago Press, 1992.

Hariman, Robert, ed. *Popular Trials: Rhetoric, Mass Media and the Law*. Tuscaloosa: University of Alabama Press, 1990.

Harris, Whitney R. *Tyranny on Trial*. Dallas: Southern Methodist University Press, 1999.

Hecht, Ben. *Perfidy*. 1961; Jerusalem, Israel: Milah Press, 1997.

Heinrichs, Terry. "Censorship as Free Speech! Free Expression Values and the Logic of Silencing in *R. v. Keegstra*." *Alberta Law Review* 36 (1998): 835–904.

Hilberg, Raul. *The Destruction of the European Jews*. Chicago: Quadrangle Books, 1967.

———. *The Politics of Memory: The Journey of a Holocaust Historian*. Chicago: Ivan R. Dee, 1996.

Hirsh, David. "The Trial of Andrei Sawoniuk: Holocaust Testimony Under Cross-Examination." *Social and Legal Studies* 10 (2001): 529–545.

Hobsbawn, Eric, and Terrence Ranger, eds. *The Invention of Tradition*. Cambridge: Cambridge University Press.

Hoess, Rudolf. *Commandant of Auschwitz*. New York: Popular Library, 1961.

Hoffman, Eva. *After Such Knowledge: Memory, History, and the Aftermath of the Holocaust*. New York: Public Affairs, 2004.

International Military Tribunal. *Trial of the Major War Criminals before the International Military Tribunal, Nuremberg, 14 November–1 October, 1946.* Nuremberg: International Military Tribunal, 1947.

Irwin-Zarecka, Iwona. *Frames of Remembrance: The Dynamics of Collective Memory*. New Brunswick, N.J.: Transaction, 1994.

Jackson, Robert H. *The Nürnberg Case*. New York: Cooper Square, 1971.

Kammen, Michael. *Mystic Chords of Memory*. New York: Vintage Books, 1993.

Kochavi, Arieh J. *Prelude to Nuremberg: Allied War Criminals Policy and the Question of Punishment*. Chapel Hill, N.C.: University of North Carolina Press, 1998.

Kranzbühler, Otto "Nuremberg Eighteen Years Afterwards." *De Paul Law Review* 14 (1965).

Krausnick, Helmut, Hans Buchheim, Martin Broszat, and Hans-Adolf Jacobsen. *Anatomy of the SS State*. Trans. Richard Barry, Marian Jackson, and Dorothy Long. New York: Walker, 1968.

LaCapra, Dominick. *History and Criticism*. Ithaca, N.Y.: Cornell University Press, 1985.

_____. *Representing the Holocaust*. Ithaca, N.Y.: Cornell University Press, 1994.

Lahav, Pnina. *Judgment in Jerusalem: Chief Justice Simon Agranat and the Zionist Century*. Berkeley: University of California Press, 1997.

Landau, Asher Felix, and David Levinson. *The Demjanjuk Trial*. Tel Aviv: Israel Bar Publishing House, 1991.

Lasson, Kenneth. "Holocaust Denial and the First Amendment: A Quest for Truth in a Free Society." *George Mason Law Review* 6 (1997): 35–86.

Lemkin, Ralph. *Axis Rule in Occupied Europe: Laws of Occupation, Analysis of Government, and Proposals for Redress*. Washington, D.C.: Carnegie Foundation for International Peace, 1944.

Linenthal, Edward T. *Preserving Memory: The Struggle to Create America's Holocaust Museum*. New York: Viking, 1995.

Lippman, Matthew. "The Trial of Adolf Eichmann and the Protection of Universal Human Rights under International Law." *Houston Journal of International Law* 5 (1982): 1–34.

Lipsitz, George. *Time Passages: Collective Memory and the American Popular Culture*. Minneapolis: University of Minnesota Press, 1990.

Lipstadt, Deborah. *Beyond Belief: The American Press and the Coming of the Holocaust 1933–1945*. New York: Free Press, 1986.

_____. *Denying the Holocaust: The Growing Assault on Truth and Memory*. New York: Plume Press, 1994.

Lookstein, Haskell. *Were We Our Brothers' Keepers?: The Public Response of American Jews to the Holocaust, 1938–1944.* New Haven, Conn.: Vintage Books, 1988.

Ludi, Regula. "Waging War on Wartime Memory: Recent Swiss Debates on the Legacies of the Holocaust and the Nazi Era." *Jewish Social Studies* 10 (2004): 116–152.

Margolian, Howard. *Unauthorized Entry: The Truth about Nazi War Criminals in Canada, 1946–1956.* Toronto: University of Toronto Press, 2000.

Marrus, Michael R. *The Nuremberg War Crimes Trial 1945–1946: A Documentary History.* Boston: Bedford, 1997.

Martin, Douglas. "Hate-Mongering Teacher Tests Canada's Patience." *New York Times,* May 26, 1983.

Maser, Werner. *Nuremberg: A Nation on Trial.* New York: Charles Scribner's Sons, 1979.

Mayer, Arno J. *Why Did the Heavens Not Darken? The "Final Solution" in History.* New York: Verso, 1988.

McNamara, Lawrence. "History, Memory, and Judgment: Holocaust Denial, the History Wars and Law's Problems with the Past." *Sydney Law Review* 26 (2004): 353–394.

Medoff, Rafael. "New Perspectives on How America, and American Jewry, Responded to the Holocaust." *American Jewish History* 84 (1996): 253–266.

Merritt, Anna J., and Richard L. Merritt. *Public Opinion in Occupied Germany: The OMGUS Surveys 1945–1949.* Urbana: University of Illinois Press.

Merritt, Richard L. *Democracy Imposed: U.S. Occupation Policy and the German Public, 1945–1949.* New Haven, Conn.: Yale University Press, 1995.

Minow, Martha. *Between Vengeance and Forgiveness: Facing History after Genocide and Mass Violence.* Boston: Beacon Press, 1998.

Moeller, Robert G. *War Stories: The Search for a Usable Past in the Federal Republic of Germany.* Berkeley: University of California Press, 2001.

Morgan, Ted. *An Uncertain Hour: The French, the Germans, the Jews, the Klaus Barbie Trial, and the City of Lyon, 1940–1945.* New York: Arbor House, 1990.

Morris, Arthur D. *While Six Million Died: A Chronicle of American Apathy.* New York: Random House, 1968.

Morris, Richard, and Peter Ehrenhaus, eds. *The Cultural Legacy of Vietnam.* Norwood, N.J.: Ablex, 1990.

Morse, Arthur D. *While Six Million Died: A Chronicle of American Apathy.* 1967; New York: Random House, 1968.

Naumann, Bernd. *Auschwitz: A Report on the Proceedings against Robert Karl Mulka and Others before the Court at Frankfurt.* New York: Frederick A. Praeger, 1966.

Newton, Verne W., ed. *FDR and the Holocaust.* New York: St. Martin's Press, 1996.

Nietzsche, Friedrich. "History in the Service and Disservice of Life." In *Unmodern Observations,* ed. William Arrowsmith, trans. Gary Brown. New Haven, Conn.: Yale University Press 1990.

Nora, Pierre. "Between Memory and History: Les Lieux de Memoiré." *Representations* 26 (1989): 7–25.

Novick, Peter. *The Holocaust in American Life.* Boston: Houghton Mifflin, 1999.

Osiel, Mark. *Mass Atrocity, Collective Memory, and the Law.* New Brunswick, N.J.: Transaction, 1997.

_____. *Obeying Orders: Atrocity, Military Discipline, and the Rule of Law.* New Brunswick, N.J.: Transaction Publishers, 1999.

Pal, Radhabinod. *Dissentient Judgment of Justice Pal: International Military Tribunal for the Far East.* Tokyo: Kokusho-Kankokai, 1999.

Peck, Sarah E. "The Campaign for an American Response to the Nazi Holocaust, 1943–1945." *Journal of Contemporary History* 15 (1980): 367–400.

Pendas, Devin O. "Displaying Justice: Nazis on Trial in Postwar Germany." Ph.D. diss., University of Chicago, 2000.

_____. "'I Didn't Know What Auschwitz Was': The Frankfurter Auschwitz Trial and the German Press, 1963—1965." *Yale Journal of Law and Humanities* 12 (2000).

Persico, Joseph E. *Nuremberg: Infamy on Trial.* New York: Penguin, 2000.

Phillips, Kendall R., ed. *Framing Public Memory.* Tuscaloosa: University of Alabama Press, 2004.

Phillips, Raymond. *The Belsen Trial.* London: William Hodge, 1949.

_____. *Trial of Josef Kramer and Forty-four Others.* London: William Hodge, 1949.

Poliakov, Leon. *Harvest of Hate.* London: Elek Books, 1956.

Rehnquist, William. *All the Laws but One: Civil Liberties in Wartime.* New York: Knopf, 1999.

Porat, Dina. *The Blue and the Yellow Stars of David: The Zionist Leadership in Palestine and the Holocaust 1939–1945.* Cambridge, Mass.: Harvard University Press, 1990.

Post, Robert C., ed. *Censorship and Silencing: Practices of Cultural Regulation.* Los Angeles: Getty Research Institute, 1998.

Reitlinger, Gerald. *The Final Solution: The Attempt to Exterminate the Jews of Europe, 1939–1945*. New York: A. S. Barnes, 1961.

———. *The SS: Alibi of a Nation, 1922–1945*. Englewood Cliffs, N.J.: Prentice-Hall, 1981.

Robinson, Jacob. *And the Crooked Shall Be Made Straight: A New Look at the Eichmann Trial*. New York: Macmillan, 1965.

Robinson, Jacob, and Henry Sachs. *The Holocaust: The Nuremberg Evidence*. New York: YIVO Institute for Jewish Research, 1976.

Rogers, A. P. V. "War Crimes Trials under the Royal Warrant: British Practice 1945–1949." *International and Comparative Law Quarterly* 39 (1990): 780–800.

Rosenbaum, Alan S., ed. *Is the Holocaust Unique*? Boulder, Colo.: Westview Press, 1996.

Rousso, Henry. *The Vichy Syndrome: History and Memory in France since 1944*. Cambridge, Mass.: Harvard University Press, 1994.

Rubenstein, William D. *The Myth of Rescue: Why the Democracies Could Not Have Saved More Jews from the Nazis*. London: Routledge, 1997.

Rückerl, Adalbert. *The Investigation of Nazi Crimes 1945–1978*. Hamden, Conn.: Archon Books, 1980.

Sarat, Austin, and Thomas R. Kearns, eds. *History, Memory, and the Law*. Ann Arbor: University of Michigan Press, 2001.

———. *The Rhetoric of Law*. Ann Arbor: University of Michigan Press, 1994.

Schwartz, Barry. "The Social Context of Commemoration: A Study in Collective Memory." *Social Forces* 61 (1982): 374–402.

Schwartz, Thomas Alan. *America's Germany: John J. McCloy and the Federal Republic of Germany*. Cambridge, Mass.: Harvard University Press, 1991.

Segev, Tom. *The Seventh Million: Israelis and the Holocaust*. New York: Hill and Wang, 1993.

Sheftel, Yoram. *Defending "Ivan the Terrible": The Conspiracy to Convict John Demjanjuk*. Washington, D.C.: Regnery, 1996.

Shklar, Judith N. *Legalism*. Cambridge, Mass.: Harvard University Press, 1964.

Simpson, Gerry J. "Didactic and Dissident Histories in War Crimes Trials." *Albany Law Review* 60 (1997): 801–839.

Smith, Bradley F. *Reaching Judgment at Nuremberg*. New York: Meridian, 1979.

Snyder, Jack, and Leslie Vinjamuri. "Trials and Errors: Principle and Pragmatism in International Justice." *International Security* 28 (2004): 5–44.

Stein, Eric. "History against Free Speech: The New German Law against the 'Auschwitz' and Other 'Lies.'" *Michigan Law Review* 85 (1986): 277–324.

Stern, Kenneth S. *Holocaust Denial.* New York: American Jewish Committee, 1993.

Sturken, Marita. *Tangled Memories: The Vietnam War, the AIDS Epidemic, and the Politics of Remembering.* Berkeley: University of California Press, 1997.

Taylor, Telford. *The Anatomy of the Nuremberg Trials.* Boston: Little, Brown, 1992.

Trunk, Isaiah. *Judenrat: The Jewish Councils in East Europe under Nazi Occupation.* New York: Macmillan, 1972.

Turner, Kathleen J., ed. *Doing Rhetorical History: Concepts and Cases.* Tuscaloosa: University of Alabama Press, 1998.

Tusa, Ann, and John Tusa. *The Nuremberg Trial.* New York: Atheneum, 1986.

Van Pelt, Robert Jan. *The Case for Auschwitz: Evidence from the Irving Trial.* Bloomington: Indiana University Press, 2002.

Weimann, Gabriel, and Conrad Winn. *Hate on Trial: The Zündel Affair, the Media, and Public Opinion in Canada.* Oakville, Ontario: Mosaic Press, 1986.

Weiss, Yfaat. "The Transfer Agreement and the Boycott Movement: A Jewish Dilemma on the Eve of the Holocaust." *Yad Vashem Studies* 26 (1988): 129–171.

White, Hayden. *Tropics of Discourse: Essays in Cultural Criticism.* Baltimore: Johns Hopkins University Press, 1985.

White, James Boyd. *The Legal Imagination: Studies in the Nature of Legal Thought and Expression.* Boston: Little, Brown, 1973.

Wiedmer, Caroline. *The Claims of Memory: Representations of the Holocaust in Contemporary Germany and France.* Ithaca, N.Y.: Cornell University Press, 1999.

Wiesel, Elie. *From the Kingdom of Memory, Reminiscences.* New York: Summit Books, 1990.

Wittmann, Rebecca E. "Indicting Auschwitz? The Paradox of the Frankfurt Trial." *German History* 21 (2003): 505–531.

_____. "The Wheels of Justice Turn Slowly: The Pretrial Investigations of the Frankfurt Trial, 1963–65." *Central European History* 35 (2002): 345–378.

Woetzel, Robert K. *The Nuremberg Trials in International Law and a Postlude on the Eichmann Case.* London: Stevens and Sons, 1962.

Wood, Nancy. *Vectors of Memory: Legacies of Trauma in Postwar Europe.* New York: Berg, 1999.

Wyman, David S. *The Abandonment of the Jews: America and the Holocaust, 1941–1945.* New York: Pantheon Books, 1984.

Yablonka, Hanna. "The Development of Holocaust Consciousness in Israel: The Nuremberg, Kapos, Kastner, and Eichmann Trials." *Israel Studies* 8 (2003): 1–24.

———. *The State of Israel vs. Adolf Eichmann*. New York: Schocken Books, 2004.

Young, James E. *The Texture of Memory: Holocaust Memorials and Meaning*. New Haven, Conn.: Yale University Press, 1993.

Zelizer, Barbie. *Remembering to Forget: Holocaust Memory through the Camera's Eye*. Chicago: University of Chicago Press, 1998.

———, ed. *Visual Culture and the Holocaust*. New Brunswick, N.J.: Rutgers University Press, 2001.

Zerubavel, Yael. *Recovered Roots: Collective Memory and the Making of Israeli National Tradition*. Chicago: University of Chicago Press, 1995.

Zimmerman, John C. *Holocaust Denial: Demographics, Testimonies, and Ideologies*. Landham, Md.: University Press of America, 2000.

Zuroff, Efraim. *The Response of Orthodox Jewry in the United States to the Holocaust: The Activities of the Vaad-Ha-Hatzala Rescue Committee, 1939–1945*. Hoboken, N.J.: KTAV Publishing House, 2000.

Index